AIM HIGHER

MCAS ENGLISH

SHEPHERD · SALINGER · CASTRO

LEVEL J

aim

advanced instructional materials

The Future of Education, Today

Beverly, Massachusetts · Middletown, New Jersey

aim higher!

STAFF CREDITS:

EDITORIAL

DIANE PERKINS CASTRO
ANNIE SUN CHOI
SHARON S. SALINGER
ROBERT D. SHEPHERD
KELSEY STEVENSON

PRODUCTION AND DESIGN

MATTHEW PASQUERELLA

OTHER CONTRIBUTORS:

AARON COHEN
NATASHA NESE

The publisher gratefully acknowledges permissions granted by the following persons and institutions for the reprinting of copyrighted material in this work:

Excerpt from PILGRIM AT TINKER CREEK by ANNIE DILLARD. Copyright © 1974 by Annie Dillard. Reprinted by permission of HarperCollins Publishers, Inc.

From LAKE WOBEGON DAYS by Garrison Keillor, Copyright © 1985 by Garrison Keillor. Used by permission of Viking Penguin, a division of Penguin Putnam Inc.

First Edition

Printed in the United States of America

04 03 02 01 00   10 9 8 7 6 5 4 3 2 1

ISBN: 1-58171-018-6

Advanced Instructional Materials
100 Cummings Center
Beverly, MA 01915
Sales Office: 1–800–552–1377
Visit our Web site at http://www.higheraim.com
    or e-mail us at learning@higheraim.com.

Who's Who?

Can you match the pictures of these Massachusetts authors with their names? See page 256 for answers.

_____ 1. Louisa May Alcott, novelist

_____ 2. Emily Dickinson, poet

_____ 3. Frederick Douglass, journalist

_____ 4. Ralph Waldo Emerson, essayist

_____ 5. Henry Wadsworth Longfellow, poet

_____ 6. Henry David Thoreau, naturalist

_____ 7. Phillis Wheatley, poet

CONTENTS

This book is dedicated to the students of Massachusetts.
You are the future. You are our hopes and dreams.

Cross-Curricular Icons Used in the Text

The Massachusetts Comprehensive Assessment System (MCAS) English Exam assesses student skills in the areas of reading and writing. These skills, though directly addressed in English classes, are used in every curricular area. In keeping with the cross-curricular nature of the MCAS, the authors and editors of this text have used icons throughout to identify the curricular areas treated in selections and examples. The following icons appear throughout the text:

 The Arts

 Geography/ Global Studies

 History and Social Science

 Language and Literature

 Mathematics

 Science

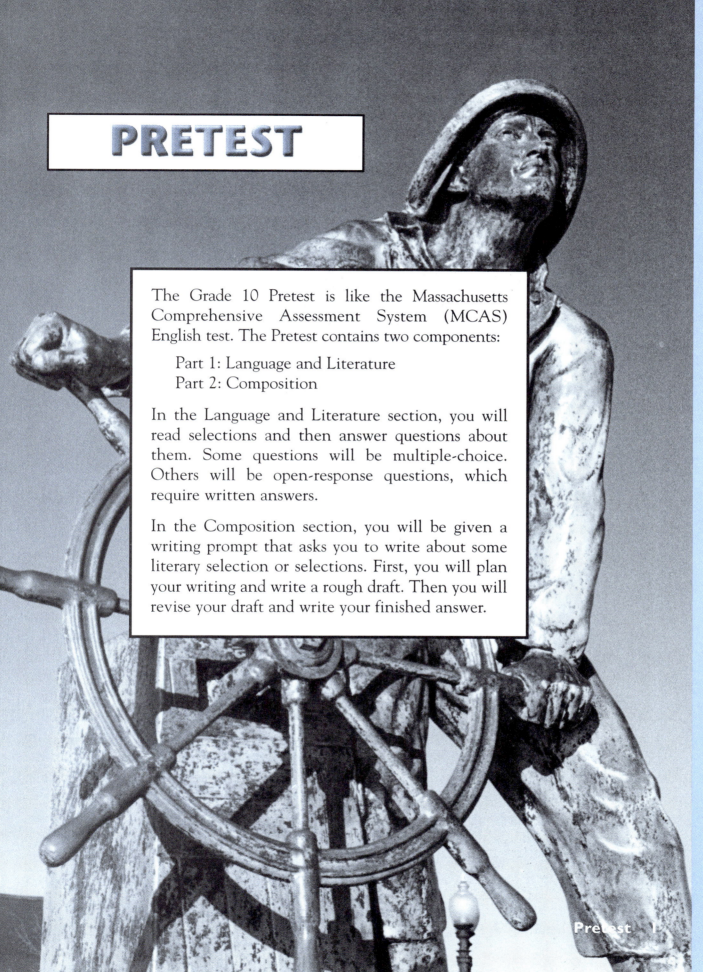

PRETEST

The Grade 10 Pretest is like the Massachusetts Comprehensive Assessment System (MCAS) English test. The Pretest contains two components:

Part 1: Language and Literature
Part 2: Composition

In the Language and Literature section, you will read selections and then answer questions about them. Some questions will be multiple-choice. Others will be open-response questions, which require written answers.

In the Composition section, you will be given a writing prompt that asks you to write about some literary selection or selections. First, you will plan your writing and write a rough draft. Then you will revise your draft and write your finished answer.

DIRECTIONS

Read this excerpt from *Pilgrim at Tinker Creek*. Then answer the questions that follow.

from

Pilgrim at Tinker Creek

by Annie Dillard

After the flood last year I found a big tulip-tree limb that had been wind-thrown into Tinker Creek. The current dragged it up on some rocks on the bank, where receding waters stranded it. A month after the flood I discovered that it was growing new leaves. Both ends of the branch were completely exposed and dried. I was amazed. It was like the old fable about the corpse's growing a beard; it was as if the woodpile in my garage were suddenly to burst greenly into leaf. The way plants persevere in the bitterest of circumstances is utterly heartening. I can barely keep from unconsciously ascribing a will to these plants, a do-or-die courage, and I have to remind myself that coded cells and mute water pressure have no idea how grandly they are flying in the teeth of it all.

In the lower Bronx, for example, enthusiasts found an ailanthus tree that was fifteen feet long growing from the corner of a garage roof. It was rooted in and living on "dust and roofing cinders." Even more spectacular is a desert plant, *Ibervillea sonorae*—a member of the gourd family—that Joseph Wood Krutch describes. If you see this plant in the desert, you see only a dried chunk of loose wood. It has neither roots nor stems; it's like an old gray knothole. But it is alive. Each year before the rainy season comes, it sends out a few roots and shoots. If the rain arrives, it grows flowers and fruits; these soon wither away, and it reverts to a state as quiet as driftwood.

Well, the New York Botanical Garden put a dried *Ibervillea sonorae* on display in a glass case. "For seven years," says Joseph Wood Krutch, "without soil or water, simply lying in the case, it put forth a few anticipatory shoots and then, when no rainy season arrived, dried up again, hoping for better luck next year." That's what I call flying in the teeth of it all.

(It's hard to understand why no one at the New York Botanical Garden had the grace to splash a glass of water on the thing. Then they could say on their display case label, "This is a live plant." But by the eighth year what they had was a dead plant, which is precisely what it had looked like all along. The sight of it, reinforced by the label "Dead *Ibervillea sonorae*," would have been most melancholy to visitors to the botanical garden. I suppose they just threw it away.) 🍎

1 Annie Dillard gives three examples of plants that show an amazing ability to cling to life even after they are seemingly dead. All of the following are examples of this ability EXCEPT

  A an ailanthus tree on a roof
  B the woodpile in the garage
  C the tulip-tree limb stranded on the bank of Tinker Creek
  D an *Ibervillea sonorae* in a glass case

2 What statement about the stranded tulip-tree limb BEST makes the main point of the selection?

  A It was dead, like the woodpile in her garage.
  B It illustrates the fact that new leaves can grow on a branch.
  C It had been thrown into the creek by the wind.
  D It shows the way plants persevere in the bitterest of circumstances.

3 Read the following phrase from the excerpt.

  I can barely keep myself from unconsciously ascribing a will to these plants, a do-or-die courage . . .

  Of which literary device is the author's urge an example?

  A simile
  B personification
  C onomatopoeia
  D alliteration

4 Why is it surprising that the ailanthus tree was rooted in and living on dust and roofing cinders?

  A Plants usually need to be rooted in earth so that their roots can take in water and nutrients.
  B Dust and roofing cinders are rare in the Bronx, a section of New York City.
  C Enthusiasts found it, rather than the people in the neighborhood.
  D Cinders are not something you would expect to find on a roof.

5 The desert plant in the display case put forth a few anticipatory shoots. What does *anticipatory* mean here?

  A doomed
  B tiny
  C strange
  D expectant

Open-Response Questions, Session 1

6   What is the author's attitude toward the *Ibervillea sonorae*? Use details from the excerpt to support your answer.

7 How are the plants described in the excerpt "flying in the teeth of it all"? Use details and information from the excerpt to support your answer.

_____

_____

_____

_____

_____

_____

_____

_____

_____

_____

_____

_____

_____

_____

_____

_____

_____

_____

DIRECTIONS

Read the following passage from "The Death of Iván Illych" and the poem "Death, Be Not Proud." Then answer the questions that follow.

from

The Death of Iván Illych

by Leo Tolstoy, translated by Sasha Cuperin

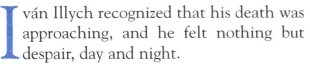

Iván Illych recognized that his death was approaching, and he felt nothing but despair, day and night.

In the deepest part of himself, in his heart's core, he knew that he was dying. He refused, however, to give admittance to the thought. He would not—could not, in fact—entertain such a simple but somehow absurd concept. Death, that unwelcome guest, was simply unacceptable in the parlor of his consciousness.

In his schooldays he had read in Kiesewetter's *Outline of Logic* this straight-forward argument:

Caius is a man.
All men are mortal.
Therefore, Caius is mortal.

The argument certainly made sense when applied to Caius, but Iván Illych could not believe it true, as well, of himself. Caius was an abstraction, and people in the abstract were, of course, mortal. Death came to them all, no doubt about it. It was a matter of logic, as any schoolboy could tell you. But Iván Illych was not some logical abstraction. He was flesh-and-blood. He was unique, different. He had been a child, delighting in his toys. He had been called Vanya. He had had a mamma and a papa and a nurse. He had had joys and delights, griefs and sorrows. It was no abstract Vanya who had played with a ball, kissed his mother, complained about the food at school. It was no abstract young man who had fallen in love, who had risen to become

P
R
E
T
E
S
T

a respectable public prosecutor. Abstract men like Caius could die, but surely not Iván Illych, that universe of thoughts and emotions and experiences. How could all those thoughts and emotions and experiences, all that he was, all that he had been or would be, simply disappear? Impossible! It could not be the case. The very thought filled Iván Illych with horror and disgust.

"Surely," he said to himself, "if I were going to die, I would have known about it. I would have felt death creeping upon me like a highwayman or a thief in a dark alleyway. I am told that I am going to die, but this cannot be so! It makes no sense. No sense at all."

Iván Illych tried not to think of it, but the effort, and his illness, tired him. It was like trying not to think of a toothache when one has, in fact, a toothache. As soon as he slammed the door in the face of the unwelcome guest, he heard again the ghastly knocking at the door of his consciousness, as if some terrible person, a bill collector—or worse, a murderer—were outside and demanding entrance.

Reading Selection #3, Session 1

Death, Be Not Proud
by John Donne

Death, be not proud, though some have callèd thee
Mighty and dreadful, for thou art not so;
For those whom thou think'st thou dost overthrow
Die not, poor Death, nor yet canst thou kill me.
From rest and sleep, which but thy pictures be,
Much pleasure; then from thee much more must flow,
And soonest our best men with thee do go,
Rest of their bones, and soul's delivery.
Thou art slave to fate, chance, kings, and desperate men,
And dost with poison, war, and sickness dwell,
And poppy or charms can make us sleep as well
And better than thy stroke; why swell'st thou then?
One short sleep past, we wake eternally
And death shall be no more; Death, thou shalt die.

8 In what sense is the word *entertain* used in the second paragraph of "The Death of Iván Illych"?

en • ter • tain 1) [Archaic] to keep up; maintain 2) to hold the interest of and give pleasure to; divert; amuse 3) to give hospitality to; have as a guest 4) to allow oneself to think about; have in mind; consider

A definition 1
B definition 2
C definition 3
D definition 4

9 Death is described as an "unwelcome guest" who is "unacceptable in the parlor" of Iván's consciousness. This kind of figure of speech is called

A personification
B antithesis
C hyperbole
D understatement

10 What does it mean that "Caius was an abstraction"?

A He was a mythological figure.
B He was a figment of Iván Illych's imagination.
C To Iván Illych, he was not a flesh-and-blood human being but just an idea.
D He did not have strong feelings about his own death.

11 "The Death of Iván Illych" is a short story, a type of prose narrative. Which of the following is ALWAYS true of a prose narrative?

A It is written from the third-person point of view.
B It tells the thoughts of the main character.
C It is a work of fiction.
D It tells a story.

12 All of the following sentences from "The Death of Iván Illych" contain similes EXCEPT

   A "I would have felt death creeping upon me like a highwayman or a thief in a dark alleyway."

   B "It was like trying not to think of a toothache when one has, in fact, a toothache."

   C "As soon as he slammed the door in the face of the unwelcome guest, he heard again the ghastly knocking at the door of his consciousness, as if some terrible person, a bill collector—or worse, a murderer—were outside and demanding entrance."

   D "Abstract men like Caius could die, but surely not Iván Illych, that universe of thoughts and emotions and experiences."

13 "Death, Be Not Proud" is an example of all of the following except

   A free verse

   B a sonnet

   C rhymed verse

   D a lyric poem

14 Which statement best expresses the poet's attitude toward death?

   A Death is "mighty and dreadful."

   B Death can conquer him.

   C Death will bring even more pleasure than rest and sleep do.

   D Death is to be feared.

15 Which line from the poem is closest in meaning to the statement "The good die young"?

   A "For those whom thou think'st thou dost overthrow / Die not"

   B "And the soonest our best men with thee do go"

   C "One short sleep past, we wake eternally"

   D "And better than thy stroke; why swell'st thou then?"

Open-Response Questions, Session 1

16 Logic tells Iván Illych one thing about death, and his emotions tell him another. What is the nature of the conflict Iván experiences between his reason and his feelings? Use details from the selection to support your answer.

_____

_____

_____

_____

_____

_____

_____

_____

_____

_____

_____

_____

_____

_____

_____

_____

_____

_____

_____

17 Use details from both selections to contrast the attitudes toward death held by the speaker of the poem and by the character in the short story.

_____

_____

_____

_____

_____

_____

_____

_____

_____

_____

_____

_____

_____

_____

_____

_____

_____

_____

_____

_____

_____

_____

STOP ⬤

PRETEST

DIRECTIONS

Read "The Story of an Hour." Then answer the questions that follow.

The Story of an Hour

by Kate Chopin

Because Mrs. Mallard was afflicted with heart trouble, great care was taken to break to her as gently as possible the news of her husband's death.

It was her sister Josephine who told her, in broken sentences; veiled hints that revealed in half concealing. Her husband's friend Richards was there, too, near her. It was he who had been in the newspaper office when intelligence of the railroad disaster was received, with Brently Mallard's name leading the list of "killed." He had only taken the time to assure himself of its truth by a second telegram, and had hastened to forestall any less careful, less tender friend in bearing the sad message.

She did not hear the story as many woman have heard the same, with a paralyzed inability to accept its significance. She wept at once, with sudden, wild abandonment, in her sister's arms. When the storm of grief had spent itself, she went away to her room alone. She would have no one follow her.

There stood, facing the open window, a comfortable, roomy armchair. Into this she sank, pressed down by a physical exhaustion that haunted her body and seemed to reach into her soul.

She could see in the open square before her house the tops of trees that were all aquiver with the new spring life. The delicious breath of rain was in the air. In the street below a peddler was crying his wares. The notes of a distant song which someone was singing reached her faintly, and countless sparrows were twittering in the eaves.

There were patches of blue sky showing here and there through the clouds that had met and piled one above the other in the west facing her window.

She sat with her head thrown back upon the cushion of the chair, quite motionless except when a sob came up into her throat and shook her, as a child who has cried itself to sleep continues to sob in its dreams.

She was young, with a fair, calm face, whose lines bespoke repression and even a certain strength. But now there was a dull stare in her eyes, whose gaze was fixed away off yonder on one of those patches of blue sky. It was not a glance of reflection but rather indicated a suspension of intelligent thought.

There was something coming to her and she was waiting for it, fearfully. What was it? She did not know: it was too subtle and elusive to name. But she felt it, creeping out of the sky, reaching toward her through the sounds, the scents, the color that filled the air.

Now her bosom rose and fell tumultuously. She was beginning to recognize this thing that was approaching to possess her, and she was striving to beat it back with her will—as powerless as her two white slender hands would have been.

When she abandoned herself, a little whispered word escaped her slightly parted lips. She said it over and over under her breath: "free, free, free!" The vacant stare and the look of terror that had followed it went from her eyes. They stayed keen and bright. Her pulses beat fast, and the coursing blood warmed and relaxed every inch of her body.

She did not stop to ask if it were or were not a monstrous joy that held her. A clear and exalted perception enabled her to dismiss the suggestion as trivial.

She knew that she would weep again when she saw the kind, tender hands folded in death; the face that had never looked save with love upon her, fixed and gray and dead. But she saw beyond that bitter moment a long procession of years to come that would belong to her absolutely. And she opened and spread her arms out to them in welcome.

There would be no one to live for her during those coming years; she would live for herself. There would be no powerful will bending hers in that blind persistence with which men and women believe they have a right to impose a private will upon a fellow creature. A kind intention or a cruel intention made the act seem no less a crime as she looked upon it in that brief moment of illumination.

And yet she had loved him—sometimes. Often she had not. What did it matter! What could love, the unsolved mystery, count for in face of this possession of self-assertion which she suddenly recognized as the strongest impulse of her being!

"Free! Body and soul free!" she kept whispering.

Josephine was kneeling before the closed door with her lips to the keyhole, imploring for admission. "Louise, open the door! I beg; open the door—you will make yourself ill. What are you doing, Louise? For heaven's sake open the door."

"Go away. I am not making myself ill." No; she was drinking in a very elixir of life through that open window.

Her fancy was running riot along those days ahead of her. Spring days, and summer days, and all sorts of days that would be her own. She breathed a quick prayer that life might be long. It was only yesterday she had thought with a shudder that life might be long.

She arose at length and opened the door to her sister's importunities. There was a feverish triumph in her eyes, and she carried herself unwittingly like a goddess of Victory. She clasped her sister's waist, and together they descended the stairs. Richards stood waiting for them at the bottom.

Someone was opening the front door with a latchkey. It was Brently Mallard who entered, a little travel-stained, composedly carrying his gripsack and umbrella. He had been far from the scene of the accident and did not know there had been one. He stood amazed at Josephine's piercing cry; at Richards's quick motion to screen him from the view of his wife.

But Richards was too late.

When the doctors came, they said she had died of heart disease—of joy that kills. 🍎

18 The news of Brently Mallard's death is the _____ of this story.

    A crisis

    B climax

    C inciting incident

    D falling action

19 As the realization that her husband is dead begins to sink in, something subtle and elusive is coming to Mrs. Mallard. What does *elusive* mean?

    A dull, uninteresting

    B quickly comprehended or understood

    C difficult to grasp

    D wrong-headed, false

20 At the end of page 15, Mrs. Mallard thinks to herself, "a kind intention or a cruel intention made the act seem no less a crime as she looked upon it in that brief moment of illumination." What act does she view as a "crime?"

    A the killing of her husband

    B the attempt by one person to control another

    C taking pleasure in the freedom made possible by her husband's death

    D her husband's love for her

PRETEST

21 Mrs. Mallard thinks, "What could love, the unsolved mystery, count for in face of this possession of self-assertion which she suddenly recognized as the strongest impulse of her being." What does this mean?

A Love is a mysterious force that cannot be comprehended.

B Love is the driving force of her life.

C Her love is overshadowed by her desire to assert herself.

D Her love is a changing, not a constant, emotion.

22 At the beginning of column 2 on page 16, the narrator says of Mrs. Mallard, "It was only yesterday she had thought with a shudder that life might be long." What was she thinking yesterday?

A that her heart condition would not cut her life short after all

B that her life would seem long because it loomed empty and meaningless

C that the prospect of living with a fatal illness was dreadful

D that life without her husband would be one long, lonely day after another

23 The doctors believe Mrs. Mallard to have died of "joy that kills" while the truth is really quite different. This mistake is an example of

A foreshadowing

B onomatopoeia

C parallelism

D irony

Open-Response Questions, Session 2

24 What is the central conflict in "The Story of an Hour"? Use details from the selection to describe the conflict. Be sure to tell whether it is an internal or an external conflict.

_____

_____

_____

_____

_____

_____

_____

_____

_____

_____

_____

_____

_____

_____

_____

_____

_____

_____

PRETEST

25 Reread paragraphs 5 and 6 of "The Story of an Hour," in which the author paints a word picture using images of spring. Identify at least four images in these lines. To which sense or senses does each image appeal?

_____

_____

_____

_____

_____

_____

_____

_____

_____

_____

_____

_____

_____

_____

_____

_____

_____

_____

Reading Selection #2, Session 2

DIRECTIONS

Read the following article about an ancient civilization. Then answer the questions that follow.

The Etruscans

by Sandrine Cantare

The Etruscans were an ancient people whose civilization flourished on the Italian peninsula about the eighth century B.C. At the height of its power, the Etruscan civilization covered an area from the Arno River to the Tiber, roughly equivalent to the modern Italian region of Tuscany. The ancient Roman civilization was greatly influenced by this earlier people, but we know surprisingly little about the Etruscans. These people became powerful and prosperous before disappearing almost completely from recorded history. Today they remain a mystery to those who would know about their culture and history.

Origins

From where did the Etruscans come? Even the ancient Greeks wondered about their origins. The Greek historian Herodotus, in the fifth century B.C., wrote that they came over the seas from Lydia in Asia Minor. Modern scholars echo Herodotus' theory, believing the Etruscans to be a people from the eastern Mediterranean who brought with them an ancient and well-developed culture. Because of the great difficulty in deciphering their language, however, the exact location of their original home and their reasons for migrating remain unknown.

Etruscan Civilization

The Etruscans built a powerful empire. At first they fortified themselves in independent city-states. These walled cities formed alliances, and their government evolved from a monarchy, or rule by kings, to an elective form of government. The government was conducted by oligarchies, or small councils of officials elected from the most wealthy and powerful families.

In the beginning, the Etruscans were primarily agrarian, meaning that they made most of their living by agriculture, but they were also powerful militarily and conquered surrounding peoples. These people they subjugated and forced to perform their agricultural labor. Supported by the labor of these conquered peoples, the Etruscans turned their time and attention to trade. It was by trade that the Etruscans built their wealth and spread their influence as far as northern Europe and Africa.

The Etruscans developed a sophisticated civilization. Their alphabet and their religion were based on Greek influences. They had a strong tradition of craftsmanship. Their art in painting and in sculpture was advanced and reflected their strong interest in the afterlife. They built elaborate necropolises, or cities of the dead, with streets and public squares. Their homes, built as they were of vulnerable materials like wood, have perished, but their tombs, built to survive the centuries, stand today. While the rest of the ancient world made sharp divisions between the spheres of activity of women and men, women in the Etruscan society enjoyed a remarkable degree of equality.

Their History

Ascension and Decline of Power. Sometime in the eighth century B.C., the Etruscans began to expand their area of influence through trade with the peoples of the Mediterranean. Etruscan merchants were as significant to the trade of the ancient world as the Greek and Phoenician traders. They reached all ports of the Mediterranean. Sometime in the middle of the sixth century B.C., the Etruscans reached the highest point of their military and commercial power, achieving control of the Tyrrhenian Sea. Etruscan traders also traveled over land, and to make trade and the movement of troops more efficient, they built many finely engineered roads. The Romans who followed them were also to conquer the known world in part by virtue of their roads.

Growth of Greek Colonies. By the next century, Etruscan power began to wane as Greek colonies in southern Italy became stronger. Greek forces from the city of Syracuse soundly defeated the Etruscan fleet in 474 B.C. at Cuma.

Emergence of Rome. A small village on the River Tiber was the home of the Romans, a Latin tribe that was greatly influenced in language, religion, and culture by the powerful neighboring Etruscan civilization. In the fifth century, the people of Rome asserted themselves militarily and gained independence.

Attacks by Land. In addition to being defeated at sea by the Greeks, the Etruscans were also attacked by land. Celts from the northern Alps invaded the Etrurian plain of the Po River. Local populations recaptured the Campania. The once flourishing power of the Etruscans dwindled until the original city-states existed as isolated pockets of the civilization, without the unifying structure that once bound them to each other and to their territories. One by one, the city-states were conquered by the growing dynamo that was Rome. The civilization of the Etruscans gradually disappeared into the civilization of Rome, which adopted many aspects of their culture.

A Whisper in History

Today, the Etruscans represent an intriguing mystery to scholars. Their written legacy is small, and because their language does not really fit into known language families, it has proved difficult to translate. Much of their life is available to us only as it can be deduced from the rare remnants of art, architecture, and implements that survive them. The most intriguing aspect of their story may be that, though they once dominated a significant portion of the ancient world, the Etruscans occupy a far smaller space in our consciousness than many another ancient civilization. 🍎

PRETEST

26 What is this article mostly about?

   A the origins of Roman civilization

   B society in ancient times

   C an ancient civilization that flourished and disappeared

   D Etruscan art and language

27 Which of the following lessons does the article as a whole teach us?

   A A society will have very little influence if its language is not understood by its neighbors.

   B Even the richest and most powerful civilizations can fade from the Earth.

   C To prosper, you must build a good system of roads.

   D The best way for a people to achieve a prominent place in history is to build lasting tombs.

28 To what modern Italian region was the area of the Etruscan civilization equivalent?

   A Rome

   B Liguria

   C Lydia

   D Tuscany

Detail of an Etruscan statue of a she-wolf, from the Museo Capitalino in Rome. The ancient Romans believed that Rome was founded by two boys, Romulus and Remus, who were abandoned in the woods and raised by a she-wolf. A Roman sculptor took this ancient Etruscan statue of a wolf and added to it smaller statues of two boys. Thus the statue became a symbol of the Roman appropriation of Etruscan culture.

29 The Etruscan alphabet was based on that of

    A Asia Minor

    B the Celts

    C the French

    D the Greeks

30 Which of the following is NOT true of the Etruscan civilization?

    A Women were repressed more than in other ancient cultures.

    B The civilization declined as the power of Rome grew.

    C Little from the Etruscan culture remains today to tell us what it was like.

    D One factor that gave the Etruscan civilization its strength was the unity of its city-states under an oligarchical government.

31 Which of the following can be inferred from the article about the Etruscans?

    A They believed that they would pass into oblivion after death.

    B They had a powerful fleet of ships as well as good roads.

    C Their language is closely related to Latin.

    D Rome attacked the Etruscan city-states at the height of Etruscan power.

Etruscan writing

Etruscan vase

32 In what ways were the Etruscans a powerful, sophisticated, and influential people? Use details from the article as evidence.

_____

_____

_____

_____

_____

_____

_____

_____

_____

_____

_____

_____

_____

_____

_____

_____

_____

_____

_____

_____

STOP ⬤

PRETEST

Reading Selection #1, Session 3

DIRECTIONS

Read the excerpt from the essay "Remarks Concerning the Natives of North America" and the poem "Boast Not, Proud English." Then answer the questions that follow.

from

Remarks Concerning the Natives of North America

by Benjamin Franklin

The Indian men, when young, are hunters and warriors; when old, counselors; for all their government is by counsel of the sages. There is no force. There are no prisons, no officers to compel obedience or inflict punishment. Hence they generally study oratory, the best speaker having the most influence. The Indian women till the ground, dress the food, nurse and bring up the children, and preserve and hand down to posterity the memory of public transactions. These employments of men and women are accounted natural and honorable. Having few artificial wants, they have abundance of leisure for improvement by conversation. Our laborious manner of life, compared with theirs, they esteem slavish and base, and the learning on which we value ourselves they regard as frivolous and useless.

An instance of this occurred at the Treaty of Lancaster, in Pennsylvania, *anno* 1744, between the government of Virginia and the Six Nations [of the Iroquois Confederacy]. After the principal business was settled, the commissioners from Virginia acquainted the Indians by a speech that there was at Williamsburg a college with a fund for educating Indian youth, and that, if the Six Nations would send down half a dozen of their young lads to that college, the government would take care that they should be well provided for and instructed in all the learning of the white people.

It is one of the Indian rules of politeness not to answer a public proposition the same day that it is made. They think it would be treating it as a light matter and that they show it respect by taking time to consider it, as of a matter important. They therefore deferred their answer till the day following;

when their speaker began, by expressing their deep sense of the kindness of the Virginia government in making them that offer:

"For we know," says he, "that you highly esteem the kind of learning taught in those Colleges, and that the maintenance of our young men, while with you, would be very expensive to you. We are convinced, therefore, that you mean to do us good by your proposal, and we thank you heartily. But you, who are wise, must know that different nations have different conceptions of things; and you will therefore not take it amiss if our ideas of this kind of education happen not to be the same with yours. We have had some experience of it. Several of our young people were formerly brought up at the colleges of the northern provinces. They were instructed in all your sciences, but when they came back to us, they were bad runners, ignorant of every means of living in the woods, unable to bear either cold or hunger, knew neither how to build a cabin, take a deer, or kill an enemy, spoke our language imperfectly, were therefore neither fit for hunters, warriors, nor counselors. They were totally good for nothing. We are, however, not the less obliged by your kind offer, though we decline accepting it. And to show our grateful sense of it, if the gentlemen of Virginia will send us a dozen of their sons, we will take great care of their education, instruct them in all we know, and make men of them." 🍎

The Iroquois False Face Society was a healing group that used grotesque wooden masks to frighten evil spirits believed to cause illness.

Reading Selection #2, Session 3

Boast Not, Proud English
by Roger Williams

[Editor's Note: Roger Williams (1603(?)–1683) was an English Puritan clergyman who emigrated to the Americas in 1631. Williams soon ran afoul of authorities in Massachusetts because of his support for religious freedom and his insistence that colonists could not simply take land from Native Americans but were required to purchase it. Most famous as the founder of Rhode Island and the Providence Plantations, Williams is also known for his pioneering work as a student of Native American language.]

Boast not, proud English, of thy birth and blood:
    Thy brother Indian is by birth as good.
Of one blood God made him, and thee, and all.
    As wise, as fair, as strong, as personal.
By nature, wrath's his portion, thine, no more
    Till Grace his soul and thine in Christ restore.
Make sure thy second birth, or thou shalt see
    Heaven ope[1] to Indians wild, but shut to thee. 🍎

---

[1] **ope.** Open

PRETEST

33 According to Franklin's essay, the commissioners from Virginia offered to

    A educate some Iroquois youth at a college in Williamsburg

    B buy some land belonging to the Iroquois

    C send their youth to be educated among the Iroquois

    D join the Iroquois in a war against the French

34 To illustrate the theme that different peoples have different customs and are no better or worse than other peoples, Franklin

    A recites a narrative poem

    B shares an anecdote

    C writes a speech

    D relates a legend

35 The Iroquois spokesperson demonstrates the absurdity and pompousness of the Virginians' offer by

    A getting angry and pointing out the prejudice implied by the offer

    B refusing to respond immediately to the offer

    C making the same offer to the Virginians that they made to the Iroquois

    D laughing at the Virginians

36 The commissioners from Virginia believed their educational system to be superior. Therefore, the reply the Iroquois make to their offer is

    A metaphorical

    B fanciful

    C allegorical

    D ironic

37 According to Franklin, the Native Americans consider the colonists' manner of life

A admirable and worthy of imitation

B slavish and base

C interesting, but not for them

D comical

38 The poem "Boast Not, Proud English" is addressed to

A Native Americans

B English people who think that they are better than the Native Americans

C English people who consider the Native Americans their brothers

D students of Native American languages

39 The repetition of *b* sounds in *birth*, *blood*, and *brother* is an example of

A onomatopoeia

B simile

C alliteration

D rhythm

40 According to the speaker of Williams's poem, if the English person is not reborn, then he will find that heaven is

A open to him but closed to Native Americans

B closed to him but open to Native Americans

C closed to all

D open to all

41 With which statement would the speaker of "Boast Not, Proud English" agree?

A English people are better than Native Americans.

B Native Americans are better than English people.

C English people are no better and no worse than Native Americans.

D English people can go to heaven, but Native American people cannot.

Open-Response Questions, Session 3

42 According to Franklin, what were the roles of men and women among the Native Americans? How did both the men and the women spend their leisure time?

_____

_____

_____

_____

_____

_____

_____

_____

_____

_____

_____

_____

_____

_____

_____

_____

_____

_____

_____

43 Many early European settlers of the Americas thought themselves superior to the Native Americans. What did Franklin and Williams think of such attitudes? Compare their positions, using details from both selections to support your answer.

_____

_____

_____

_____

_____

_____

_____

_____

_____

_____

_____

_____

_____

_____

_____

_____

_____

_____

_____

_____

DIRECTIONS

Read the following article about developments in the science of genetics. Then answer the questions that follow.

Well Hello, Dolly

by Andrea Azaria

In July 1996, the first successful birth of a cloned mammal, a sheep named Dolly, took place at the Roslin Institute in Edinburgh, Scotland. In the spring of 1998, Dolly, who was named after the country singer Dolly Parton, gave birth to a lamb named Bonnie, who was conceived the old-fashioned way. A year later, she gave birth to triplets—two male lambs and one female—also from the same father as Bonnie.

Cloning, a process that creates an identical copy of a creature, one with the same genes, had previously been done with plants and with such lower animals as frogs but was believed to be impossible with higher animals such as mammals. Mammals, such as sheep, pigs, monkeys, and human beings, bear live offspring and produce milk to feed their young. Previous attempts to clone mammals had been completely unsuccessful, but Ian Wilmut of the Roslin Institute succeeded in cloning the sheep. Wilmut took a cell nucleus from

the udder of an adult Finn Dorset sheep and inserted it into the egg of a Poll Dorset sheep. He then placed the egg into the womb of a Scottish Blackface sheep. Five months later, the Scottish Blackface gave birth to Dolly, a lamb that was a genetically identical copy of the original Finn Dorset.

Scientists around the world heralded Wilmut's accomplishment as a great step forward in the science of genetics, which studies how traits of animals and plants are passed down from generation to generation. Geneticist Ian McKinnagh called Wilmut's achievement, "Just breathtaking. Absolutely astonishing."

Political reaction to this development has been mixed, however. The cloning of Dolly raises fears that scientists might attempt to clone human beings, making identical copies of living adults. Governments around the world are struggling with how to regulate this procedure with its vast and largely unknown ramifications.

Although Dolly was born healthy and has given birth to healthy offspring, concerns have been raised about the long-term consequences for cloned organisms. Recent studies have shown that Dolly's cells appear to be the same age as those of the older sheep from which she was created. In that case, the implications regarding the aging process in cloned animals could be frightening.

While fear of cloning humans raises the prospect of armies of identical super soldiers fighting for some terrorist regime, scientists point to potential benefits of the new technology. Cloning sheep, pigs, cows, and other mammals could produce herds of identical, high-quality livestock. Another possibility is that by combining cloning with another technology known as recombinant DNA, scientists might be able to create copies of animals to produce organs for transplant, such as hearts and livers, or to yield vital drugs based on animal products, such as human growth hormone, insulin, and interferon, for the treatment of disease.

While debate rages over the uses and abuses of cloning, research into and experimentation with cloning continue unabated. Only time will tell what new doors will be opened in the twenty-first century. 🍎

44 What is the name of the scientist who first successfully cloned a mammal?

A Wilmut

B Parton

C Roslin

D McKinnagh

45 What is the branch of science that studies how characteristics of plants and animals are passed on from generation to generation?

A heredity

B genetics

C cloning

D recombinant DNA

46 Which of the following statements is true?

A The first organism ever to be cloned was a sheep.

B Dolly was an identical copy of the Scottish Blackface sheep that gave birth to her.

C The Roslin Institute is located in Edinburgh, Scotland.

D Dolly has given birth to four cloned lambs.

47 Which of the following conclusions can be inferred from the article?

   A Government safeguards will prevent unscrupulous scientists from using the technology of cloning for selfish or evil purposes.

   B All three sheep involved in Dolly's cloning were females.

   C All scientists favor further experimentation with cloning.

   D The cloning of human beings will be a reality within ten years.

48 Apart from ethical considerations, what concerns about cloning have been raised as a result of Dolly's creation?

   A Dolly was born with birth defects, leading to the fear that there might be a high percentage of birth defects in cloned animals.

   B Dolly's cells appear to be older than those of a normal sheep her age, suggesting that there are many unknowns regarding the aging process in cloned animals.

   C Dolly has been unable to conceive normally, raising questions about the reproductive fitness of cloned animals.

   D Dolly is unusually prone to infection, raising concerns that cloning results in a weakened immune system.

49 All of the following were mentioned in the article as possible positive spin-offs of cloning technology EXCEPT

   A producing herds of high-quality livestock

   B creating copies of animals with organs suitable for transplant

   C getting drugs such as insulin from cloned animals

   D creating clones of people who are highly intelligent

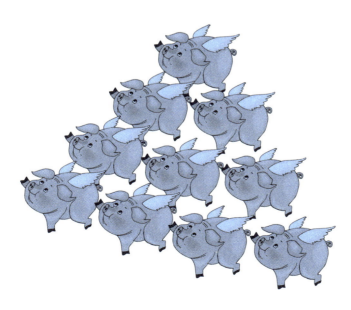

Open-Response Question, Session 3

50 Do you think that experimentation with cloning should be encouraged or discouraged? Use information from the article to support your opinion.

STOP

PRETEST

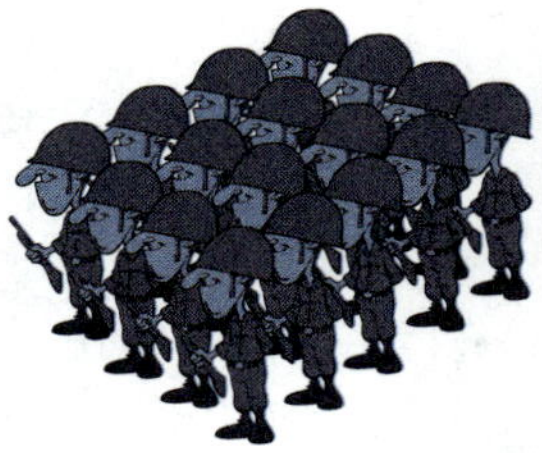

Composition

DIRECTIONS

You may use a dictionary during the Composition portion of the exam.

Session 1: You will have forty-five minutes for this session. During this session, you should

- plan what you are going to write (make notes, or make an outline or web)
- write a first draft on two pages of lined paper

If you have not finished your rough draft by the end of Session 1, you should be close to finishing. Most of your time during Session 2 should be spent revising your draft and producing your final composition.

Session 2: You will have another forty-five minutes for this session. During this time, you should make changes that improve your composition and then write your final composition on the pages provided in this book. When you correct your draft, remember the characteristics that the person who scores your test will be looking for in your composition (see below).

Scoring Guidelines

Your composition will be given two scores. The first score will be for your ideas and how well you organize and explain them. The second score will be for spelling, grammar, punctuation, and capitalization.

PLANNING PAGE

You may use this page to plan what you are going to write for your composition. You might wish to make notes, an outline, or a word web. Then write the first draft of your composition on two pages of lined paper. You will have about forty-five minutes for this session.

Writing Prompt

In this excerpt from a play about the overthrow of a weak and misbehaving king, the speaker is the king, Richard II. He has just been overthrown by his cousin, Bullingbrook.

After you read this speech, respond to the writing assignment that follows.

from
The Tragedy of Richard II
by William Shakespeare

 Let's talk of graves, of worms, and epitaphs[1],
Make dust our paper, and with rainy eyes
Write sorrow on the bosom of the earth.
Let's choose executors and talk of wills;
And yet not so, for what can we bequeath[2]
Save our deposéd[3] bodies to the ground?
Our lands, our lives, and all are Bullingbrook's,
And nothing can we call our own but death,
And that small model of the barren earth[4]
Which serves as paste[5] and cover to our bones.
For God's sake let us sit upon the ground
And tell sad stories of the death of kings:
How some have been depos'd, some slain in war,
Some haunted by the ghosts[6] they have deposed,
Some poisoned by their wives, some sleeping kill'd,
All murthered[7]—for within the hollow crown
That rounds[8] the mortal temples of a king

---

[1] **epitaphs.** Inscriptions on gravestones
[2] **bequeath.** Leave after death
[3] **deposéd.** Removed from power, especially from the throne
[4] **model . . . earth.** Clay figure
[5] **paste.** Pie crust
[6] **ghosts.** Ghosts of kings
[7] **murthered.** Murdered
[8] **rounds.** Encircles

Keeps Death his court, and there the antic[9] sits,
Scoffing his state and grinning at his pomp,
Allowing him a breath, a little scene,
To monarchize,[10] be fear'd, and kill with looks,
Infusing him with self[11] and vain conceit,
As if this flesh which walls about our life
Were brass impregnable[12]; and humor'd[13] thus,
Comes at the last and with a little pin
Bores thorough[14] his castle wall,[15] and farewell king!
Cover your heads, and mock not flesh and blood
With solemn reverence, throw away respect,
Tradition, form, and ceremonious duty,
For you have but mistook[16] me all this while.
I live with bread like you, feel want,
Taste grief, need friends: subjected[17] thus,
How can you say to me I am a king? 🍎

---

[9] **antic.** Jester
[10] **monarchize.** Act as king
[11] **self.** Ideas of his own importance
[12] **impregnable.** Safe from entry by force
[13] **humor'd.** Entertained
[14] **thorough.** Through
[15] **castle wall.** The king's flesh
[16] **mistook me.** Failed to see the truth about me
[17] **subjected.** Made a subject (to human needs)

Writing Assignment: What is the theme of this selection? In your response, explain how metaphor, personification, and irony are used to reinforce this theme.

Now write an essay in response to this question on two pages of your own lined paper.

Session 2

In this session, you have another forty-five minutes to change and correct the draft of the composition you wrote in Session 1 and to write the final copy of your composition. Use proofreading marks to make corrections to your draft. Keep in mind the guidelines that the person who scores your test will be looking for (see page 39). Write your final composition on the lines below and on the following pages.

_____

_____

_____

_____

_____

_____

_____

_____

_____

_____

_____

_____

_____

STOP ⬣

LESSONS

LESSON 2.1 *Understanding Standardized Tests*

During World War II, the people who ran the United States armed services had a problem. They needed to figure out which of their new soldiers would make the best officers. They could easily tell, from what they were doing in basic training, which young men and women were the strongest, which were the best at taking orders, which could hold up under pressure, and so on. However, they needed to know more. In particular, they needed to know which soldiers were most able to learn and to think clearly.

In response to this need, they created the first standardized tests taken by large numbers of Americans. A **standardized test** is one that is given to lots of people to compare their abilities or to compare what they have learned.[1] Such tests are commonplace in the modern world.

___
[1] Technically, a standardized test is one that has been developed using sophisticated statistical methods to establish norms for responses to the test questions; however, in popular usage, the term refers to any widely used exam of set format. Exams such as MCAS English, which measure achievement relative to fixed standards or criteria, are technically known as **criterion-referenced examinations**.

Kinds of Standardized Tests

Standardized tests come in two varieties: aptitude tests and achievement tests.

An **aptitude test** tells what general abilities a person has. It is not supposed to measure particular knowledge that a person has gained. Instead, it tells how capable someone is of learning. For example, an aptitude test for becoming a typist might measure whether you can read and how quickly and carefully you can move your fingers—two basic skills that typists have to have. Someone who could move his or her fingers very quickly and carefully might have a lot of aptitude, or general ability, for learning how to type. IQ tests are one kind of aptitude test. They are supposed to measure a person's **general intelligence**— how carefully, clearly, and quickly he or she can think.

UNDERSTANDING THE MCAS ENGLISH EXAM

An **achievement test** tells what someone has already learned in some area. For example, after studying typing for a year, you might then take an achievement test to find out how fast you can type. The **Massachusetts Comprehensive Assessment System (MCAS) English exam** is an achievement test that measures what you have learned about reading and writing in English. If you work hard and do the lessons in this book, you should have no problem succeeding at this test. An achievement test measures what you have learned. If you apply yourself and have a positive attitude, you are bound to learn enough to pass the test with flying colors.

Why Are Standardized Tests Important?

Throughout your life you will take many standardized tests. You already know that you must take the MCAS exams in high school. If you plan to go to college, you will most likely take the **Scholastic Aptitude Test (SAT)** or the **American College Testing (ACT) Assessment Test,** which many colleges require of students applying for admission. Specialized schools, such as schools of nursing, may require applicants to show aptitude for the field of study by performing well on standardized tests.

If you plan, instead, to take a job immediately after high school, you will find standardized tests in the world of work too. For example, if you want to sell real estate, to do electrical work or plumbing, or to repair or install computers and computer networks, you will have to take standardized tests to become licensed or certified to do these jobs. Many states now require automobile mechanics to take achievement tests.

Professionals, such as accountants, therapists, medical assistants, doctors, pharmacists, and lawyers, have to pass standardized tests before they are allowed to practice.

For those who want to find out what kind of work they might enjoy and do well in, standardized tests are available that match ability and interest with the skills and environments of suitable occupations. Even dating services sometimes use standardized tests to match people!

The ability to take tests well is a skill that can be learned. Learning this skill can help you throughout your life, making it easier for you to fulfill your dreams. Studying the lessons in this book will help you to do well not only on the MCAS English exam and but also on the other tests you will come across in your life.

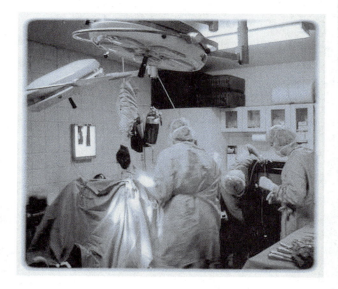

To work in many fields, one must first become licensed or certified. Doing so usually involves passing a standardized examination in the field. Automotive repair, computer network administration, electronics, law, medicine, and teaching are just a few of the career fields with standardized tests as entry requirements. All lawyers, for example, must pass a standardized test called a bar exam. Some states require prospective teachers to pass a standardized teacher certification exam.

Overcoming Test Anxiety

Anxiety is a feeling of uneasiness or worry about something that might happen in the future. We naturally feel anxious when we are confronted by new challenges or unknown situations. A little bit of anxiety can be a good thing. It can help to focus our attention, to make us alert and ready to act. Too much anxiety, however, can be extremely negative. Anxiety can keep us from performing as well as we usually do. One of the reasons that people feel anxiety is fear of failure. If we are worried about performing, we may get in our own way and forget how to do the tasks we need to perform.

Many people feel anxious when called upon to perform in front of an audience—to give a speech, perform in a play, or play in a game with spectators watching. Some people also feel anxious about performing on tests. Nervousness, shaking, inability to concentrate, negative thoughts, and an inability to remember known facts are signs of this kind of anxiety. Unfortunately, anxiety can cause people to do badly on tests. Fortunately, there are ways to deal with anxiety. Combat your test anxiety by taking the steps described in the chart below and on the next page.

Combating Test Anxiety: Strategies That Work

Follow these strategies to overcome anxiety about taking standardized tests:

1. **Prepare.** The most important thing you can do to combat anxiety is to be prepared for the test. If you are prepared, you will do well on the test, and therefore you have nothing to fear. The best way to prepare is to do the lessons in this book. If you do these lessons, you will know what to expect on the test.

2. **Practice.** This book teaches many skills that will help you to succeed on standardized tests in reading and writing, but no book can give you all the practice that you need. Begin now to practice your writing skills by writing something every day. Keeping a journal is one way to practice writing. Write a few sentences, or better, a paragraph every day. The following are some suggested topics for your journal writing:

   - One of the day's events
   - Your feelings or opinion on some controversial issue
   - Topics that you are studying in other classes
   - Something you really enjoy doing
   - A short review of a story, movie, TV show, computer game, book, or CD

- Your reactions to an event in the news
- Your plans for the weekend
- Your hopes and dreams for the future

In addition, you should begin now to practice your reading every day. Magazines and newspapers are a good place to start. Read one or two pieces from magazines or newspapers every day. Keep a list in your journal of new vocabulary words that you run across in your reading. Also write in your journal your responses to what you have read.

3. **Think Positively.** Negative thoughts can cause people to fail, but positive thoughts can cause them to succeed. Researchers who study test-taking have found that when students believe that they will do well, their scores go up! If you start to have negative thoughts about yourself, remember something positive about you. Think, "I am doing what I can to prepare myself for this test." Remind yourself of times when you have succeeded at difficult tasks.

   Set aside a "worry time." Allow yourself fifteen minutes a day for worrying. During that time, let yourself worry about whatever you want. If you start to worry during the rest of the day, tell yourself, "This is not my time to worry. I can worry about this at 7:15," or whatever your time is.

4. **Sleep and Eat Well Before the Test.** Get plenty of sleep the night before the test. Eat nutritious meals the night and morning before the test. Don't skip breakfast. Resting and eating well will help you be in peak condition during the exam.

5. **Don't Be Thrown by Something You Don't Understand.** Remember, no one is expected to get a perfect score, and there will be a few items on every test that most people will not understand. When you come across something that you don't understand, remain calm, reread that part of the test carefully, and try to figure out what is being said. Use the strategies described in this book to make your best guess. Then go on to items that you do understand.

6. **Practice Relaxation Techniques.** Some people are helped by such techniques as breathing slowly and deeply or by closing their eyes and imagining pleasant, quiet scenes.

Your Turn

A   Answer the following questions about Lesson 2.1.

1   Standardized tests were first given to large numbers of Americans by

     A   colleges and universities

     B   the Peace Corps

     C   accountants, doctors, and lawyers

     D   the armed services

2   A test that measures a person's ability to learn to type is an example of an

     A   aptitude test

     B   achievement test

     C   oral examination

     D   IQ test

3   A test given at the end of a typing class to measure how much a person has learned is an example of an

     A   aptitude test

     B   achievement test

     C   oral examination

     D   IQ test

4   A standardized test that people might take if they plan to apply to an undergraduate college program is the

     A   Graduate Record Examination (GRE)

     B   Bar Exam

     C   Scholastic Aptitude Test (SAT)

     D   Graduate Management Admissions Test (GMAT)

5   Anxiety is

     A   a feeling of uneasiness or worry about something that might happen in the future

     B   anger about having to do something that one doesn't want to do

     C   fear of physical harm

     D   a feeling of confidence

6   The most valuable thing that a person can do to combat test anxiety is

     A   not to think about the test

     B   to prepare well for the test

     C   to take the test at another time

     D   to ignore the parts of the test that are confusing

B   No two people are exactly the same. Every person has special, unique abilities. Number a sheet of paper from 1 to 4. Then, list four things that you do well—four aptitudes that you have. Next, think about the aptitudes that you have listed. Given these, what sort of job or career do you think might be best for you in later life? On your own paper, write a paragraph explaining what job or career you think you might be good at and why.

C   What will you do to prepare yourself to take the MCAS English exam? Write a plan that includes supporting details from this lesson.

D   Standardized tests are quite controversial. Do some research and hold a debate, in class, on the pros and cons of standardized testing.

LESSON 2.2 MCAS English: The Elements of the Exam

All tenth-graders in Massachusetts are required to take a test of English language skills: the **Massachusetts Comprehensive Assessment System English exam.** This test, commonly referred to as **MCAS English,** is a criterion-referenced achievement examination.[1]

Purpose of the Exam

This exam measures the ability of Massachusetts students in reading and writing. It is used to measure the achievement of individual students, schools, and school districts. Graduation depends, in part, on how well the individual student performs on the exam. The exam also allows teachers to see how well their schools are meeting the reading and writing goals of the commonwealth, as described in the Massachusetts Curriculum Framework developed by the Massachusetts Department of Education.

Format of the Exam

The Language and Literature component of the MCAS English exam presents short articles, stories, or other selections called **passages.** After you read each passage, you answer questions about its contents.

There are two kinds of questions on this part of the exam. Each of the **multiple-choice questions** asks something about the selection and offers four possible answers. From these choices, you must pick the one that BEST answers the question. The **open-response questions** on the exam ask for written responses.

Format of the Composition Sessions

The Composition component of the exam requires students to respond to a writing prompt. The Composition exam is divided into two forty-five-minute sessions separated by a break. In these sessions, you will be asked to write about some literary work or works. In the first session, you will plan your response and write your first draft. After the break, you will read over your answer and revise it for conformity and completeness—how well it meets the requirements of the task—and for correct use of standard English writing conventions—grammar, usage, spelling, punctuation, and capitalization. You will have at least one dictionary in the classroom to help you correct your work. You will then write out your final answer.

Your Turn

Imagine that you are a school administrator. Write a letter to be sent to parents or guardians. The letter should announce that tenth-grade students will be taking the MCAS English exam. It should also explain the purpose and format of the examination.

---

[1] **criterion . . . examination.** See footnote, page 47.

LESSON 2.3 *General Strategies: Multiple-Choice Questions*

Many of the questions you will encounter on the MCAS English exam will be in the multiple-choice format. This lesson will teach you the general skills you will need to answer such questions confidently.

A multiple-choice question consists of three parts: a **direction line,** which tells you what to do; a **leader line,** which may be a question to answer or a sentence to complete; and several answers. On the MCAS English test, you are given four answers from which to choose. Your job is to pick the BEST answer from those provided.

The chart below shows some typical multiple-choice formats.

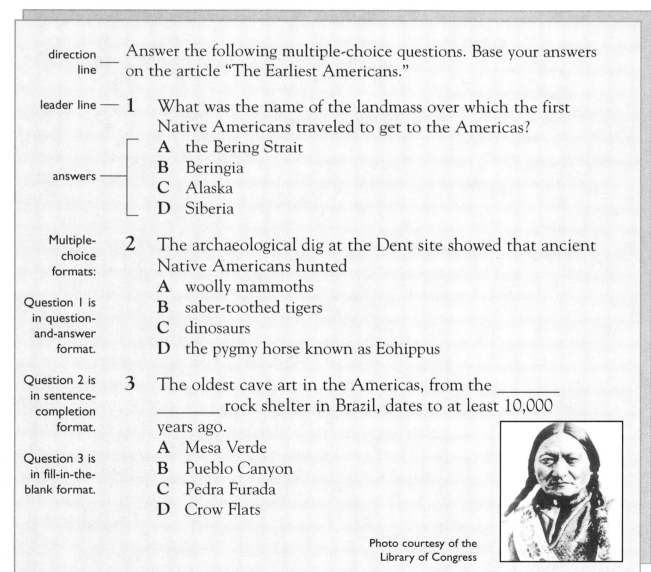

direction line — Answer the following multiple-choice questions. Base your answers on the article "The Earliest Americans."

leader line — **1** What was the name of the landmass over which the first Native Americans traveled to get to the Americas?

answers —
    A the Bering Strait
    B Beringia
    C Alaska
    D Siberia

Multiple-choice formats:

2 The archaeological dig at the Dent site showed that ancient Native Americans hunted
    A woolly mammoths
    B saber-toothed tigers
    C dinosaurs
    D the pygmy horse known as Eohippus

Question 1 is in question-and-answer format.

Question 2 is in sentence-completion format.

3 The oldest cave art in the Americas, from the _____ _____ rock shelter in Brazil, dates to at least 10,000 years ago.
    A Mesa Verde
    B Pueblo Canyon
    C Pedra Furada
    D Crow Flats

Question 3 is in fill-in-the-blank format.

Photo courtesy of the Library of Congress

Winning Strategies
for Multiple-Choice Questions

When answering multiple-choice questions, keep the following tips in mind:

- If you do not immediately know the answer to a question, go on to the other questions and come back later to the one you cannot answer. Answering the other questions might provide a clue to the answer or help to jog your memory.

- Before looking at the answers, decide what *you* think the answer is. Then see if your answer is among the possible responses.

- Eliminate obviously wrong answers first. Then choose the one that seems most likely from the answers that remain.

- Even if you are not sure of an answer, always make your best guess. There is no additional penalty on the MCAS English exam for wrong answers, and if you guess, there is at least a 1-in-4, or 25 percent, chance of choosing the correct answer.

  If you eliminate one wrong answer and then guess, your chances of choosing the correct answer are 1 in 3, or 33 percent.

  If you eliminate two wrong answers and then guess, your chances of choosing the correct answer are 1 in 2, or 50 percent.

  If you eliminate three wrong answers, then the remaining answer has to be the correct one!

- Remember that on multiple-choice tests, you are supposed to choose the BEST answer to the question. If one answer is partly right, look for another that is completely right.

- If the multiple-choice question is a sentence completion or fill-in-the-blank type, then check your answer by reading the whole sentence, with the answer in it, silently to yourself. (Example: "The archaeological dig at the Dent site showed that early Native Americans hunted woolly mammoths.")

- Pay particular attention to negative words in leader lines, such as NOT or EXCEPT. (Example: "Which of the following was NOT a signer of the United States Declaration of Independence?")

- Also pay attention to any words or phrases that tell how many, such as *all*, *many*, *most*, *some*, *none*, or *a few*. (Example: "According to the speaker, *all* Americans really enjoy . . .")

Your Turn

A   Read the article "The Birth of the Net" below. Then answer the multiple-choice questions that follow.

"The Birth of the Net"
from The Complete Student's Guide to the Internet
by Allyson Stanford

The Internet is a vast system of computers, scattered around the world, that are connected to one another in a single, gigantic network. Another name for the Internet, given to it by Al Gore, is the information superhighway. Computers can be hooked up to the Internet by means of ordinary telephone lines, by cables like those used for cable television, or by wireless connections, which make use of signals that travel through the air.

Almost any computer can be connected to the Internet, from the large mainframe computers and powerful workstations used by universities and corporations to the small personal computers and laptops used by individuals. Most people connect to the Internet from personal computers, using ordinary telephone lines and special pieces of hardware known as modems.

The Internet began as a special network created by the United States government to connect researchers and officials working on projects for the Department of Defense. In 1955, President Dwight D. Eisenhower created the Advanced Research Projects Agency, also known as ARPA, to fund and coordinate defense-related scientific projects in the United States. In 1969, the Advanced Research Projects Agency created a network known as the ARPANet to connect computers at the defense department to computers at research centers and universities around the country. The ARPANet used high-speed transmission lines to connect computers at the University of California at Los Angeles, the Stanford Research Institute, the University of California at Santa Barbara, and the University of Utah in Salt Lake City. In the years that followed, the ARPANet merged with other networks used to connect the Department of Defense with laboratories around the world, such as the European Center for Nuclear Research, Lawrence Livermore Laboratories, the Argon National Laboratory, and Los Alamos. This early version of the Internet was

used almost exclusively by scientists—physicists and rocket scientists, for example—to exchange information related to defense projects such as building and testing new missiles.

The early Internet was almost completely text based. In other words, those scientists could use it to send words and numbers but not sounds, pictures, video, and the like. By the early 1980s, people were starting to use the term *Internet* to describe the system of connected defense and research computers.

What makes the Internet different from previous networks is that every computer on the Internet is connected to every other computer instead of being connected to one gigantic computer at a central location. The Department of Defense gave the Internet this kind of peer-to-peer organization in response to worries about what might happen to a centralized supercomputer in the case of a nuclear war. In such a war, if the enemy bombed the central computer, then the whole system would go down. By using a peer-to-peer organization, the Department of Defense made sure that, even if some computers and their connections were destroyed, the others would still be able to send and receive messages. So, the Internet, with its ability to store, serve, send, and receive messages using any computer on the network, was an outgrowth of the Cold War.

The most important event in the history of the Internet occurred in 1979. In that year, Dr. Tim Berners-Lee of the European Center for Nuclear Research, also known as CERN, came up with the idea for the World Wide Web, which is one part of the Internet. The basic idea for the Web is simple. People create pages and store these on special computers known as servers. Each server and each page has its own unique address on the network. When a person creates a page for the World Wide Web, that page can contain links to any other page stored elsewhere in the world on a computer connected to the Internet. In other words, the World Wide Web is a system of pages stored on computers around the world that are connected to each other by links. By using a mouse to click on a link, one can instantly go to a page stored on a computer across the state, the country, or the world.

The wonderful thing about the World Wide Web is that pages can contain not only text but also sound, pictures, and movies. Anyone with a computer hooked up to the Internet can create a World Wide Web page and link it to other pages.

Because of Tim Berners-Lee's creation of the World Wide Web, the Internet has grown tremendously in the past few years. What started out to be a network for connecting a few scientists is now the Internet, connecting more than 100 million users worldwide. By the year 2000, the number of people connected to the Internet is expected to grow to over 300 million. Soon the entire world will be connected, and when that happens, the differences between the haves and the have-nots will dwindle.

The Internet has grown so rapidly because people can use it for so many different purposes. They can go onto the World Wide Web to do research; to shop; to pay bills; to send electronic mail, or e-mail; to talk to other people in electronic chat rooms; to catch up on the latest news; or just to entertain themselves. Whatever people are interested in—sports, books, music, movies, clothes, politics, just about anything—can be found today on the part of the Internet known as the World Wide Web.

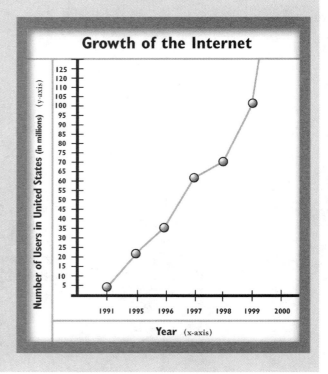

Now answer the following questions.

1 The Internet is a

   A large system of interconnected computers that spans the globe

   B system of telephone lines and modems

   C very fast television

   D service that sells connection time to computer users

2 Why was the Internet given a peer-to-peer structure instead of a centralized structure?

   A Designers wanted to be able to control it from a central location.

   B Designers wanted to create a single supercomputer.

   C Designers wanted to make sure the Internet could survive nuclear bombing.

   D Designers were worried that nonscientists might use the system.

3 Which of the following statements is true?

   A The main purpose of the ARPANet was to connect scientific researchers.

   B The most important thing the ARPANet did was enable people to shop online.

   C The best application of the ARPANet was replacing television with online movies.

   D The main purpose of the ARPANet was to warn ordinary Americans about missile attacks.

4 One use of the World Wide Web that is NOT mentioned in the article is

   A shopping

   B paying bills

   C videoconferencing

   D sending electronic mail

5 According to the article, why has the Internet grown so rapidly?

   A because so many people can use it for so many different purposes

   B because every computer is connected to every other computer

   C because it is text based

   D because World Wide Web pages have largely replaced movies and television

6 Most people connect to the Internet using _____ and telephone lines.

   A typewriters

   B telephones

   C modems

   D workstations

B Use the multiple-choice questions above to follow the directions below.

1 Find one example of a question-and-answer-type question, one sentence-completion-type question, and one fill-in-the-blank-type question.

2 Find one example of a question that contains an obviously wrong answer. How does identifying this answer as obviously wrong improve your chances of guessing the correct answer?

3 Find one example of an answer that is partly right. Why is another one of the answers better?

4 Find one example of a question that contains the word *most* (a word that tells how many). How would the answer to the question be different if the word *most* were changed to *some*?

5 Find a question that contains the negative word NOT. How does the use of this word affect the answer to the question?

C Write six multiple-choice questions based on the article "The Birth of the Net." Write two of the question-and-answer-type questions, two of the sentence-completion type, and two of the fill-in-the-blank type.

D Work with other students in a small group to write a multiple-choice test about a story, poem, or play that you have read in class, or write some multiple-choice questions about the selection given below. Exchange tests with another group. Take the tests. Then, meet with the other group to discuss the test questions. Explain which questions were well written, which were too easy, which were tricky, and so on. Use what you have learned in this lesson to critique the test created by the other group.

"Our Place on the Planet: Biodiversity and Human Ends" by Héctor A. Sánchez

The world teems with life—with billions of creatures, great and small. From viruses far tinier than the point of a pin to giant sequoias over 300 feet tall, life appears in an amazing variety of forms. To date, scientists have identified over 1,400,000 different species of plants, animals, fungi, and micro-organisms. The actual number of species, however, is probably far greater. Harvard biologist E. O. Wilson estimates that the total number of different species on the Earth today might run as high as 100 million, or 71.4 times the number known to science. As Wilson points out, one can pick any tree at random in the Brazilian rain forest, shake it, and a number of new species, never before seen by a human being, will fall to the ground. In 1939,

Life comes in an amazing variety of forms.

fishermen near the Comoro Islands off the coast of Africa pulled up in their nets a Coelacanth—a fish previously believed to have been extinct for over 300 million years. A teaspoonful of dirt contains some 30 billion bacteria, most representing species as yet unknown to science. The world is full of a remarkable variety of life forms—insects that live buried in the Antarctic ice, tube worms that live in the absolute darkness at the deepest depths of the ocean, algae that live in boiling hot springs—and most of these creatures—most of those that share this planet with us—are unknown.

We humans tend to think of ourselves as special, but we represent a very small number of the creatures on the planet. Most of the known species of living creatures are insects. Scientists have identified over 750,000 species of insects, including almost 300,000 species of beetles and over 100,000 species of ants and wasps. The next largest group of creatures is the plants. Almost 250,000 separate plant species have been identified, mostly flowering plants known as angiosperms. The higher animals, including human beings, make up only about 20 percent of the known species on Earth. Human beings are one species among a possible 100 million on the planet—a staggeringly large

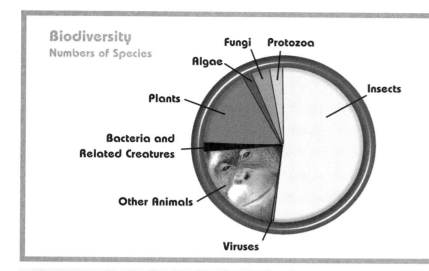

Biodiversity
Numbers of Species

Fungi Protozoa

Algae

Plants

Bacteria and
Related Creatures

Other Animals

Insects

Viruses

Known Species

1. Insects: 751,000 (53.15%)
2. Protozoa: 30,800 (2.18%)
3. Fungi: 69,000 (4.88 %)
4. Algae: 26,900 (1.90 %)
5. Plants: 248,400 (17.58 %)
6. Bacteria: 4,800 (.34 %)
7. Viruses: 1,000 (.07 %)
8. Other Animals: 281,000 (19.89 %)

number, if you think about it—and yet we act as though the entire Earth belonged to us.

In some sense, it does. Human beings are doubtless the smartest of all creatures on Earth. We, alone, have created language, civilization, technology, books, and computers. We have figured out how to live in most places on the globe, from the hottest deserts to the frozen Arctic. We have conquered the land, the sea, and the skies. Our voices and our computer data travel around the globe at the speed of light. Recently, we have taken the first tentative steps away from our birthplace, the Earth, and toward the stars. These are all impressive accomplishments, and we have reason to be proud of our species.

However, it is important for us to understand that with our abilities come responsibilities. We alone among the millions of species on the planet have the power to change the environment in dramatic ways. In the twentieth century our technologies have advanced to such a point that they can have dramatic impact on the other creatures with which we share the planet. When, in the 1970s, the World Bank financed a road into the

Brazilian rain forest, loggers followed, cutting down hundreds of thousands of square miles of trees—habitats for hundreds of thousands of species that we may never know. In the 1960s and '70s, the waters off the coast of Peru were almost entirely fished out, causing the collapse of an entire ecosystem. The World Wildlife Fund estimates that as much as 92 percent of the wetlands along the coast of California has been filled in or destroyed by humans. All this activity has enormous cost. We are now in a period of mass extinctions of species around the globe, and many of these extinctions have come about as a result of human activity.

In the seventeenth century, European settlers on the island of Mauritius, in the Indian Ocean, killed off the large, flightless bird known as the dodo. On the Hawaiian Islands alone, over 70 species of birds have been hunted to extinction by humans. When the first people arrived in the Americas, tens of thousands of years ago, they found pygmy horses, antelopes, camels, woolly mammoths, saber-toothed tigers, ground sloths, and enormous dire wolves. All were hunted to extinction. In New Zealand, the giant, flightless birds known as moas were also hunted, eaten, and made extinct. When people first came to Australia, over 30,000 years ago, they killed off such interesting native creatures as marsupial lions, Australian rhinos, and a species of giant kangaroo over eight feet tall. In the past 2,000 years, a fifth of the world's bird species have become extinct, and in recent years, the total number of songbirds in North America has dropped by 50 percent. According to the World Wildlife Fund, we are currently losing about 110 species to extinction

Lesson 2.3—General Strategies: Multiple-Choice Questions 59

Sea turtles are among the many animals on endangered species lists around the world.

every day. The Endangered Species Act, passed by the United States Congress in 1974, protects over 1,000 endangered and threatened species.

What is causing these extinctions? The biggest single cause is destruction of habitat. When people fill in wetlands, plow under prairies, or cut down forests, species lose habitats that they depend upon for their livelihoods. It is estimated that 47.1 million acres of rain forest are being cut down every year, putting over 250,000 flowering plants at risk for extinction. The second biggest cause of extinctions is displacement by introduced species. For example, in the 1950s people introduced the perch to the Nile River. The perch preyed on native fish, driving many to extinction. Other causes of extinctions include pollution and overharvesting or hunting.

We are in the middle of one of the most massive extinctions in geological history, and most of these extinctions are caused by humans. Still, there are those who ask, "Why should we care?" What does it matter if a few hundred thousand plants and animals, mostly small creatures such as bacteria and fungi, disappear? There are many answers to these questions, many reasons why it is important for people to protect biodiversity. First, other animals and plants provide us with needed medicines. Aspirin, for example, was first extracted from willow leaves, and digitalis, used to treat heart failure, came from the foxglove plant. Taxol, a drug  used to treat several kinds of cancer, comes from the Pacific yew tree, and several exotic plants are being studied for treatment of acquired immune deficiency syndrome (AIDS). Over

150 medicines currently in use are taken from animal sources, including insulin for treatment of diabetes. Forty percent of all medicines are taken from or modeled on naturally occurring substances, yet many species now disappearing have not been tested for their medicinal value.

Second, biodiversity is important to the human food supply. By crossbreeding corn with newly discovered varieties found growing wild in Mexico, agricultural scientists were able to create varieties resistant to a corn blight that destroyed 15 percent of the U.S. corn crop each year. In the 1970s, a virus destroyed much of the rice crop in India and Southeast Asia, threatening millions with famine. The crisis was ended by crossbreeding Asian rice with a newly discovered wild variety. Recombinant DNA techniques promise to make it even easier for scientists to harvest genes from newly discovered species to make better, stronger, more disease resistant plants and animals for food.

The African elephant is one species currently threatened with extinction due to loss of habitat and hunting by humans. This magnificent creature, one of the most intelligent of all animals, mourns its dead and was recently discovered to communicate using sounds too low for human ears to hear.

There are other reasons, as well, for protecting the diversity of life on the planet. Many threatened species, such as the Atlantic salmon and the Peruvian sardine, are important economically. In addition, and this is no small reason, other creatures provide humans with recreation and with the pleasure of their company. To a large extent, it is up to us to reverse the current trend toward extinction and so preserve the magnificent variety of life on Earth as a legacy for our children and for generations to come.

LESSON 3.1 *Previewing the Selection*

The MCAS English exam consists of informative and literary passages followed by questions about those passages. To be successful on the exam, you need to be able to read the passages well. **Previewing** a passage, or looking it over before you read it in depth, can improve your understanding considerably. The following chart describes some of the advantages of previewing.

> **Previewing a passage will help you to . . .**
>
> 1. **understand** what kind of passage it is (a story, a fable, a news report, etc.)
> 2. **determine** how the passage is organized
> 3. **identify** the subject matter of the passage
> 4. **focus** your attention on the task at hand
> 5. **establish** a meaningful context for your in-depth reading

The Parts of a Piece of Writing

To preview a passage properly, you need to be familiar with the elements that passages typically contain. The following chart describes these elements. Of course, not every selection has all of these parts.

> **Elements Commonly Found in Short Pieces of Writing**
>
> 1. The **title** of a piece will often tell you, generally, what it is about. The title may tell you not only what the subject of the piece is but might also suggest the work's main idea. Usually, a piece on the test will be a complete, self-contained work, such as a short fable or a news story. It might, however, be an **excerpt** or **selection** from a longer work, such as a novel or a book-length work of nonfiction.
>
> 2. The name of the **author** usually appears after the title.
>
> 3. The **text** of a piece of writing is simply the words that make it up.
>
> 4. On the MCAS English exam, there will typically be a short introduction telling you a little bit about the selection. Then there will be directions telling you to read the piece. Often, this direction line will identify the type of piece you will be reading, as in "Read the *article* and then answer the questions that follow."

USING READING STRATEGIES

Elements Commonly Found in Short Pieces of Writing (cont.)

5. **Headings** are the subtitles that appear within the piece. These mark the major parts of a piece and can indicate the major topics and supporting ideas in the piece.

6. **Illustrations** are any pictures or graphics reproduced with a work. Maps, pie charts, drawings, and photographs are all examples of illustrations.

7. Often writers and publishers emphasize **key terms**—words that are especially important, that are unique to the subject, or that are defined in the text—by printing them in special type. Such key terms might be **boldfaced**, written in *italics*, underlined, or highlighted in a different color.

8. **Footnotes** might appear at the bottom of pages, presenting definitions of difficult or unfamiliar words or other important clarifying information. If these appear at the end of a selection, they are called **endnotes.**

9. If the piece you are reading is prose, then it will probably be written in paragraphs. A **paragraph**, of course, is a group of related sentences, the first line of which is usually indented. Often, a paragraph will contain a **topic sentence** (which may be the first sentence) that expresses its main idea. It may also contain a **clincher sentence** at the end that sums up the paragraph.

10. Most pieces will contain three major parts: an **introduction** at the beginning that grabs the reader's attention and introduces the subject and the main idea, or **thesis;** a **body** that presents material to support the thesis; and a **conclusion** that sums up the selection or makes a final statement about the subject.

Words to Know

boldface	illustration
caption	introduction
clincher sentence	italics
conclusion	key term
direction line	paragraph
endnote	selection
excerpt	text
footnote	thesis
heading	title
highlighted	topic sentence

Previewing

Before reading a passage for the test in depth, you should first preview it. Previewing consists of four steps: scanning, skimming, questioning, and calling on prior knowledge. The entire process of previewing a passage should not take you more than a few minutes.

1. Scanning. When you **scan,** you look quickly through a passage to find specific parts or specific information. Begin your preview by scanning the passage, looking for these parts: the title; the author's name; the direction line; any boldfaced, highlighted, or italicized words; headings; illustrations; and captions. Once you locate a part, glance quickly at it to get the gist of it. Then go on to the next part.

2. Skimming. When you **skim,** you read quickly through a piece of text to get its most important points. Skim the first and the last paragraphs of the passage and the first and last sentences of body paragraphs in the passage.

3. Questioning. Steps 1 and 2, above, will give you an overview of the passage as a whole. As you scan for elements and skim the introduction, body, and conclusion, ask yourself these questions:

a. What kind of selection is this?

b. What is this selection about? That is, what is the author's topic?

c. What is the main idea, or thesis, of the selection?

d. What are the major supporting ideas or subtopics?

e. What is the author's conclusion? (This may or may not be clear to you from a quick preview. It should become clear when you read the selection in depth.)

f. What can I expect this article to tell me about the topic?

4. Calling on Prior Knowledge. Of course, all new learning builds on the body of knowledge and experience that you already have. As you preview the selection, think about what you already know and feel about the topic. For example, if the selection is about rescue dogs, you might recall already having learned about these dogs' superior sense of smell, their ability to be trained, and their loyalty. You might contrast this in your own mind with the difficulty that you have in training your own dog. This might lead you to pose questions such as "How are dogs trained to perform rescues?" or "Can any dog become a rescue dog?" Thinking briefly about what you already know about the topic can help you to read the selection in a more active, engaged manner.

Your Turn

Preview the selection on the following pages, without reading it carefully. First scan the selection for the title, author's name, direction line, headings, key words, illustrations, and captions. Then skim the introduction, the conclusion, and the first sentences of paragraphs. Finally, on your own paper, make a list of five questions that you expect the selection to answer, based on your preview. After reading the selection carefully, answer your questions or write "Question not answered by selection."

USING READING STRATEGIES

Preview the following article.

Old Saying, New Meaning: Everything in Moderation

by Anita Shriver

Glance at some of the popular magazines sold at your local supermarket checkout counter, and you'll see that Americans are obsessed with dieting and fitness. Every week, as I stand waiting for the cashier to ring through my low-fat sorbet, mineral water, and celery sticks, those magazine covers stare back at me, announcing articles with titles like "Ten Days to a New You," "Better Abs for a Better Life," "Use It and Lose It," and "The Do-or-Die Diet." Usually, there is at least one book on dieting or fitness on the *New York Times* nonfiction bestseller list, and the health and fitness sections of bookstores are among the largest. You would think, given all the ink spilled on these subjects, that Americans would be the healthiest people on Earth and the most knowledgeable about nutrition and exercise. If you were to think that, you would be wrong. The problem is that much of what is written about diet and exercise is produced to sell products—weight machines, food supplements, weight-loss plans, and the like—and there's a lot of misinformation out there.

The Dangers of Dieting and Fitness Fads

All the books and magazines published in America on these subjects reflect a national concern: Many Americans feel that they are not eating right, that they are not in good condition, that they are overweight, and so on. Worry about these matters makes us easy prey for the latest exercise or dieting fads. Unfortunately, these fads can be dangerous. For example, in recent years, a low-carbohydrate[1] diet has been widely promoted for weight loss, but such a diet can raise cholesterol[2] levels and make the dieter less healthy. Another fad that has swept the United States in recent years is

---

[1] **carbohydrate.** Any of a number of organic compounds contained in food, including sugars, starches, and celluloses
[2] **cholesterol.** A substance found in animal products, such as meat and milk, that, if consumed in excess, can cause plaque build-up in blood vessels and lead to heart attacks and strokes

intense athletic activity—hours of grueling mountain biking, rock climbing, jogging, and other vigorous, calorie-burning activities. However, for people who are not in good shape, such activities can actually be dangerous, leading, for example, to heart attacks.

The Value of Moderation

The point is that in regard to both diet and exercise, scientific evidence supports the conclusion that your grandmother's old saying, "everything in moderation," is the best advice. That's the recommendation of a new report, jointly published by the Department of Agriculture (USDA) and the Department of Health and Human Services (HHS), called **Nutrition and Your Health: Dietary Guidelines for Americans.** Let's consider exercise and nutrition in turn.

Sensible Exercising. Exercise is good for you, don't get me wrong; however, it is important to exercise sensibly. Before beginning any strenuous exercise routine, make sure to get a physical checkup to ensure that you're up to it. Start slowly, and build up your stamina over time. Then, keep your exercise routine within reasonable limits. The USDA and HHS recommend *30 minutes of vigorous, high-intensity activity at least three times a week* to promote cardiovascular[3] fitness. However, for the rest of the week, and this is the big news, the recommendation is for *moderate activity daily*. In other

---

[3] **cardiovascular.** Having to do with the heart and the blood vessels as a unified bodily system (the circulatory system)

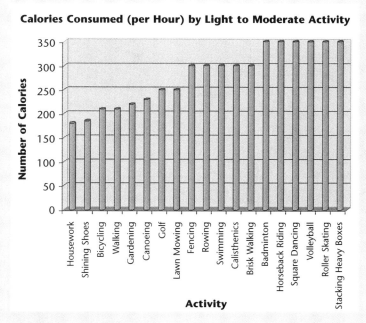

Calories Consumed (per Hour) by Light to Moderate Activity

A **calorie** is a unit used to measure the energy produced by food when it is used by the body. Of course, not all food is converted to energy. Some is turned into waste products, and some is made into bodily tissues. If a person consumes many more calories than he or she needs for energy or for normal bodily maintenance and growth, then the excess will be stored in the body as fat. As the chart shows, even moderate activities can burn lots of calories and keep a person trim.

words, extreme, grueling daily workouts are not necessary. As a 1995 Mayo Clinic Health Letter suggests: "It's time to exercise. So get out and mow the lawn. Or play a game of badminton. Or, better yet, call a friend and hit the links." As the chart on the previous page shows, moderate physical activity, such as taking a brisk walk, gardening, doing calisthenics, or even doing housework can burn calories. Daily moderate activity can also go a long way, the USDA and HHS suggest, toward keeping you healthy.

Sensible Eating. With regard to diet, moderation is also in order. The USDA/HHS report suggests that people should eat a wide variety of foods, including lots of fruits, vegetables, and grains, and maintain a diet low in fat, saturated fat, and cholesterol. For adults, *no more than 30 percent of daily calories, averaged over several days, should come from fat.* Crash diets and rapid weight loss should be avoided, as these can be extremely stressful on the system, and diet plans should be undertaken only on the advice and under the monitoring of a physician. A good guideline for eating well is the **USDA Food Pyramid,** which suggests eating *lots of bread, cereal, rice, pasta, vegetables, and fruit and adding two or three servings of dairy products and two or three servings of meat products.*

All of this just goes to show you that your grandmother's advice wasn't so bad after all. "Everything in moderation"—remember that phrase and forget the fads from the books and articles.

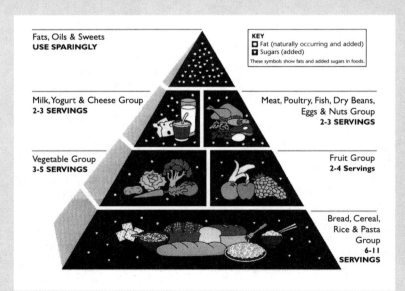

The **Food Pyramid** was created by the USDA as a guide to sensible, moderate eating. As the pyramid suggests, a person's diet should contain large amounts of bread, cereal, rice, and pasta; smaller amounts of vegetables and fruits; still smaller amounts of dairy products, meats, beans, and eggs; and very small amounts of fats, oils, and sweets.

Source: U.S. Department of Agriculture

LESSON 3.2

Identifying the Main Idea

As you have seen, the MCAS English exam evaluates reading comprehension. **Comprehension** is the ability to make sense of what you read. There are many types of reading comprehension questions on the test. Each of the next few lessons discusses one type of reading comprehension question.

A Closer Look at the Exam: Questions About Main Ideas

Review the selection from the Pretest on pages 21 through 23. Then review the following questions:

26 What is this article mostly about?

    A the origins of Roman civilization

    B society in ancient times

    C an ancient civilization that flourished and disappeared

    D Etruscan art and language

27 Which of the following lessons does the article as a whole teach us?

    A A society will have very little influence if its language is not understood by its neighbors.

    B Even the richest and most powerful civilizations can fade from the Earth.

    C To prosper, you must build a good system of roads.

    D The best way for a people to achieve a prominent place in history is to build lasting tombs.

One Student's Response

As she looked at question 26, Yolanda quickly realized that the question was asking about the subject of the selection as a whole. Answer A could not be correct because the selection mentions Roman civilization only a couple of times. Likewise, answer B could not be correct because societies other than the Etruscan are not described. Finally, answer D could not be correct because art and language are discussed only in portions of the selection. Thus, the correct answer must be C.

When answering question 27, Yolanda first read through all the possible answers. When she got to answer C, she thought, "Well, the selection does teach us that the Etruscans were able to trade and make war because they built good roads." Then Yolanda remembered that the question asked about "the article as a whole." The whole article wasn't about the usefulness of the roads, so answer C could not be correct. Yolanda also realized that answer A could not be correct because the essay never says that the Etruscans' neighbors didn't understand their language. She ruled out answer D, because the Etruscans do not have a prominent place in history. Yolanda did

USING READING STRATEGIES

find references throughout the selection that described how the civilization had prospered and faded; therefore, she reasoned, the correct answer must be B.

Understanding Main Ideas, Subjects, and Themes

Questions 26 and 27 are both examples of questions about the main idea. A **main idea** is any idea that is particularly important or central in a written work. Reading comprehension tests often ask questions about the main idea. Some of these questions ask about the subject of the selection. The **subject,** or **topic,** is what the selection as a whole is about. Question 26, for example, asks about the subject.

Another type of main idea question asks about the theme of the selection. A **theme** is a lesson that the selection teaches or a major point that the selection makes. Question 27 asks what lesson the selection as a whole teaches, so it is a question about the theme.

To find the overall subject or theme of a selection, use the reading strategy known as **skimming.** Run your finger back and forth, quickly, along the lines of the whole selection. Notice such parts as the title, the headings, the introduction, the first and last sentences of paragraphs, and the conclusion. Then ask yourself, "What is the selection mostly about?"

Yolanda's responses to questions 26 and 27 suggest some excellent strategies for answering multiple-choice questions about main ideas.

Strategies

- Examine the question for words and phrases that tell you that it is asking about the selection as a whole. A question of this kind may contain such key words and phrases as *main idea, subject, theme, as a whole, in general, mostly,* or *for the most part.*

- Begin by looking through all the answers. Eliminate all the answers that are obviously incorrect. Then concentrate on the remaining answers.

- If a question is asking about the overall main idea, subject, or theme of the selection, then make sure that the answer you choose deals with the selection as a whole, not with just a part of the selection.

- Remember that a statement can be true but still not express the main idea.

Your Turn

Read each passage and then answer the questions that follow.

Jim Thorpe was born on an Indian reservation in Oklahoma in 1888. He had remarkable athletic ability in many sports. When he played football, trying to catch him was like trying to catch a shadow. At the 1912 Olympic games, he won both the decathlon and the pentathlon. After the Olympics, he played professional baseball and football. In 1950, the Associated Press named him the greatest football player and all-around male athlete of the first half of the twentieth century.

1 What is this selection mostly about?
   A the Olympic Games of 1912
   B life on an Indian reservation
   C an amazing all-around athlete
   D the decathlon and pentathlon

2 Which sentence expresses the main idea of the selection?
   A Thorpe had remarkable athletic ability in many sports.
   B Jim Thorpe was born on an Indian reservation in Oklahoma in 1888.
   C At the 1912 Olympic Games, Jim Thorpe won both the decathlon and the pentathlon.
   D When he played football, trying to catch him was like trying to clutch a shadow.

Begin by making a ball of clay and pressing it flat until you have a circle about three inches in diameter. Then make more balls of clay and rub them together between your palms to create clay ropes about a quarter of an inch thick. Starting at the outside of the circle, lay down the ropes of clay, working your way around the circle and laying rope upon rope. As you lay down the ropes of clay, press down slightly to seal the clay ropes together. In this manner, build up the sides of your bowl. Once the sides are as tall as you want, you are ready to paint your bowl. Then you can glaze and fire it.

3 Which phrase best captures what this selection is mostly about?
   A glazing pottery
   B using a pottery wheel
   C making a simple clay bowl
   D creating clay ropes

4 What would be a good title for this paragraph? (Hint: This is another way of asking which phrase best identifies the subject.)
   A The Uses of Clay
   B An Introduction to Ceramics
   C Types of Pottery
   D Creating a Clay Bowl

Light given off by living things is called "bioluminescence." Nature is full of bioluminescent creatures. One of the most familiar is the firefly, or lightning bug, that flashes its tiny light on summer evenings. Glowworms are any of various wormlike insects or insect larvae that glow in the dark. There are a few glowing fungi, including certain toadstools and molds. The foxfire fungus, for example, grows on decaying wood. Many light-creating life forms exist in the oceans. Some deep-sea fish use lights to attract mates or prey. Some kinds of plankton—very small animals and plants found in great numbers in the oceans—are bioluminescent. At times they can be seen lighting up the wakes of boats.

5 Which of the following would be the best title for this paragraph?
   A Glowworms
   B Light
   C Bioluminescence in Animals
   D Bioluminescence in Living Creatures

6 Which sentence from the paragraph best expresses its main idea?

- **A** Light given off by living things is called "bioluminescence."
- **B** Nature is full of bioluminescent creatures.
- **C** Glowworms are any of various wormlike insects or insect larvae that glow in the dark.
- **D** Many light-creating life forms exist in the oceans.

There was once a man who had five sons who were always bickering. He decided to teach them a lesson. He tied five sticks together in a bundle. Then he challenged his sons to break the bundle of sticks. Each one tried to break the bundle of sticks over his knee and declared that it could not be done.

Then the father untied the bundle, gave one stick to each son, and told them to break the sticks. The sticks snapped like matches.

"You see," said the father, "when a man stands alone, he can be broken easily, but when he is united with others, nothing can break him."

7 Which statement best describes what this story is mostly about?

- **A** There is always conflict among brothers.
- **B** Sticks tied in a bundle are hard to break.
- **C** Some brothers like to break sticks.
- **D** A man teaches his sons that there is strength in unity.

8 Which of the following sayings, or proverbs, best expresses the theme of this story?

- **A** Boys will be boys.
- **B** Two heads are better than one.
- **C** United we stand; divided we fall.
- **D** Don't put all your eggs in one basket.

Probability is the fascinating branch of mathematics that deals with chance. An example of a problem in probability is the question "What is the probability of getting a head with one flip of a dime?" There are two equal possibilities, so the probability is one half, or .5. Another example is the question "If a man was born in January, what is the probability that he was born on January 13?" Since there are 31 days in January, the probability would be one in 31, or 1/31.

9 Which would be the best title for this paragraph?

- **A** What Is Probability?
- **B** How to Win at Coin Tossing
- **C** Guessing a Person's Birthday
- **D** Beginning Mathematics

10 What is this selection mostly about?

- **A** the probabilities of coin tosses
- **B** birthdays
- **C** games of chance
- **D** what probability means

LESSON 3.3 *Scanning for Details*

A Closer Look at the Exam: Questions About Supporting Details

Review the selection on the Pretest on pages 21 through 23. Then review the following test questions.

28 To what modern Italian region was the area of the Etruscan civilization equivalent?

   A Rome

   B Liguria

   C Lydia

   D Tuscany

29 The Etruscan alphabet was based on that of

   A Asia Minor

   B the Celts

   C the French

   D the Greeks

One Student's Response

When Alphonse read question 28, he remembered reading in the beginning paragraphs about the area covered by the Etruscan civilization. He looked quickly through the first paragraph and spotted the words *modern Italian region*. He read the sentence and discovered that the Etruscan region was comparable to modern Tuscany. Then he knew that answer D was correct.

When Alphonse read question 29, he remembered that somewhere in the passage there was information about the Etruscan alphabet. He figured that French wasn't the answer because he knew that modern French culture developed centuries after ancient times. Therefore, he looked through the selection for the other groups. When he found the word *alphabet,* he stopped and read closely the sentences containing and surrounding the word. These told him that the correct answer was D, "the Greeks."

Understanding Supporting Details

Questions 28 and 29 ask you about **supporting details** from the selection. Supporting details are facts, statements, examples, and illustrations that demonstrate or elaborate upon the main idea. A reading method that you can use to answer questions about supporting details is **scanning.** When you **scan,** you move your eyes quickly along a line or down a page to find particular information. One way to scan is to move your finger, an index card, or a ruler along the line or down the page and to follow the object with your eyes. As you scan, look for a key word or phrase that tells you that you

USING READING STRATEGIES

are close to the information you are seeking. Once you find the key word or phrase, stop and read closely. Alphonse scanned the passage to find the words *Italian region, Asia Minor, Celt, Greek,* and *alphabet.* When he found them, he stopped and read closely to find the answers.

Strategies

📖 When reading a paragraph, first identify the main idea. Then look for details that support the main idea.

📖 To find a particular supporting detail, scan the passage for a key word or phrase. Then read closely to find the answer you need.

📖 Use your finger, an index card, or a ruler to keep your place as you scan down a page.

Your Turn

Read each selection. Then scan the selection to find answers to the questions about supporting details.

In 1998, James Cameron's film *Titanic* won the Academy Award for Best Picture. The film broke box office records and was one of the most expensive films ever made, costing over $280 million to produce. The movie tells the story of the *Titanic*, a luxury cruise ship that sank in 1912. As shown in breathtaking detail in the film, on its first voyage the *Titanic* hit an iceberg and began taking on water.

As water filled the hold of the ship, the front part, or bow, sank into the ocean. After a short while, the ship snapped in two. The back part, or stern, of the ship rose upward and then it, too, sank into the ocean. All told, 1,513 people aboard the *Titanic* lost their lives.

As terrible as the *Titanic* disaster was, it was not the deadliest event ever to occur at sea. Early in 1945, World War II was drawing to a close. The Germans were suffering heavy casualties against the advancing Russian army. In January of that year, a German luxury liner called the *Wilhelm Gustloff* set sail from Danzig (now Gdansk), Poland, carrying 6,050 refugees from the advancing Russian army. As the ship headed for the open sea, it took on additional passengers who arrived by small boat.

On January 30, shortly before midnight, the Russian submarine S–13 torpedoed the *Wilhelm Gustloff*. Three torpedoes hit the ship, which sank about fifteen minutes later. Only 964 passengers were rescued, and many of those later died. It is estimated that the sinking of the *Wilhelm Gustloff* led to the deaths of as many as 7,000 people, over four and a half times as many people as went down with the *Titanic*. 🍎

1. James Cameron's film *Titanic* cost over
   A $280 million
   B $360 million
   C $420 million
   D $530 million

2. When did the *Wilhelm Gustloff* sink?
   A 1998
   B 1954
   C 1945
   D 1912

3. The *Wilhelm Gustloff* was torpedoed by
   A an American submarine
   B a Russian submarine
   C a German submarine
   D a Japanese submarine

4. The *Wilhelm Gustloff* set sail from
   A Halifax, Nova Scotia
   B Heidelberg, Germany
   C Lisbon, Portugal
   D Danzig, Poland

5. The number of people rescued after the *Wilhelm Gustloff* went down was
   A 7,000
   B 6,050
   C 1,513
   D 964

A glance at the surface of the moon shows that meteor impacts in our part of the solar system are pretty common. The Earth itself is not covered with craters because most meteors burn up in the Earth's atmosphere and because geological processes have destroyed the evidence of past impacts. Here and there on the surface of the Earth, giant craters can nonetheless be seen. One example is the large impact crater near Winslow, Arizona, which measures about 1.2 kilometers across.

As the Arizona crater demonstrates, the Earth is sometimes hit by large meteors. In 1908, for example, a meteor 50 meters in diameter exploded above the ground in the Tunguska region of Siberia and knocked down trees over an area of 2,000 square kilometers. According to scientists, a meteor of that size strikes the Earth, on average, once every three hundred years.

The Tunguska meteor was not the largest one that has ever hit the Earth. At the end of the Cretaceous Period, about 65 million years ago, most of the life on Earth, the dinosaurs included, was destroyed when a meteor 10 kilometers in diameter hit the Yucatán peninsula in Mexico. The impact threw enough debris into the air to block the sunlight for many months and to kill most of the planet's plants and animals.

Fortunately for us, the larger outer planets of the solar system, Saturn and Jupiter, provide some protection against meteors. The gravity of a large planet like Jupiter or Saturn acts like an enormous slingshot, throwing large meteors that enter the solar system

USING READING STRATEGIES

back out again so that they do not hit the Earth. If not for these large planets, the Earth would be hit by large meteors quite often, and life on our planet would not exist. 🍎

6 The Earth is not covered with meteorite craters because

A meteor impacts in our area of the solar system are very rare

B over time the action of geological forces has destroyed the evidence of past impacts

C impacts occur only in a very limited area of the Earth's surface

D most meteors that enter the Earth's atmosphere go into orbit around the Earth

7 Scientists estimate that the diameter of the Yucatán meteor was

A 1.2 kilometers

B 50 meters

C 10 kilometers

D 2,000 kilometers

8 When did the Tunguska meteor impact occur?

A about 65 million years ago

B about three hundred years ago

C in 1908

D cannot be determined

9 All of the following occurred as a result of the meteor impact in the Yucatán EXCEPT

A Debris from the impact blocked sunlight for many months.

B Most of the plant life on Earth was destroyed.

C New species of dinosaurs evolved as a result of mutations brought about by the impact.

D Most of the animals on Earth died.

10 What helps prevent meteors from crashing into Earth?

A An electromagnetic field around the Earth blocks most meteors from entering the atmosphere.

B The gravity of Jupiter and Saturn acts like a giant slingshot, throwing large meteors back out of the solar system.

C The gravity of the sun attracts meteors away from the Earth.

D The moon attracts meteors, keeping them from hitting the Earth.

The giant, ringed planet Saturn. Photo courtesy of the National Aeronautics and Space Administration (NASA)

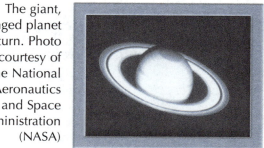

LESSON 3.4   *Decoding Vocabulary*

A Closer Look at the Exam: Questions About Vocabulary

Review the selection from the Pretest on pages 21 through 23. Then read the following questions based on sentences in the selection.

1   "One by one, the city-states were conquered by the growing dynamo that was Rome." What is a *dynamo*?

   A   a forceful thing or person
   B   a democracy
   C   a very wealthy nation
   D   a conglomerate

2   "These people they subjugated and forced to perform their agricultural labor." What does *subjugated* mean?

   A   introduced
   B   enlightened
   C   envied
   D   enslaved

One Student's Response

To answer the first question, Adam looked back at the paragraph in the selection that talked about the overthrow of the Etruscans by Rome. Nothing in the paragraph mentioned the wealth or form of government of Rome, so he ruled out answers B and D.

The paragraph stated that the weakened city-states were conquered by the growing dynamo. It seemed that the weakened city-states were being contrasted to the growing dynamo, so Adam concluded that a dynamo is the opposite of something weak. He decided that answer A, a forceful thing or person, made the most sense.

Adam did not know the word *subjugated* in question 2, but the sentence in which the word was found gave him some clues as to its meaning. The peoples the Etruscans subjugated were "forced to perform their agricultural labor." Adam reasoned that this action did not go along with introducing or envying people, so he eliminated answers A and C. He did not know what *enlightened* meant, but he did know that to *enslave* a person means to force him or her to work for you. Therefore he chose the correct answer, D.

Using Context Clues to Determine the Meanings of Words

One type of question you will frequently encounter on the MCAS English exam is the vocabulary question. In addition, you will have to figure out the meanings of other important but unfamiliar words as you read the selections on the exam. You will often be able to figure out the meaning of a

USING READING STRATEGIES

word from its **context,** that is, from what comes before and after the word. The hints that the context gives you about word meanings are called **context clues.**

Sometimes a writer will clarify the meaning of a difficult word by using different words to state the same concept, as in the following example:

> *Conifers* are common in the North Woods. However, not all the trees of this area are *evergreens*.

This type of context clue is called **restatement.** In a restatement, a meaning is repeated using different words. In this case, the concept *conifers* is repeated using a different word, *evergreens*, which means the same thing.

Sometimes, a restatement appears immediately after the word that it is explaining and is set off by commas. Such a restatement is known as an **apposition.** Here is an example:

> *Conifers, or evergreens*, are common in the North Woods.

Sometimes, an apposition is a whole phrase, as in this example:

> *Conifers, trees that do not lose their leaves in the fall*, are common in the North Woods.

Sometimes, a restatement is a **synonym,** a single word that has the same meaning. *Evergreen*, for example, is a synonym for *conifer*. Here is another example:

> Shaw's character Professor Higgins is sometimes described as a *misogynist*, but other critics claim that Higgins isn't really a *woman-hater*.

Misogynist and *woman-hater* are synonyms. Notice that a synonym does not have to appear immediately after a word.

Sometimes two phrases or sentences contain parallel, or similar, ideas. If you know the meaning of one phrase, you can guess the meaning of the other. This type of context clue is called a **comparison.** Here is an example:

> The first piece the orchestra played was ridiculously sad and mournful. The second piece was likewise *lugubrious*.

The word *likewise*, in the example, tells you that the first piece and the second piece are being compared. Since the first piece was "ridiculously sad and mournful," then the second piece must have been also. You can therefore conclude that *lugubrious* must mean "ridiculously sad and mournful."

A similar type of context clue is **contrast,** in which two opposite ideas are stated, as in this example:

> Jubal's ideas were not very *pragmatic*; rather, they were idealistic.

Here, the contrast word, *idealistic*, is an **antonym,** or word with a meaning opposite to *pragmatic*, the word being contrasted. The word *rather* suggests that *pragmatic* and *idealistic* are opposites.

Another way to discover the meaning of a word is through **examples.** If a passage provides examples of an unfamiliar word, try to figure out what the examples have in common, and from that you may be able to deduce what the word means, as in this sentence:

> *Conifers*, such as firs, spruces, pines, and cedars, are common in the North Woods.

Sometimes, the context of an unfamiliar word does not contain a simple, direct context clue such as an antonym, a synonym, or examples. Nonetheless, you can often figure out the meaning of the word by reasoning from the information provided by the context. Simply read the context and ask yourself what meaning would make sense given everything else that the passage tells you. The process of making such an educated guess is called **inference.** Consider this example:

The first great English lexicographer was Samuel Johnson. In his work, the first great dictionary of the English language, Johnson defined *lexicographer* as "a harmless drudge."

The passage tells you that Johnson was "the first great lexicographer" and that he created "the first great dictionary of the English language." Therefore, a *lexicographer* must be someone who makes dictionaries, a specialist in the histories and meanings of words. Here is another example:

Maria would not be able to see her friends or her parents for several months. No wonder she felt *melancholic*.

Even if you do not know what *melancholic* means, you can guess how someone might feel if she were unable to see her parents and friends for several months.

Recognizing Word Parts

You can sometimes figure out the meaning of a word you don't know by using your prior knowledge. Many words are composed of parts, and if you know the meanings of the parts of a word, you can figure out the meaning of the whole. Consider the following example:

The ground shifted during the earthquake, causing a 30-degree *declination* of the stretch of Highway 23 near exit 5A.

Declination is an uncommon word, one that probably is not familiar to you. However, if you recognize that it is made up of two parts, the base word *decline* and the suffix *–ation*, which is used to make nouns, you can guess that *declination* means something like *downturn*.

The following chart describes some of the common parts of which words are made:

Word Parts

- **Prefixes** are parts added to the beginnings of words.

  predetermined
  underappreciated

- **Suffixes** are parts added to the ends of words.

  merri**ment**
  under**ling**

- **Base words** are ordinary words that can be combined into **compound words** or to which prefixes and suffixes may be added.

  moon + walk = **moonwalk**
  sub + zero = sub**zero**

- **Roots**, like base words, can be compounded or can be expanded with prefixes or suffixes; however, roots cannot stand alone.

  in + spec + tion = in**spec**tion

Some Common Prefixes and Suffixes

Prefix	Meaning	Example	Definition
ante–	before	antebellum	before the war
anti–	against	antisocial	avoiding contact with others
bi–	two, twice	bicycle	two-wheeled
bio–	life	biography	written story of someone's life
co–	with	cooperate	work with
contra–	against, not	contraindicated	not indicated or advisable
extra–	outside	extracurricular	outside the curriculum
inter–	between	interpersonal	between people
intra–	within	intramural	within the walls of one school
macro–	large	macroclimate	climate over a large area
micro–	small	microscopic	very small
mini–	small, short	miniseries	small (or short) series
multi–	many	multicultural	representing many cultures
neo–	new	neoclassical	revival of classical style
post–	after	postwar	after the war
pre–	before	preview	see before
pro–	forward, ahead	proactive	taking initiative, acting first
pseudo–	false	pseudonym	fictitious name
semi–	half, partly	semiconscious	partly, not fully, conscious
sub–	under	submarine	under the sea
super–	over, above	superconducting	conducting very well
trans–	across	transport	carry across
ultra–	beyond	ultrasonic	beyond hearing range

Suffix	Meaning	Example	Definition
–archy	form of rule	monarchy	rule by a king
–ate	become, like	rejuvenate	make young again
–able, ible	capable of	bearable	capable of being borne
–cide	killing	insecticide	substance that kills insects
–fold	multiplied by	tenfold	ten times as much
–ism	doctrine, belief	patriotism	belief in one's country
–itis	inflammation	rhinitis	inflammation of the nose
–less	without	spineless	without strength of character
–logy	science of	musicology	science or study of music
–tude	state, quality	fortitude	strength

Some Common Roots and Word Families

Root	Meaning	Examples
anim	living	animate, inanimate
anthro	human	anthropology, philanthropy
arche, archae	old, ancient	archaeology, archaic
bibl, biblio	book	bibliography, bibliophile
chron, chrono	time	chronology, geosynchronous
cogn	know	cognition, incognito, recognition
corp	body	corpus, corporeal, corps
cred	know, believe	credulous, creed, incredible
crypt, crypto	hidden, secret	cryptic, encryption, cryptography
dem, demo	people	democracy, endemic
duc, duct	carry, lead	conduct, deduction, induce
ge, geo	Earth	geology, geothermal, geosynchronous
gnos, gnosis	know, knowledge	diagnosis, agnostic, prognosticate
graph	write	polygraph, graphic, graphologist
homo	same	homogeneous, homonym
log, logy	word, thought, study	sociology, neologism, dialog
lum	light	illuminate, luminous
mand	command	mandate, reprimand
mit, mis	send	transmit, transmission, missile, admit
path	sadness, suffering	pathological, sympathetic
phil	love	philanthropy, philharmonic
port	carry	import, export, portable, portage
scrib	write	inscribe, inscription, subscribe, scribe
scope	see, look	periscope, microscopy, oscilloscope
spec	see	inspection, speculate, spectacle
tact, tang	touch	tactile, tangible, tangential
tele	far, across distance	teleportation, telephone, telegraph
therm	heat	thermal, thermodynamic, thermometer

A group of words that all share the same root, such as *asterisk, astrology, astronomy,* and *disaster,* is called a **word family.** The Greek root *aster* means "star."

USING READING STRATEGIES

Eponyms

Sometimes you can figure out the meaning of a word because it is based on a famous or familiar name. A person from whose name a word has been created is known as an **eponym.** For example, if you read that "Writing the new tax code was a *Herculean* task," you can be safe in assuming that the word *Herculean* comes from the name of the mythical ancient strongman Hercules. A *Herculean* task would therefore be one that is very difficult, requiring great strength, ability, hard work, or endurance.

Strategies

- When you encounter a new word in your reading, write it down in a vocabulary journal, along with its definition. Review your list from time to time to build your vocabulary.

- Notice the relationships among words and phrases in a passage. Be alert to clues to meaning provided by the context in which unfamiliar words appear.

- Notice the use of key words such as *and*, *also*, and *likewise* that signal comparisons.

- Notice the use of key words such as *however*, *in contrast*, *rather*, and *on the other hand* that signal contrasts.

- Be alert to restatements, appositions, synonyms, and antonyms.

- Use your knowledge of word parts, including prefixes, suffixes, base words, and roots, to determine the meanings of unfamiliar words containing these parts.

- Relate words based on names, such as *Herculean* or *titanic*, to the real or imaginary person from whose name the word was taken.

Your Turn

A   Read the passages below and use context clues to determine the meanings of the words indicated.

Angelo makes sporadic attempts to discipline himself to do his homework. From time to time, he buckles down and works hard. His sister Vanessa, on the other hand, is consistently diligent. She does her homework as soon as she gets home from school and always gives it her best effort.

1   Angelo makes sporadic attempts to discipline himself. What does *sporadic* mean?

   A   impressive

   B   useless

   C   occasional

   D   effective

2   Vanessa is a very diligent student. What does *diligent* mean?

   A   lazy

   B   courteous

   C   fastidious

   D   industrious

When Karen flew over the Grand Canyon, she suffered an attack of acrophobia, an abnormal fear of being in high places. Shelley is afraid of being in public places; she has agoraphobia. Garrett has always been terrified of spiders; he suffers from arachniphobia. Ever since he received a near-fatal bee sting that made him unable to breathe, Luke has had apiphobia.

3   A person who is excessively fearful of going to the mall suffers from

   A   acrophobia

   B   agoraphobia

   C   apiphobia

   D   arachniphobia

4   Someone who is terrified of climbing a ladder has

   A   acrophobia

   B   agoraphobia

   C   apiphobia

   D   arachniphobia

The camp counselor acted judiciously when he refused to let the boys go down the rapids in the canoes. He also used good judgment in making them set up camp before it started to rain.

5   The camp counselor acted judiciously. What does *judiciously* mean?

   A   as a spoilsport

   B   using good judgment

   C   in a bossy way

   D   timidly

Alicia and Alvin were both late for school this morning. Alicia's explanation was plausible, but Alvin's sounded pretty unlikely to me.

6   Alicia's explanation was plausible. What does *plausible* mean?

   A   seemingly true

   B   funny

   C   imaginative

   D   improbable

Some well-known aphorisms are: "Haste makes waste," "Live and learn," "Look before you leap," and "Knowledge is power."

7   This sentence gives several examples of aphorisms. The examples suggest that an *aphorism* is

   A   a statement containing rhyming words

   B   a phrase with alliteration

   C   a political slogan

   D   a short saying giving practical wisdom

The surgeon failed to read the patient's chart carefully and made an egregious mistake: He removed her kidney instead of her gall bladder.

8   The surgeon made an egregious mistake. What does *egregious* mean?

   A   relatively minor

   B   extremely capable

   C   remarkably clever

   D   extraordinarily bad

He is by far the most contentious candidate in the campaign; he is constantly getting into disputes with the other candidates.

9 The restatement in this passage suggests that *contentious* means

A popular
B argumentative
C knowledgeable
D independent

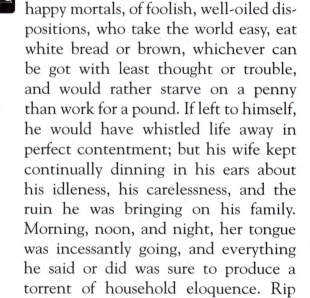 Rip Van Winkle . . . was one of those happy mortals, of foolish, well-oiled dispositions, who take the world easy, eat white bread or brown, whichever can be got with least thought or trouble, and would rather starve on a penny than work for a pound. If left to himself, he would have whistled life away in perfect contentment; but his wife kept continually dinning in his ears about his idleness, his carelessness, and the ruin he was bringing on his family. Morning, noon, and night, her tongue was incessantly going, and everything he said or did was sure to produce a torrent of household eloquence. Rip had but one way of replying to all lectures of the kind, and that, by frequent use, had grown into a habit. He shrugged his shoulders, shook his head, cast up his eyes, but said nothing. 🍎

10 Read the passage above from Washington Irving's short story "Rip Van Winkle." Then use context clues to determine the meaning of *incessantly*.

A constantly
B pleasantly
C persuasively
D slowly

B Identify the parts of each of the following words. Then write a definition for the word.

1 *bidirectional*

2 *interspecies*

3 *sevenfold*

4 *macroscopic*

5 *pseudoscience*

C Use an analysis of the word parts to give a probable meaning for each of the following words. Refer to the charts in this lesson as necessary. Then, look up each word in a dictionary to make sure that the meaning you have come up with is correct.

1 *corporeal,* based on the root *corp*

2 *inanimate,* based on the root *anim*

3 *credulous,* based on the root *cred*

4 *graphology,* based on the roots *graph* and *logy*

5 *tangible,* based on the root *tang* and the suffix *–ible*

D Look up each of the following words in a dictionary and tell both who the eponym is and what the word means.

1 *bowdlerize*

2 *quisling*

3 *sandwich*

4 *narcissism*

5 *arachnid*

LESSON 3.5 *Understanding Graphics*

I n your reading, both on examinations and in everyday life, you will often encounter such visual materials as tables, graphs, maps, illustrations, and diagrams. Such visual materials, variously referred to as **graphics, graphic aids, informative graphics,** or **infographics,** are common in newspapers, in magazine articles, on the Web, on television news programs, in textbooks, and in many other media. When you encounter such a graphic, you need to be able to **analyze** it—to examine it closely, noting its parts, the relations among the parts, and the relations of the parts to the whole. This lesson will review some of the most important types of infographics that you will encounter in your reading. In Lesson 6.2, you will learn about other types of graphics that you can use to plan your own writing.

Understanding Line Graphs

A **line graph** contains two parts: an **x-axis,** running across (horizontally), and a **y-axis,** running up and down (vertically). A line graph is used to show how one **variable** (a changing element, such as number of products or people) changes with respect to another variable (such as time or cost). The line graph below shows the growth in the number of users of the Internet in the United States over the past few years.

A line graph

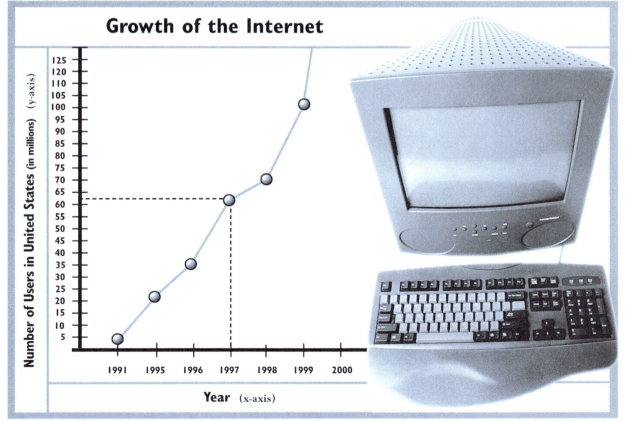

Growth of the Internet

Number of Users in United States (in millions) (y-axis)

Year (x-axis)

USING READING STRATEGIES

In most cases, a line graph shows how the amount or number of something corresponds to a changing variable. In the example on the previous page, the graph shows the number of people using the Internet for each of seven years. To read the line graph, all you need to do is to trace two straight lines. Trace a vertical line from the x-axis (year) to where it intersects the line on the graph. Then trace a horizontal line from that point to the y-axis (number of users). The dotted lines on the graph show that in 1997 the number of Internet users in the United States was about 62 million. Notice that line graphs are good for showing trends. What trend does this line graph show with regard to Internet usage?

Understanding Bar Graphs

A bar graph, like the one below, also contains an x-axis running across (horizontally) and a y-axis running up and down (vertically). The independent variable (years in the sample graph) is given on the y-axis. From each independent variable, a bar extends horizontally across the graph. Values for the dependent variable (millions of people) are given on the x-axis. To read the graph, you simply draw a line, like the dotted line in the graph below, from the end of the bar to the x-axis. Reading the x-axis at the point where the dotted line intersects it, we can see that the projected, or estimated, population of Brazil in the year 2010 is 202 million people.

Brazil: Projected Population Growth 1995-2015

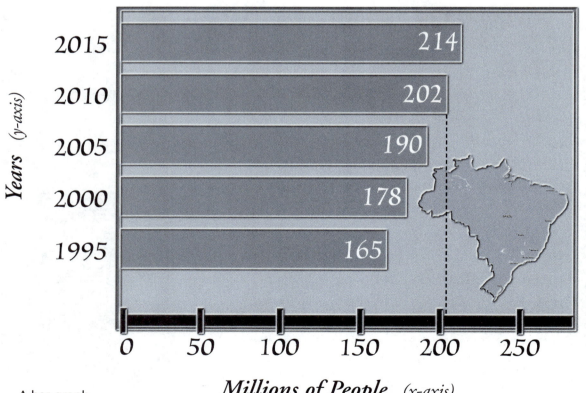

A bar graph

Understanding Column Graphs

A **column graph** is similar to a bar graph, except that the independent variables appear on the x-axis, and the horizontal bars are replaced by vertical columns. To read the value of each of the independent variables, you trace with your finger a horizontal line from the end of the column to the y-axis. The column graph below shows that it definitely pays to stay in school. What trend does the chart show, as one moves across it from left to right?

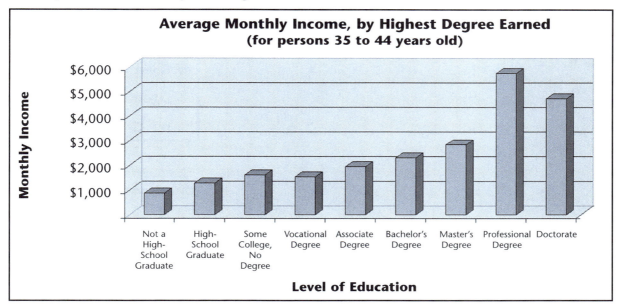

A column graph

Source: Statistical Abstract of the U. S., 1995

Understanding Pie Charts

A **pie chart** takes its name from its shape. It is circular and is divided into wedges, like a pie. The wedges represent the "parts of the pie," that is, the relative percentages of the whole taken up by each of a number of variables. The pie chart to the right simply shows the relative sizes of various groups of species. Looking at the chart, you can tell at a glance that the number of insect species is considerably larger than the number of plant species.

The pie charts on the next page both give the amounts of the variables as **percentages,** or parts out of one hundred.

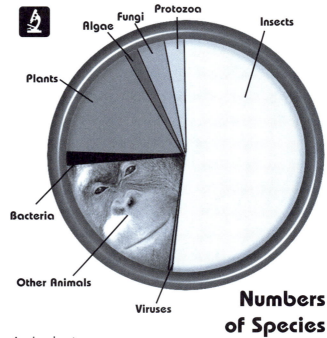

A pie chart

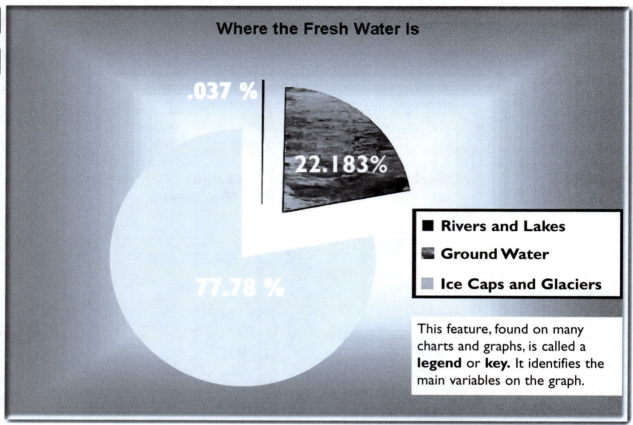

Where the Fresh Water Is

.037 %

22.183%

77.78 %

- ■ Rivers and Lakes
- ▨ Ground Water
- ▨ Ice Caps and Glaciers

This feature, found on many charts and graphs, is called a **legend** or **key.** It identifies the main variables on the graph.

A pie chart showing the relative percentages of fresh water on the Earth found in rivers and lakes, in the ground, and in ice caps and glaciers

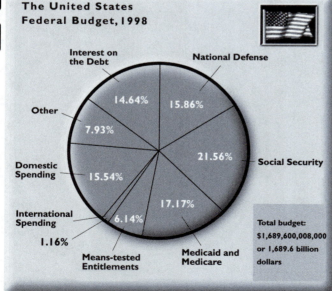

The United States Federal Budget, 1998

Interest on the Debt — 14.64%

National Defense — 15.86%

Other — 7.93%

Social Security — 21.56%

Domestic Spending — 15.54%

International Spending — 1.16%

6.14%

Means-tested Entitlements

Medicaid and Medicare — 17.17%

Total budget: $1,689,600,008,000 or 1,689.6 billion dollars

A pie chart showing categories of expense as percentages of the U.S. federal budget

In a pie chart, the circle represents the whole of something. In the pie chart above, the circle represents all of the fresh water on Earth. In the pie chart to the left, the circle represents the entire federal budget for the United States. In other words, the circles represent 100 percent of the fresh water and of the budget, respectively.

In both pie charts on this page, each part is given as a percentage, or part of 100. So, for example, the fresh water found in ice caps and glaciers is 77.78 percent (%) of all the fresh water on Earth, or 77.78 parts out of 100. Domestic spending accounts for 15.54 percent of the federal budget, or 15.54 parts out of 100.

To calculate the expense for domestic spending, you can multiply the amount of the total budget ($1,689,600,000,000) times the percentage for domestic spending (15.54%, or 0.1554).

Sometimes pie charts give amounts as ordinary numbers rather than as percentages. See the example to the right.

Understanding Tables

Another common kind of infographic is the table. A **table** consists of information arranged in **rows** and **columns,** with headings identifying the information. To read a table, simply locate a heading for the variable that is of interest or importance to you and then run your finger down and across, or across and up, as necessary. For example, to find out from the table below how many threatened reptiles there are, run your finger across to the column heading *Reptiles* and then down to the row heading *Threatened.*

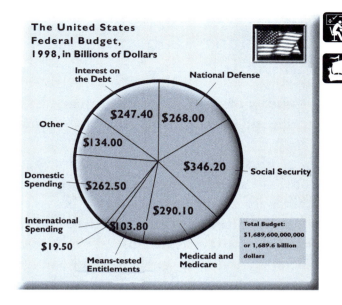

A pie chart showing categories of expense in the U.S. federal budget in billions of dollars

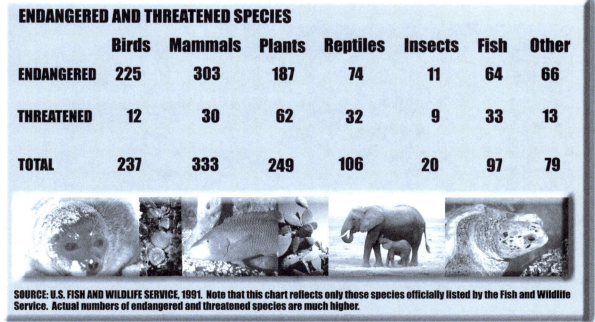

ENDANGERED AND THREATENED SPECIES

	Birds	Mammals	Plants	Reptiles	Insects	Fish	Other
ENDANGERED	225	303	187	74	11	64	66
THREATENED	12	30	62	32	9	33	13
TOTAL	237	333	249	106	20	97	79

SOURCE: U.S. FISH AND WILDLIFE SERVICE, 1991. Note that this chart reflects only those species officially listed by the Fish and Wildlife Service. Actual numbers of endangered and threatened species are much higher.

A table

USING READING STRATEGIES

Other Visual Materials: Illustrations, Diagrams, Plots, and Maps

Other common types of infographics include illustrations, diagrams, plots, and maps.

An **illustration** is any kind of drawing, painting, sketch, or other artwork that accompanies, enhances, and/or provides information about written material. Often, illustrations have **captions,** special text accompanying and explaining them. A caption may include the name of the illustrator, the title of the piece, copyright information about the piece, and additional information.

A **diagram** is an illustration that shows the parts of something. Usually a diagram has labels that identify the parts.

A **plot** is an illustration that shows the physical layout of something. Common types of plots include floor plans and blueprints.

Maps are scale drawings that show the relative sizes and locations of physical features, such as oceans, rivers, forests, mountain ranges, islands, and highways, as well as the locations and relative sizes of geopolitical entities such as cities, states, and countries. Maps often contain **legends** or **keys** that show the relative size, or **scale,** of the map (e.g., one inch = ten miles) and may contain special **icons,** little symbols that indicate such features as cities, recreation areas, or monuments.

The term **chart** is used to describe a wide variety of infographics, including tables, pie charts, and labeled diagrams (such as the charts hanging in butcher shops that show the parts of animals).

A diagram, or labeled illustration, shows the parts of something.

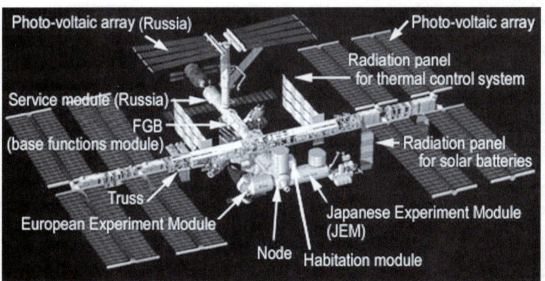

Diagram of the International Space Station (ISS). Courtesy of the National Aeronautics and Space Administration (NASA)

Analyzing Infographics

🪐 Read the **title** of the graphic to make sure that you understand what the graphic represents.

🪐 If the graphic has a **caption**, study this caption for further information about the graphic.

🪐 Locate the **variables** or **headings** on the graphic.

🪐 If the graphic has a **legend** or **key,** study it to make sure that you can locate the important parts of the graphic.

🪐 Study the graphic for interesting or important **relationships** among the headings or variables. Look for relationships such as *greater than*, *smaller than*, *equal to*, *percentage of*, *part of*, and so on. Also look for trends.

🪐 If the graphic is a **diagram,** look for labels that identify its parts.

🪐 For **line graphs**, trace with your finger a line from the main variable axis to the line. At the point where your finger crosses the line on the graph, trace a straight line to the axis that gives the value for the other variable.

🪐 For **bar graphs** and **column graphs,** trace with your finger a line from the end of the bar for the main variable to the axis that gives the value for the other variable.

🪐 For **pie charts,** determine whether the amounts shown on the graph for each variable are given in percentages, in ordinary numbers, or simply as wedges showing relative size. Determine how the wedge for each variable relates to the whole represented by the pie.

🪐 For **tables,** read the table by tracing with your finger imaginary lines from the headings above the columns and to the left of the rows. The values appear at the intersection of these imaginary lines.

USING READING STRATEGIES

Your Turn

A Use the information from the infographics in this lesson to answer the following questions.

1 What was the approximate number of users of the Internet in the United States in 1996?

2 What was the total change in the number of users of the Internet in the United States between 1991 and 1998?

3 What is the projected population of Brazil in the year 2015?

4 By how much is the population of Brazil expected to grow between the year 2000 and the year 2015?

5 What is the approximate average monthly income of a 35- to 44-year-old high-school graduate? Of the average person with a college bachelor's degree?

6 How much greater, on average, is the monthly income of someone with an associate degree than the monthly income of someone who is not a high-school graduate?

7 How much of the Earth's fresh water is found in rivers and lakes? Where can most of the Earth's fresh water be found?

8 Ice caps, glaciers, and groundwater account for what percentage of the Earth's fresh water?

9 Which type of animal accounts for about half of the species known to science?

10 Social Security payments accounted for what percentage of the 1998 federal budget? What percentage of the budget was set aside for defense? Which costs American taxpayers more, foreign aid (international spending) or interest on the debt?

11 How many endangered and threatened bird species were recognized by the U.S. Fish and Wildlife Service in 1991? How many fish? How many plants?

12 What was the total number of endangered and threatened species listed by the U.S. Fish and Wildlife Service in 1991?

13 Is the number of threatened mammal species listed by the U.S. Fish and Wildlife Service less than, more than, or about the same as the number of threatened reptile species?

14 What abbreviation is used to designate the International Space Station?

15 On the diagram of the International Space Station, is the habitation module located above or below the Japanese Experiment Module?

B   An excellent way to learn about charts and graphs is to create some yourself. Use the information from the table on endangered and threatened species on page 87 to create two graphs. The first should be a bar graph showing the number of endangered animals of various kinds. The second should be a column graph showing the number of threatened animals of various kinds. In your graphs, use a different color for each bar or column and create a legend for each graph showing which animal corresponds to which color.

C   Choose one of the following topics and write a paragraph supporting an opinion with information from a chart or graph from this lesson.

1   The Situation: You are President of the United States and wish to decrease the amount of money that the federal government spends. Your Task: Write a paragraph to be read during a radio address to the American people in which you explain which part or parts of the budget you would like to cut. Refer to the information given in the pie chart on page 87.

2   The Situation: Suppose that your younger brother says to you, "I don't care about high school or about going to vocational school or to college. I just want to have fun." Your Task: Write a short note to your brother explaining why it is in his best interest to stay in school and get a degree. Refer to the information given in the graph on page 85.

D   Work in a small group to find in popular magazines and newspapers examples of the following kinds of infographics:

1   Line Graph

2   Bar or Column Graph

3   Pie Chart

4   Table

5   Diagram

6   Map

7   Line Graph

8   Bar or Column Graph

Find at least one example of each kind. Excellent sources for such graphics include newspapers like the *New York Times*, the *Miami Herald*, the *Boston Globe*, and *USA Today* and magazines like *U.S. News and World Report*, *Newsweek*, and *Time*. Bring the graphics you find to class and share them with your classmates in a group presentation.

USING READING STRATEGIES

E   Imagine that your family is taking a road trip to the imaginary state of Paddywack. You will pick up and drop off your rental car in Wynona. Your little sister wants to go to the natural water slides on the Crafty River in the town of Xanadu. You want to visit the amusement park in Def Jam Springs. Your mother wants to purchase a hand-loomed rug in Weaversville. Your grandmother wants to visit her Cousin Millie in Crumblyville.

Your father wants to visit Megalopolis, the state capital. He also wants to use as little gasoline as possible. It's up to you to plan your route through the state of Paddywack.

Example: If you wanted to go from Megalopolis through the Valley of Doom to Weaversville, your directions would read: Take 9 South to 240 West to 933 South through the Valley of Doom to Weaversville.

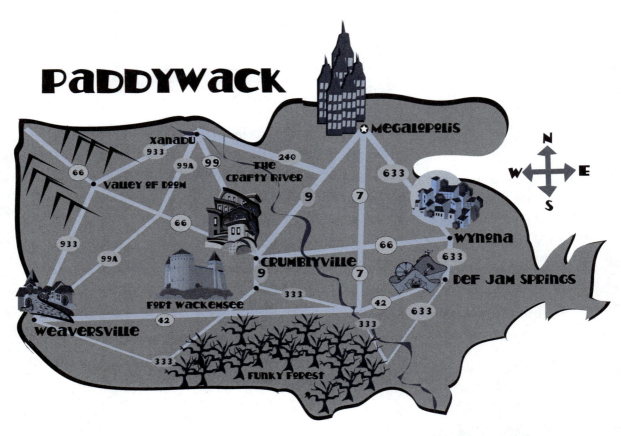

LESSON 3.6 *Reading Actively*

To be successful on the MCAS English exam, you need to be able to read well. A good reader takes an active approach, which involves thinking carefully about the material being read. An active reader asks questions, makes inferences and predictions, and summarizes to himself or herself during the reading process.

Asking Questions

Asking questions as you read keeps you focused. Ask yourself questions that are relevant to the material. Then, as you read, look for answers to your questions.

Suppose that you are reading a **narrative,** or story. You will want to ask questions that have to do with **motives** (reasons why characters act as they do): "Who might want to poison the butler?" You will also want to consider **relationships**: "Why can't Mr. O'Leary ask his own sons for help, instead of going to the bank?" You should note the nature of any **conflicts** in the story (struggles in which the characters are involved). After reading the whole piece, you should ask yourself about the **theme** of the story: "What lesson did the characters learn?"

In passages that describe events, you might want to ask yourself questions about sequence and about cause and effect. **Sequence** is the order in which things happen. Narratives will often (but not always) describe events in the order that they occurred. A passage that describes a process, like how to build a bird feeder, will detail a sequence of events. **Key words,** such as *first*, *next*, *then*, *later*, *before*, *after*, *last*, and *finally*, give you clues about the order of events in a passage: *First*, you draw a plan for your bird feeder. *Then*, you find the right materials. *After that*, in the proper sequence, you measure, cut, and connect the pieces. *Next*, you paint. *Later*, you fill with bird seed. *Finally*, you hang the feeder. To get the most out of such an article, you should ask questions like "What do I need to do before I start building?" and "What happens next?"

An article about the events leading up to a war would involve sequence, because the events that occurred are ordered in time. Even more important in such a passage, however, would be issues of **cause and effect**. A **cause** is anything that makes something else happen. The **effects** are the results produced. If you are reading about the rise of Nazism in prewar Germany, you might ask yourself a question like "Why did the German people accept a dictator?" Then you will be prepared to follow the reasoning as the author relates the chain of events that he or she believes led to this development. It is important not to confuse sequence with cause and effect. One event may happen in conjunction with (at the same time as) or right after another but not be caused by it. When you read a description of a series of events, ask yourself whether there is actually a cause-and-effect link or whether the events happened independently. Questions you might ask yourself as you read this kind of passage include "What causes this?" and "What effect will this have?"

USING READING STRATEGIES

Making Inferences: Induction and Deduction

Sometimes, as you read, you find that not everything is stated explicitly in the text. Some parts you have to figure out on your own, following clues that the author has provided. When you figure something out using reasoning, you are making an **inference**. Questions on the MCAS English exam may ask you to draw conclusions that are not explicitly drawn in the passages. To do that, you consider the information that is given, put those facts together, and use logical reasoning to figure out the answers. You will often be able to eliminate choices that are obviously wrong and use reasoning to choose among the answers that remain.

There are two methods of reasoning that you can use to draw inferences from **premises**, the information that you are given. These two methods of reasoning are **induction** and **deduction.**

When you reason **inductively,** you draw a general conclusion from particular facts. For example, suppose that you are reading a short story. In the first part of the story, a minor character hides her purse when a character named Andy shows up. Later in the story, when money is missing from a cash register drawer, a character tells the boss, "Maybe Andy took it." From facts like these, you might draw the general conclusion that "People don't trust Andy." Such a general conclusion would be an example of induction.

When you reason **deductively,** you start with a general statement, or premise, and draw a specific conclusion from it. The most famous example of deductive reasoning is this:

All human beings are mortal.
Socrates is a human being.
Therefore, Socrates is mortal.

Notice that this argument is deductive because it starts with a general premise (All human beings are mortal) and draws a specific conclusion (Socrates is mortal). In a **valid deduction,** like the one above, the conclusion (the last sentence) has to be true if the premises (the first two sentences) are true.

Suppose that you are reading a story and you learn that a particular character is a doctor. From this general fact, you can draw many specific conclusions, using deduction. For example, if the character is a doctor, then he or she went to medical school; is pretty smart; probably makes a good income; and knows a lot about sickness, injuries, the human body, medicines, and so on. So, if the character happens to witness an automobile accident, you can expect, based on your deductions, that the character is in a position to help. As you can see, using deductive reasoning as you read can help you to understand more about characters and events.

Making Predictions

One way to draw an inference as you are reading is to make a **prediction**, a guess about what will happen later in the piece of writing. If you are reading a nonfiction selection, you might make predictions to yourself about where the selection is leading. For example, suppose that you are reading a piece about Mars exploration. In the first part of the selection, the author tells about ways to change the Martian atmosphere to make it breathable, about how mining and construction might be done on Mars by robots, and about the development of cheap, reusable spacecraft. Based on this material, you might predict that the author will then discuss the possibility of establishing permanent colonies on Mars. As another example, suppose that you are reading a story and the narrator mentions, in passing, that the main character has a fear of fire. You might predict that fire will play a role later in the story. For example, the character might have to overcome this fear to rescue a family member.

Making predictions as you read can make your reading more enjoyable. As you read further, you can find out whether your predictions come true, how close they are to the mark, and so on.

Summarizing

Another way to remain actively involved as you are reading is to **summarize** as you go. From time to time, as you read, put together a few facts that you've learned into a statement that summarizes those facts, or draws them together into one compact form. Suppose, for example, that in the beginning of a story, you learn these facts about a character:

Although he works in a busy office, he always eats lunch alone.

He never volunteers to speak at company meetings, and when called upon to speak, he stutters, shuffles his papers, and has little to say.

When an attractive new employee asks him if he would like to go to dinner sometime, he turns red and makes an excuse not to go.

Based on these facts, you might decide that the character is a loner or is shy and afraid of people. As you can see, summarizing is a type of induction—drawing a general conclusion from specific facts.

Making Judgments

As part of the normal reading process, you form **judgments,** or opinions, about what you are reading. If you think to yourself, "This is boring," or "This is great," you are making both an observation about your interest in the subject and a judgment about the quality of the writing. When you are reading actively, you will want to make the process of judgment more conscious. If, for example, you are reading a piece of writing that is intended to persuade you to do something or to adopt a particular view, you will want to judge whether the author's arguments are valid and based on true facts. Questions you might ask yourself include the following:

- "Is this true?"
- "Is this the whole story?"
- "Does the author have some reason to be biased about this subject?"
- "Has the author presented evidence strong enough to convince me?"

When you are reading stories, you will want to make judgments about the characters. Do you approve or disapprove of a character's actions? Why, or why not?

USING READING STRATEGIES

Strategies for Active Reading

When you read selections during the MCAS English exam, read actively, following these guidelines:

📖 Begin by previewing the selection. Follow the steps outlined in Lesson 3.1, Previewing a Selection.

📖 As you read, remain focused on the text. Do not let your mind wander to other matters.

📖 As you read, ask yourself questions about what you are reading. Make inferences of all kinds—inductions, deductions, predictions, and summaries. Also make judgments about the facts, opinions, people, and events that you are reading about. Evaluate the facts upon which these judgments are based.

Remember that a good reader thinks continually during the reading process. One way to conceptualize active reading is to imagine that you are holding a dialogue, or conversation, with the text, much as you would with another person. The author makes his or her statements of facts and opinions, his or her inferences, predictions, summaries, and judgments, and so do you. Some people mistakenly think of reading as a passive process in which a person just sits back and takes in what the author says. Nothing could be further from the truth. A good reader actively engages the text while reading and thus gains a lot more from the experience.

Your Turn

A Choose a partner. Then choose a short story from a literature anthology—one that you have not read before but that you think you would enjoy. If the story has questions that follow it, ignore those. Instead, read the story actively. Keep a Reading Log as you read the story. Simply get a piece of paper and, as you read, write down the questions, inferences, predictions, summaries, and judgments that occur to you. When you are finished with the story, exchange your Reading Log with your partner and discuss its contents with him or her. This exercise will help you to understand not only the story but the different ways in which different readers approach a text.

B Repeat Exercise A, but this time do it with a nonfiction selection, such as a long newspaper or magazine article.

LESSON 4.1 Literary Genres, Elements, and Techniques

Many of the selections that you will encounter on the MCAS English test will be works of literature. At this level in your schooling, you have probably already studied literature for many years. Therefore, much of what you will read about in this chapter will be review.

Genres of Literature

One way to understand something is to categorize it. Dividing literature into categories allows us to examine similarities and differences among literary works and gives us a vocabulary to use in literary discussion. The different categories into which literature can be divided are called genres. A **genre** is simply a type of literary work. Genre has to do with the form a literary work takes (novel, drama, poem); with its subject matter (mystery, romance, science fiction); or with its purpose (parody, rebuttal speech, satire).

On the MCAS English test, you will be asked to write about a number of literary selections. You will most likely be given at least one prose passage and one poem to read. You might also encounter a selection from a **drama,** or play. A prose passage on the exam will most likely be a portion of some **narrative,** a piece of writing that tells a story. Narratives can be fiction or nonfiction. A work of **fiction** tells about imaginary people and characters. A work of **nonfiction,** such as a memoir or biography, tells about real people and characters. Make sure that you are familiar with the types, or genres, of narratives, poems, and plays described in the chart on the following pages.

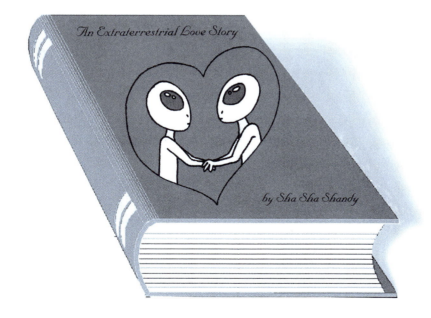

An Extraterrestrial Love Story

by Sha Sha Shandy

(*Romantic Science Fiction*)

Classifying Literary Works
Genres of Prose Narrative, Drama, and Poetry

Prose Narratives

Short Story. A short story is a brief work of fiction. The passage from "The Death of Iván Illych" in the Pretest is part of a short story by the Russian writer Leo Tolstoy.

Novel. A novel is a long piece of fictional prose. Within the category "novel" are many genres by subject matter, such as comedy of manners, Gothic novel, mystery, picaresque, romance, and science fiction. Elaborate plots involving many characters are characteristic of novels.

Narrative Essay. An **essay** is a short piece of nonfiction writing that explores a single subject from the author's point of view. A narrative essay tells a story. In an **autobiographical essay** or **memoir,** a writer tells a true story from his or her own life. In a **biographical essay,** a writer tells a true story from someone else's life. A **narrative personal essay** is written to make a specific point and uses a true story, in which the writer may play a major or a minor role, to illustrate the point.

Journal or **Diary.** A journal or diary is a day-to-day account and may be true (as in the case of *The Diary of Anne Frank*) or fictional (as in the case of *The Diary of Adrian Mole*, by Sue Townsend, or *The Diary of Adam and Eve*, by Mark Twain).

Myth. A myth is a story dealing with a god or goddess. Often myths explain the origins of natural phenomena. For example, the Greek myth of Arachne explains the origin of spiders.

Legend. A legend is a story, which may be partially or wholly true, about a hero or heroine. The stories about King Arthur are legends but are almost entirely fictional.

Tall Tale. A tall tale is a story with wildly exaggerated characters and events. The American stories about Pecos Bill and Paul Bunyan are examples of tall tales.

Fable. A fable is a short tale, usually with animal characters, told to illustrate a moral, or point about how people should behave.

Folk Tale. A folk tale is a short story that was originally passed down orally from generation to generation. Tales that were not originally written down are part of what is known as the oral tradition. Folk tales developed as they were passed on, rather than being created at one time by an individual author.

Anecdote. An anecdote, often true, is a very brief story told to make a point.

Drama

Comedy. A play in which the main character or characters meet a happy fate is called a comedy. Note that the term *comedy* is sometimes used of other types of work, such as long narrative poems, with happy endings (Dante's *Divine Comedy* is an example). In popular, nontechnical contemporary usage, a *comedy* is any work in which humorous elements predominate.

Tragedy. A drama in which the main character suffers an unhappy fate, generally because of a flaw in his or her own character, is called a tragedy.

Poetry

Narrative Poem. A narrative poem is a verse that tells a story. Narrative poems may be short, like most ballads, or long, like epics. A **ballad** is a rhymed narrative poem, generally written in four-line or six-line stanzas. An **epic** is a long story, usually in verse, relating events that occur on a grand scale. It relates the adventures of heroes, gods, and monsters and incorporates myths and legends.

Dramatic Poem. A dramatic poem is a verse that presents the speech of one or more characters in a dramatic situation. In a dramatic monologue, one character speaks, usually to another character who is silent. In a dramatic dialogue, two characters speak.

Lyric Poem. A lyric poem is a short, highly musical verse that expresses the thoughts and emotions of a speaker.

Elegy. An elegy is a long poem mourning someone's death.

UNDERSTANDING LITERARY SELECTIONS

The chart on the preceding pages is far from complete. In addition to the genres listed on the chart, there are many other genres of literature. For example, there are many genres of **nonnarrative prose,** prose works that do not tell stories. Some of these include the **persuasive essay,** in which a writer attempts to persuade readers to adopt an opinion or to take a course of action; the **informative essay,** in which a writer provides information about a subject; the **descriptive essay,** in which a writer paints a portrait, in words, of a subject; and **satire** (which can appear in prose, drama, or poetry), in which a writer pokes fun at or puts down someone or something.

Literary Elements and Techniques

If you are asked to analyze a literary passage on the MCAS English test, the directions might tell you to refer in your answer to the literary elements and techniques used by the author. **Literary elements** are the building blocks, or parts, of a work. **Literary techniques** are special ways of using language to communicate ideas or to achieve particular effects. Suspense might be an element of a story and foreshadowing the technique the author used to achieve it. It is important for you to know what the major literary elements and techniques are and to be able to recognize them in works of literature. The charts below and on the following pages explain the major literary elements and techniques.

Literary Elements and Techniques
Found in All Genres of Literature

1. **Image.** An image is a word or phrase that names something that can be seen, heard, touched, tasted, or smelled. The collection or group of images in a work is called its **imagery.** Example: "Ice covered the ground, and a cold wind whistled through the tree limbs."

2. **Setting.** The setting is the time and place in which the action of a literary work occurs. Setting is created by details that suggest a particular time and/or place.

3. **Mood.** The mood is the emotional quality evoked by a literary work. Mood is created by imagery, word choice, events, and other literary elements. Words that can be used to describe mood include *gloomy, sad, joyful, reflective, suspenseful,* and *frightening.*

4. **Subject.** The subject is the matter that a work is about. Common subjects of literary works include childhood, diversity, wonder, aging, nature, individuality, love, discrimination, struggle, death, courage, hope, and freedom.

5. **Theme.** A theme is a main idea in a literary work. For example, a work on the subject of aging might have as its theme the idea that elderly people can still be young in their thinking.

6. **Character.** A character is a being who takes part in the action of a literary work.

7. **Suspense.** Suspense is a feeling of curiosity or expectation, often tinged with anxiety, created by questions about what the outcome will be in a literary work.

8. **Tone.** Tone is the attitude adopted by the author, speaker, or narrator of a literary work toward the subject and/or reader of the work; it may also be the attitude of a speaker, narrator, or character in the work toward one or more other characters.

9. **Voice,** or **Style.** A writer's voice, or style, is the sum of all the characteristics that make his or her work sound unique. Hemingway is famous for a style that makes use of short, simple sentences with few embellishments. Faulkner is famous for a style that makes use of long, complicated sentences full of fancy flourishes.

10. **Flashbacks** and **Foreshadowing.** A flashback takes the reader to an earlier part of the story. Foreshadowing hints about events to come.

Figurative Language, or Figures of Speech

(expressions with a meaning other than or beyond the literal)

11. **Hyperbole.** A hyperbole is an exaggeration for effect. Example: "I'm so hungry, I could eat a horse!"

12. **Irony.** Irony is a contradiction, such as a difference between appearance and reality or a difference between what is said and what is meant. In the selection from "The Death of Iván Illych" in the Pretest, it is ironic that Illych should believe that all people must die but not be willing to believe that he himself must eventually die.

13. **Metaphor.** A metaphor is a figure of speech in which one thing is described as if it were another. Example: "My love is a red, red rose."

14. **Simile.** A simile is a type of metaphor, a comparison using *like* or *as*. Example: "My love is like a red, red rose."

15. **Personification.** Personification is a figure of speech in which a nonhuman thing is described as though it were human. Example: "The old car coughed, cried out once, and then gave up the ghost." One kind of personification is the **apostrophe,** in which a speaker or character addresses an inanimate object. Example: "O wild West Wind, thou breath of Autumn's being!"

16. **Symbol.** A symbol is something that stands both for itself and for something beyond itself. Roses are traditional symbols of love and beauty. A dove is a traditional symbol of peace.

(continued)

UNDERSTANDING LITERARY SELECTIONS

17. **Synesthesia.** Synesthesia is a figure of speech in which two different senses are combined. Example: "Jack wore a noisy red sweater."

18. **Understatement.** An understatement is an ironic expression in which something of importance is emphasized by being spoken of as though it were not important. Example: "The Emperor was dealing with a few minor matters like war on his borders and food riots in the streets of his cities."

Techniques Involving Sound

(commonly, but not exclusively, found in poetry)

19. **Alliteration.** Alliteration is the repetition of initial consonant sounds. Example: ". . . the <u>b</u>ass <u>b</u>oat, <u>b</u>obbing <u>b</u>eautifully"

20. **Onomatopoeia.** Onomatopoeia is the use of words or phrases that sound like the things that they describe. Examples: buzz, chop, clatter, mumble, clank, meow.

21. **Rhythm.** Rhythm is the pattern of beats, or stressed and unstressed syllables, in a line. The following line is made up of unstressed syllables followed by stressed syllables:

⏑ / ⏑ / ⏑ / ⏑ / ⏑ /

Is this the face that launched a thousand ships?

Oh, just a few minor matters like war on my borders and food riots in the streets of my cities.

Literary Elements and Techniques
Peculiar to Poetry

Rhyme Scheme (the pattern of rhymes in a poem)

1. **Rhymed verse** is poetry with a regular rhyme scheme.
2. **End rhyme** is rhyming at the ends of lines, as in

   For never was a story of more w<u>oe</u>
   Than this of Juliet and her Rome<u>o</u>.

3. **Internal rhyme** is rhyming within lines, as in "I s<u>ee</u> a bumbleb<u>ee</u>."
4. **Slant rhyme** is a near rhyme, as in "What did the w<u>ind</u>/Seek to f<u>ind</u>?"

Meter (the rhythmical pattern in a poem)

5. **Free verse** is poetry that does not have a set pattern of rhythm or rhyme.
6. **Metrical verse** is poetry with a regular rhythmical pattern.

Stanza Form

7. A **stanza** is a group of lines in a poem.
8. A **couplet** is a two-line stanza.
9. A **triplet,** or **tercet,** is a three-line stanza.
10. A **quatrain** is a four-line stanza.
11. A **quintain** is a five-line stanza.
12. A **sestet** is a six-line stanza.
13. A **heptastich** is a seven-line stanza.
14. An **octave** is an eight-line stanza.
15. A **sonnet** is a poem with fourteen lines having any of a number of different standard rhyme schemes.

Lesson 4.1—Literary Genres, Elements, and Techniques 103

UNDERSTANDING LITERARY SELECTIONS

Your Turn

A   Read the poems on the following page: John Donne's "Death, Be Not Proud," which you saw in the Pretest, and Christina Rossetti's "A Birthday." Then do the following.

1   Find an example of apostrophe in "Death, Be Not Proud."

2   Explain why "Death, Be Not Proud" can be called a sonnet.

3   Tell what kind of poem "Death, Be Not Proud" and "A Birthday" are—narrative, dramatic, or lyric—and explain why.

4   Find three similes in "A Birthday."

5   Find an example of personification in "Death, Be Not Proud."

6   Answer these questions: Is "A Birthday" free verse? rhymed verse? metrical verse?

7   Find two examples of metaphor in "Death, Be Not Proud."

8   Find one example of irony in "Death, Be Not Proud."

9   Find examples of repetition in "A Birthday."

10   Find one example of alliteration in "Death, Be Not Proud" and one example in "A Birthday."

11   Explain the tone of the speaker in each of these poems.

12   What is the stanza form of "A Birthday?"

13   In line 4 of "A Birthday," the speaker mentions fruit. Of what might this fruit be a symbol?

14   What is the theme of "A Birthday?" Of "Death, Be Not Proud"?

B   Work with other students in a small group to find in literary anthologies and other sources one example of each of the genres defined in this lesson. Create a chart listing each genre and the title and author(s) of the work that is an example of each one.

Example:

Genre	Work
Short Story	"The Devil and Daniel Webster," by Stephen Vincent Benét

C   Work with other students in a small group to find in literary anthologies and other sources one example of each of the figures of speech, rhetorical techniques, and techniques involving sound defined in this lesson. Create a chart listing each technique and an example of it.

Example:

Technique	Example
Hyperbole	"And I will love you still, my dear, / When all the seas run dry." —Robert Burns "To a Red, Red Rose"

Death, Be Not Proud

by John Donne

Death, be not proud, though some have callèd thee
Mighty and dreadful, for thou art not so;
For those whom thou think'st thou dost overthrow
Die not, poor Death, nor yet canst thou kill me.
From rest and sleep, which but thy pictures be,
Much pleasure; then from thee much more must flow,
And soonest our best men with thee do go,
Rest of their bones, and soul's delivery.
Thou art slave to fate, chance, kings, and desperate men,
And dost with poison, war, and sickness dwell,
And poppy or charms can make us sleep as well
And better than thy stroke; why swell'st thou then?
One short sleep past, we wake eternally
And death shall be no more; Death, thou shalt die. 🍎

A Birthday

by Christina Rossetti

My heart is like a singing bird
    Whose nest is in a watered shoot;
My heart is like an apple tree
    Whose boughs are bent with thickset fruit;
My heart is like a rainbow shell
    That paddles in a halcyon sea;
My heart is gladder than all these
    Because my love is come to me.

Raise me a dais of silk and down;
    Hang it with vair and purple dyes;
Carve it in doves and pomegranates,
    And peacocks with a hundred eyes;
Work in it gold and silver grapes,
    In leaves and silver fleurs-de-lys;
Because the birthday of my life
    Is come, my love is come to me. 🍎

UNDERSTANDING LITERARY SELECTIONS

LESSON 4.2 *Reading a Lyric Poem*

On the MCAS English test, you will most likely encounter at least one poem. In most cases, the poem will be a **lyric**—a short poem that expresses a speaker's emotions and thoughts in concrete, precise, musical language.

Students usually have more problems with poetry than with any other kind of literature. However, reading poetry doesn't have to be difficult. With the right approach, you'll find that reading poetry is not that difficult; in fact, reading poetry (and writing it) can be a lot of fun.

In the Renaissance era, four to five hundred years ago, well-to-do, powerful people—kings and queens, lords and ladies—often sent lyric poems to one another. These poems were like personal letters. Today, people still sometimes write lyric poems for the same purpose. In fact, the simplest way to think about a lyric poem is to consider it a kind of letter from the poem's speaker. Like a letter, the poem tells us what someone thinks and feels. Let's look at an example:

Have You Forgotten?
by James Worley

The curiosity of cats, observed,
can enable men to retrieve infancy:
some sights and sounds and the
     movements bridging them
entice the kitten and the child alike:
the drip of faucets, the slide of sinkside
     streams,
the play of light reflected to a wall,
the crumpled paper breathing on the
     floor—
have you forgotten? watch a cat!
return! 🍎

When reading a poem, don't be put off by the division of the poem into lines. Remember that most poems, like stories, are written in sentences. Don't worry about the line breaks. Simply read each sentence in the poem separately, and try to **paraphrase** it, or put it into your own words. Let's try this with James Worley's poem.

The first statement in the poem is "The curiosity of cats, observed, / can enable men to retrieve infancy." In other words, if we observe, or watch, how curious cats are, we can become like children again. The second statement in the poem is "[S]ome sights and sounds and the movements bridging them / entice the kitten and the child alike." In other words, children and kittens are enticed, or attracted, by the same sights, sounds, and movements. The poem then presents a list of the kinds of things that kittens and children are attracted to: dripping faucets, streams of water sliding down

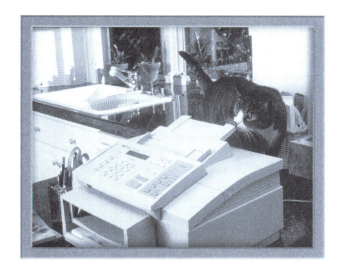

the sides of sinks, light reflected and "playing" on a wall, crumpled paper "breathing" on the floor. The speaker then asks the reader a question, "[H]ave you forgotten?"

Finally, the poem promises that if you watch a cat, you can "return," or go back to a childhood frame of mind. In other words, if you do not remember what it was like to be a child, if you do not remember how to take joy in the tiny, little events occurring all around you, simply watch a cat, and you'll remember a time when you, too, enjoyed all the little miracles in life.

The first step in understanding a poem, then, is to paraphrase it, or put its sentences into your own words. If you wish, you can jot the notes for your paraphrase down in the margins of the Student Test Booklet that you are given for the MCAS exam.

Sometimes, when attempting to paraphrase, you will encounter words in poems that you don't understand. For example, you might not have known the meaning of the word *entice* in line 4 of "Have You Forgotten?" When reading a poem on your own, you can look up such difficult words in a dictionary. When you are reading a poem during the test, it will be helpful to be able to figure out such words from their context.

For information on using context clues to determine the meanings of unfamiliar words, see Lesson 3.4.

The next step toward understanding a lyric poem is to ask yourself about the speaker and about the subject. Imagine that you are an anthropologist in the year 2225 and that you have just dug up a box. In the box you have found a journal, and in the journal you have found the poem "Have You Forgotten?" What does the poem tell you about its speaker? Who was this person? What was this person speaking about? What did this person think and feel? To answer questions like this, you need to look for clues in the poem. Again, if you wish, you can list in the margins of your Reading Book things that the poem reveals about the speaker:

The speaker . . .

—is interested in cats

—is probably a man because of the reference, in line 2, to "men"

—must be older, no longer a child, because he speaks about "retrieve[ing] infancy"

—thinks that people ought to observe cats

—thinks that observing cats will make it possible for people to "retrieve infancy"

—seems to feel that retrieving infancy, or becoming like a child again, is a good thing

—is very observant about little things (dripping faucets, light playing on the wall, etc.)

—wants us to watch cats so that we can remember what we were like when we were children and full of curiosity ourselves

UNDERSTANDING LITERARY SELECTIONS

After you have paraphrased the poem, have identified the subject, and have listed the characteristics, interests, ideas, and feelings of the speaker, you are ready to state the poem's **theme,** or main idea. In a lyric poem, the theme is the main message that the speaker wants to communicate:

Theme: Watching cats can help people to regain the sort of curiosity—wonder about and interest in ordinary things—that they had when they were children.

Finally, look for the special literary techniques used in the poem. These techniques include such features as rhythm, rhyme, alliteration, metaphor, and simile. If you have forgotten what any of these terms mean, go back to the previous lesson and review them.

Literary Techniques in the Poem "Have You Forgotten?"

Alliteration
—<u>c</u>uriosity of <u>c</u>ats
—<u>s</u>lide of <u>s</u>ink<u>s</u>ide <u>s</u>treams

Rhyme
—sl<u>ide</u> of sinks<u>ide</u>

Metaphor
—movements connecting sights and sounds are compared to bridges

Personification
—light is said to "play"
—crumpled paper, moving on the floor, is described as "breathing"

Finally, think about these techniques and ask yourself how they reinforce the poem's meaning. The alliteration and rhyme in the poem make it more musical and thus more memorable. Describing movements as bridges reinforces the idea that watching a cat serves as a kind of bridge back to one's own childhood. Personifying the light and the paper on the floor tell us that if we exercise our curiosity, then little things in the world will seem more interesting. They will "come alive."

Reading a Poem During the Exam

If one of the works that you are asked to read for the test is a poem, begin by reading the poem through quickly a couple of times. Then examine the poem, following the steps outlined on the chart on the next page.

Steps To Understanding a Lyric Poem

🍁 First, paraphrase the poem. That is, restate it to yourself, sentence by sentence, in your own words.

🍁 Second, look for clues in the poem that tell you what the speaker is speaking about—his or her subject.

🍁 Third, based on clues in the poem, identify what the poem reveals about the speaker's interests, ideas, and feelings.

🍁 Fourth, identify the main idea, or theme, that the speaker of the poem is expressing.

🍁 Fifth, note any special literary techniques used in the poem, such as vivid imagery or metaphors.

🍁 Sixth, think about how these techniques reinforce the poem's theme.

Feel free to use the margins of your Reading Book to take notes on any of the information gleaned by following the steps described above. See the example to the right.

Paraphrase:
- If we watch how curious cats are, we became like children again
- Both children + kittens are attracted by some sights, sounds, movements
- List of sights, sounds, movements
- If you've forgotten what it was like as a kid, you can remember by watching a cat

subject = Watching Cats

ncy:
movements bridging them
like:
inkside streams,
vall,
on the floor—
at! return!

Speaker:
- likes cats
- probably a man
- must be older, not a child
- thinks people should observe cats
- thinks being childlike a good thing
- is observant

Theme:
Watching cats can help people to regain curiosity, wonder they had as children

Techniques:
Alliteration
— curiosity of cats
— sinkside

Metaphor
— movements like bridges

Personification — light "plays"
— paper "breathing"

Your Turn

A   Choose one poem from the next page and do the following on your own paper:

1   First, paraphrase the poem. That is, restate it, sentence by sentence, in your own words.

2   Second, look for clues in the poem that tell you what the speaker is speaking about—his or her subject. List that subject.

3   Third, based on clues in the poem, make a list telling what the poem reveals about the speaker's interests, ideas, and feelings.

4   Fourth, state the main idea, or theme, that the speaker of the poem is expressing.

5   Fifth, make a list of the literary techniques used in the poem.

6   Sixth, make a few notes to yourself about how these techniques reinforce the poem's theme.

B   Write a paragraph explaining the theme, or main idea, of the poem that you chose for Exercise A. Begin your paragraph with a topic sentence that states the title, author, and theme of the poem, like this:

The theme of James Worley's poem "Have You Forgotten" is that by observing the playful curiosity of cats, we can remember the wonder that we felt about the world when we were very young.

After your topic sentence, write at least five or six additional sentences that present evidence from the poem to support your topic sentence. Use **transitions,** such as *first, second, third, then, next, finally, in conclusion,* and so on, to connect your ideas.

Poems for Practice

Brahma[1]

by Ralph Waldo Emerson

If the red slayer thinks he slays,
    Or if the slain think he is slain,
They know not well the subtle ways
    I keep, and pass, and turn again.

Far or forgot to me is near;
    Shadow and sunlight are the same;
The vanished gods to me appear;
    And one to me are shame and fame.

They reckon ill who leave me out;
    When me they fly, I am the wings;
I am the doubter and the doubt,
    And I the hymn the Brahmin[2] sings.

The strong gods pine for my abode,
    And pine in vain the sacred Seven;[3]
But thou, meek lover of the good!
    Find me, and turn thy back[4] on heaven.

Alone

by Edgar Allan Poe

From childhood's hour I have not been
As others were—I have not seen
As others saw—I could not bring
My passions from a common spring—
From the same source I have not taken
My sorrow—I could not awaken
My heart to joy at the same tone—
And all I lov'd— I lov'd alone—
Then—in my childhood—in the dawn
Of a most stormy life—was drawn
From ev'ry depth of good and ill
The mystery which binds me still—
From the torrent, or the fountain—
From the red cliff of the mountain—
From the sun that round me roll'd
In its autumn tint of gold—
From the lightning in the sky
As it pass'd me flying by—
From the thunder, and the storm—
And the cloud that took the form
(When the rest of Heaven was blue)
Of a demon in my view—

Ralph Waldo Emerson

Edgar Allan Poe

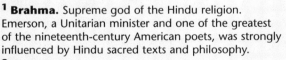

[1] **Brahma.** Supreme god of the Hindu religion. Emerson, a Unitarian minister and one of the greatest of the nineteenth-century American poets, was strongly influenced by Hindu sacred texts and philosophy.

[2] **Brahmin.** Member of the highest caste of Hindu society, the priestly caste

[3] **the Sacred Seven.** Lesser gods. Hindus are polytheistic, believing in many gods, but all, according to Hindu belief, are subordinate to and part of the one supreme god.

[4] **turn thy back.** According to Hindu philosophy, all things, good and bad, are part of Brahma, and people should therefore embrace life in all its complexity. Emerson's line suggests turning away from simplistic ideas and embracing a more inclusive spirituality.

LESSON 4.3 *Reading a Narrative*

Most likely, more than one of the selections that you will read for the MCAS English test will be a short narrative. A **narrative** is any literary work that tells a story. Types of narrative that you are likely to find on the test include very brief short stories or passages taken from short stories, novels, auto-biographies, or memoirs. Although these kinds of narrative differ in important respects, you can follow the same steps when reading them and answering questions about them for the test. That's because all narratives have at least some elements in common. The chart below and on the next page describes some of the elements that are common to narratives.

Elements of a Narrative

1. **Setting.** The setting is the time and place in which the action occurs.

2. **Mood.** The mood is the overall emotional quality evoked by the work or part of the work (melancholy, hopeful, nostalgic, etc.).

3. **Tone.** The tone is the attitude adopted by the author or narrator toward the subject or toward the reader (angry, satirical, playful, etc.).

4. **Narrator.** The narrator is the voice telling the story. In stories told from the **first-person point of view,** the narrator uses words such as *I* and *we* and may participate in the action of the story. In stories told from the **third-person point of view,** the narrator uses words such as *he, she,* and *they* and does not take part in the action of the story.

5. **Character.** The characters are the figures who take part in the action of the narrative. These include **main characters,** such as the protagonist and antagonist, and **minor characters,** who play smaller roles. A character who changes is known as a **dynamic character.** A character who does not change is known as a **static character.** A **flat, stock,** or **stereotypical** character is one that is one-dimensional and not fully developed.

6. **Protagonist.** The protagonist is the main character in the selection. Usually, the main character experiences some conflict, or struggle, and goes through some important change.

7. **Antagonist.** Some stories have an antagonist, a person or force that struggles with the protagonist.

8. **Conflict.** The central conflict is the major struggle experienced by the protagonist. This conflict may be **external** (between the character and an outside force) or **internal** (within the character).

9. **Plot.** The plot is the series of events in the narrative. The **exposition** provides background information. The **inciting incident** introduces the central conflict. The inciting incident is followed by the **rising action,** in which the central conflict is developed. The **climax** is the high point of interest or suspense in the story. The **crisis,** or **turning point,** is a point in the story at which something decisive happens to determine the future course of events in the narrative and the working out of the conflict. The events that occur after the turning point are called the **falling action.** The falling action ends with the **resolution,** the point in the story at which the central conflict is resolved. The **dénouement,** literally the untying, tells the final outcome of loose ends in the plot. (See Freytag's Pyramid below for a representation of plot.)

10. **Motive.** A motive is something that moves a character to act in a certain way. For instance, a character might be motivated by a desire for wealth or affection.

Bear in mind that a given narrative might not contain all of these parts. Consider, for example, the passage from "The Death of Iván Illych," which is one of the readings for the Pretest (pages 7–8). Since this is just a passage from the middle of a short story, it does not contain some of the elements of short stories, such as the inciting incident, a climax, and a resolution of the central conflict.

The key thing to remember about narratives is that almost all of them revolve around a **central conflict,** or struggle. Usually, by facing this central conflict, the main character grows and changes in some way. The character learns something, and what the character learns becomes the **theme,** the main idea or central point of the narrative.

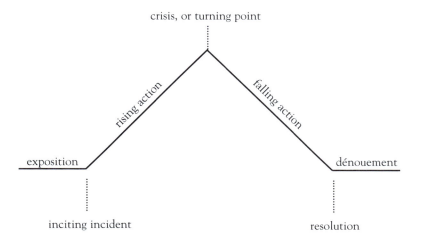

Freytag's Pyramid: Note that the climax can occur before or after the crisis or can be the same event as the crisis.

UNDERSTANDING LITERARY SELECTIONS

On the test, read the questions and the writing prompts carefully. As you look back at the passage, look for elements in the narrative that relate to the subject of the question or prompt. Suppose that you were responding to the following writing prompt:

Explain the theme of the selection from "The Death of Iván Illych," pointing out literary techniques used in the selection to present this theme.

Your topic sentence would state the theme of the selection. The rest of the paragraph would give details from the selection showing how specific literary elements were used to present the theme. Here is an example:

One Student's Response

Chantal wrote the following paragraph in response to this prompt:

In "The Death of Iván Illych," the theme of the story is the difficulty of facing one's own death. The central conflict in this passage is that the protagonist, Iván, cannot accept that he is dying. The author uses personification and metaphor to show Iván's attitude toward death. Iván thinks of death as an "unwelcome guest" who is "unacceptable in the parlor of his consciousness." He also calls death "a highwayman," "a thief," "a bill collector," and "a murderer." It is ironic that Iván, who is a public prosecutor and therefore used to

logical arguments in court and who remembers an argument about death from a logic textbook, can't accept the logical truth that he too must die.

Notice the following characteristics of Chantal's paragraph:

1. She has used literary terms, such as *protagonist*, *central conflict*, *irony*, *personification*, *metaphor*, and *theme*.

2. She has paid particular attention to aspects of the selection that deal with the subject in the writing prompt (death).

3. Chantal includes quotations from the selection as examples to back up the points made in her answer.

4. The paragraph contains a one-sentence summary of what the passage reveals about the subject of the writing prompt (the attitude of the character toward death).

Your Turn

Reread "The Story of an Hour" on pages 14 through 16 of the Pretest. Then fill in the following story map:

Story Map

Title of Story: _____ "The Story of an Hour"

Author of Story: _____

Characters:

Protagonist:

_____

Other Characters:

_____

_____

Setting:

Details that reveal time and place:

_____

_____

Influence of the setting on the main character: _____

_____

_____

_____

Plot of the Story:

Inciting Incident:

_____

Central Conflict:

_____

_____

Rising Action:

_____

_____

Turning Point:

_____

_____

Resolution:

_____

_____

Central Conflict
☐ **Internal**   ☐ **External**

How does the protagonist change in the course of the story?

_____

_____

_____

_____

Theme: What does the story tell us about feelings of repression experienced by married women in the nineteenth century?

_____

_____

_____

_____

_____

Literary Techniques:

Meaning of Symbols:
  the window: _____
  spring: _____

Irony:

_____

_____

_____

_____

UNDERSTANDING LITERARY SELECTIONS

LESSON 4.4 Two Types of Criticism: Analysis and Evaluation

In everyday speech, when people use the word *criticism*, they usually mean some sort of negative commentary. In literary studies, however, criticism is not necessarily negative. **Criticism** is simply any careful, reasoned response to a literary work. When you write about works of literature in your responses on the MCAS exam, you will be practicing, in a rudimentary way, the art of criticism.

There are many, many different approaches to criticism. Each approach represents particular views about the relationship between the reader and a text and about which elements of a literary work are important to consider. Some common approaches to criticism are described in the chart on the following page. However, a full treatment of these is beyond the scope of this text, and knowledge of them is not essential for success on the MCAS exam.

What is essential is that you understand that whatever approach a critic takes, he or she usually does analysis, evaluation, or both. When you encounter an open-response question about a literary work on the MCAS exam, think about whether the question is asking you to analyze or to evaluate and respond accordingly.

Analyzing a Literary Text

Analysis is the process of dividing something into its parts and then studying how the parts are related to one another and to the whole. When you analyze a literary text, you look at its elements and techniques and see how these are related.

Here is an example of a question that asks you to do an analysis:

> What is the central conflict in this story, how is it introduced, and how is it resolved?

To answer this question, you need to analyze the central conflict, or struggle, faced by the protagonist by dividing it into its parts: the inciting incident that introduces the conflict and the resolution in which the conflict is brought to a conclusion.

Here is another example of an analysis question:

> Who is the main character in this story, and what sets her apart from the other characters?

To answer this question, you need to identify the main character and then think about the qualities of that character—the characteristics that set her apart from other characters in the story. These qualities might include the character's appearance, her background, the nature of her relationships with other characters, her motivations, or any of a wide number of other characteristics.

Here is yet another example of an analysis question:

> What is the mood of this selection, and how is that mood created?

To answer this question, you need to identify the elements of the selection that create its mood, or overall emotional effect.

Literary Criticism
Some Common Approaches

Biographical criticism relates elements of a literary work to events in the life of the author.

Didactic criticism deals with the moral, ethical, or political messages in literary works.

Feminist criticism looks at a text from the point of view of what it reveals about gender roles and/or the relative status of men and women.

Formal criticism explains a literary work in terms of its genre or type.

Freudian criticism relates a literary work to the psychoanalytic theories advanced by Sigmund Freud and his followers, with particular emphasis on unconscious motivations; wish fulfillments; and suppressed, unresolved conflicts from childhood.

Historical criticism relates a literary work to the time and place in which it was produced.

New Criticism, a critical movement whose heyday was the mid-twentieth century, emphasizes close analysis of texts and criticism based only on the elements and techniques used in the text, not on matters outside the work itself such as politics, historical context, or authors' biographies.

Reader-response criticism holds that the meaning of a literary text lies not in the text itself but in the subjective experience that the reader has when reading. A radical but related approach, **deconstructionist criticism,** holds that a text itself has no independent meaning or reality but is constructed by the reader in the process of reading.

Structuralist criticism views a literary work from the point of view of essential "binary opposites" involved in or implied by the work, such as good/evil, sacred/profane, real/illusory, natural/artificial, literary/nonliterary, and so on. The idea behind structuralist criticism is that people, including authors, inherit languages that predispose them to view the world in terms of certain opposing categories, ideas, or forces and that these predispositions determine, to a great extent, the content and structure of a work.

These might include elements of the setting (an old house with creaky doors and floorboards, a thunderstorm, night, darkness, fog, etc.); specific imagery used in the selection ("the ghastly reflections of yellowed candlelight in the broken window-panes," "cobwebs," "the scurrying of mice"); a suspenseful twist in the plot; the tone assumed by the narrator; and the diction that the narrator uses.

In each of the examples just given, the question requires that you look back over the selection to find particular elements. Identifying elements and thinking about how they relate to a particular concern or question is what analysis is all about.

Evaluating a Literary Text

Evaluation is the process of arriving at a judgment, or opinion, of someone or something. Suppose that you are walking out of a movie and a friend asks, "What did you think of it?" Your friend is asking you for an evaluation, in this case, for an overall evaluation of the film. To answer your friend, you might simply say, "It was great" or "I hated it," but when you answer evaluation questions on the MCAS exam, you will have to be much more specific, identifying particular aspects of the selection that support your evaluation. Here is an example of an evaluation question:

Should Mr. McKuen have refused his neighbor's offer? Why, or why not?

This question asks you to make a judgment about the actions of a character, Mr. McKuen. You have to form an opinion about whether Mr. McKuen should have acted as he did and then support your opinion with evidence from the selection.

Distinguishing Between Analysis and Evaluation

As you have learned in this lesson, two functions of criticism, and two different tasks that you will need to carry out when answering written questions on the MCAS exam, are **analysis** and **evaluation**. To summarize the differences between the two:

Analysis involves gathering related facts from the selection and then generalizing, or drawing an inference, based upon those facts. A written answer to an analysis question might begin with the generalization, or inference, and then present facts to support it. The result of the analysis—the conclusion drawn based upon consideration of various elements of the selection—is an **interpretation.**

Evaluation involves making a judgment, or statement of opinion, about some aspect of the work or about the work as a whole and then supporting that judgment with facts. A written answer to an evaluation question might begin with the judgment and then present facts to support it.

> Analysis = related facts and
>   generalization about them
> Evaluation = judgment supported
>   by facts

Your Turn

A Read the selection from Washington Irving's "The Legend of Sleepy Hollow," a tale about a headless horseman. Then follow the directions given after it.

[T]his sequestered glen has long been known by the name of SLEEPY HOLLOW, and its rustic lads are called the Sleepy Hollow Boys throughout all the neighboring country. A drowsy, dreamy influence seems to hang over the land, and pervade the very atmosphere. Some say that the place was bewitched by a high German doctor during the early days of the settlement; others, that an old Indian chief, the prophet or wizard of his tribe, held his powwows there before the country was discovered by Master Hendrick Hudson. Certain it is, the place still . . . holds a spell over the minds of the good people, causing them to walk in a continual reverie. They are given to all kinds of marvelous beliefs; have trances and visions, and see strange sights, and hear music and voices in the air. The whole neighborhood abounds with local tales, haunted spots, and twilight superstitions; stars shoot and meteors glare oftener across the valley than in any other part of the country, and the Night Mare, with her whole nine fold, seems to make it the favorite scene of her gambols. 🍎

Write a paragraph in response to the following analysis question about this passage from Irving's story:

How does Washington Irving create suspense in his opening description of the valley known as Sleepy Hollow?

Follow these steps:

1 First, review the passage and make a list, on your own paper, of elements in Irving's description of the setting that contribute to creating suspense.

2 Next, write a sentence that states, generally, the idea that the author creates suspense at the beginning of his story in his description of the valley. In this first sentence for your paragraph, make sure to use both the author's name and the full title of the story. Place the title in quotation marks.

3 Then, on your own paper, write your paragraph. Use the sentence that you wrote in step 2, above, as the first sentence and topic sentence of your paragraph. In the body sentences, present the details from the list you made in step 1. You can present details by quoting or by paraphrasing (putting them in your own words). Make sure to use quotation marks around any direct quotations. As you write, use transitions at the beginnings of sentences to connect your ideas. Transitions that you might use include *in addition, furthermore, another example, yet another example, first, then, next, finally, in short,* or *in summary.*

B Washington Irving's "The Legend of Sleepy Hollow" is usually thought of as a spooky story for children. Imagine that you are an editor at a publishing house that is preparing an anthology of stories for children aged seven to ten. Based on the passage that you have just read from Irving's story, write a paragraph evaluating the suitability of the story for the anthology. State your judgment about whether the story is suitable for seven-to-ten-year-olds in your topic sentence. Then support your opinion with evidence.

LESSON 5.1 Aspects of Nonfiction Selections

Most of the passages that you will encounter on the MCAS English test will be nonfiction selections. Newspaper articles, essays, speeches, textbooks, and travel guides are just some examples of the many different **genres,** or **forms,** of nonfiction writing (see the list on page 124). In this lesson you will learn about some of the important features of nonfiction, including the subject, thesis, mode, purpose, and method of organization.

Subject and Thesis

The **subject** of a piece of writing is what the selection as a whole is about. The **thesis** is its main idea. When reading a nonfiction selection on the MCAS exam, make sure that you ask yourself, "What is the subject?" or "What is this piece about?" and "What is the author's main idea, or thesis?"

The thesis is often expressed in a **thesis statement,** a single sentence, or sometimes two or three sentences, stating the main idea of the essay or composition. In rare cases the main idea might be implied rather than directly stated. The thesis statement usually appears in the introduction. It might be restated in different words in the conclusion. An author might, for example, take the end of slavery in the United States as a subject for an informative essay. The thesis advanced in the essay might be that slavery was not ended by one person or group in one fell swoop but was ended gradually, in stages, over time. The thesis statement in the introductory paragraph of such an essay might read like this:

Slavery in the United States did not die suddenly but gradually, over a period of years, beginning with measures to limit the spread of slavery before the war, followed by the Emancipation Proclamation during the war, and ending with the Thirteenth Amendment to the Constitution.

Mode, Purpose, and Aim

Traditionally, textbook authors have classified nonfiction writing based upon its mode. A **mode** is simply a kind of writing done for a particular purpose. The **purpose** is what the writer wishes to accomplish. The modes of writing traditionally discussed in writing texts are **narration, description, persuasion,** and **exposition.**

The Traditional Modes

📖 **Narrative writing** has as its main purpose relating events. Biographies, autobiographies, histories, and news reports all employ narration. Sometimes narration makes use of **dialogue,** or speech.

📖 **Descriptive writing** has as its main purpose presenting a portrayal of a subject in words. Rarely is a piece of writing purely descriptive.

The Traditional Modes (cont.)

📖 **Persuasive writing** has as its primary purpose convincing the reader to adopt some point of view or to take some action. Campaign speeches and editorials are examples of persuasive writing.

📖 **Expository writing** has as its major purpose presenting information. Sometimes this mode is referred to as **informative writing**. Textbooks, technical manuals, directions, recipe books, and encyclopedia articles are all examples of exposition.

In an influential work called *A Theory of Discourse*, James Kinneavy offered an alternative to this traditional way of classifying writing. According to Kinneavy, writing can be classified based on the standard communication model, which views every act of communication as involving a sender who encodes a message about a subject into a set of symbols and then transmits that message to a recipient.

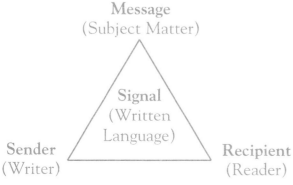

The communications triangle

Based on the communications triangle, Kinneavy classifies writing into four types, each with a different **aim,** or emphasis.

Kinneavy's Modes, or Aims

📖 **Expressive writing** has as its major purpose expressing the writer's state of mind, personal feelings, attitudes, ideas, values, or beliefs. The emphasis in this kind of writing is on the sender of the message.

📖 **Expository writing** has as its major purpose presenting information. The emphasis in this kind of writing is on the subject.

📖 **Persuasive writing** has as its major purpose changing the reader's mind or moving the reader to action. The emphasis in this kind of writing is on the receiver of the message.

📖 **Literary writing** has as its major purpose to create an imaginary world to entertain or instruct. The emphasis in this kind of writing is on the symbols—on the words themselves and the forms that they take.

Neither way of classifying writing is completely satisfactory because, in the real world, the modes and aims overlap. Narrative writing usually contains elements of description. Literary writing is often narrative and descriptive and is frequently expressive in Kinneavy's sense. Nonetheless, in many pieces of writing, one of these modes or aims predominates, and so it is useful to refer to pieces of writing using these terms, and you may have occasion to do so when you prepare written responses for the MCAS exam.

Organization

A writer doesn't simply put his or her ideas down in random order, because a willy-nilly presentation of ideas would be extremely confusing to a reader. Often, writers of nonfiction make use of overall organizational plans, arranging their ideas for presentation in a logical sequence. The following chart describes some common **methods of organization** used in nonfiction.

Methods of Organization

- **Chronological Order.** Events are presented in time order, or in order of occurrence.

- **Spatial Order.** Details are presented in order of appearance, for example, from top to bottom, from left to right, or from near to far.

- **Degree Order.** Details or ideas are presented according to the degree to which they embody some quality, such as value, familiarity, or importance. For example, ideas might be presented, in order, from most important to least important.

Methods of Organization (cont.)

- **Comparison/Contrast Order.** In comparison/contrast writing, an author discusses the similarities and/or differences between two or more subjects. If the writing is in **subject order,** the author discusses one subject and its characteristics and then the next subject and its characteristics. If the writing is in **characteristics order,** the author first compares or contrasts both subjects with regard to one characteristic (such as quality), then moves on to the next characteristic (such as price), and so on, through the piece.

- **Cause-and-Effect Order.** The writer presents one or more causes followed by their effects or one or more effects followed by their causes.

- **Classification Order.** The writer breaks his or her subject into smaller subjects, groups them, and then discusses each in turn.

- **Thesis, Antithesis, Synthesis Order.** The writer presents an idea (the **thesis**), presents an opposing idea (the **antithesis**), and then presents a compromise or a new idea that combines the two (the **synthesis**).

This chart of types of organization is far from complete, because writers are extremely inventive about coming up with logical ways to organize their work. Often, writers use a combination of these methods of organization. Sometimes, they use a **part-by-part organization** in which each idea is connected logically to the one that precedes it and the one that follows it, but the whole piece of writing follows no overall organizational pattern.

Whatever method of organization the writer uses, his or her piece will generally contain three parts: an **introduction** that presents the main idea or thesis, a **body** that elaborates on the main idea, and a **conclusion** that sums up the piece.

Reading a Nonfiction Selection

As you read, ask yourself the following questions:

📖 What is the title? Who is the author?

📖 What is the subject of the selection?

📖 What is the author's thesis, or main idea?

📖 What is the primary purpose of the piece of writing? to entertain? to inform? to persuade? to describe?

📖 What is the primary mode of the piece of writing? Is it narrative, descriptive, persuasive, or expository?

In addition, pay attention to any of the following that you encounter:

—Names of people and places

—Significant facts and figures

—Significant events and their order of occurrence, including dates

—Conflicts, issues, and arguments pro and con

—Similarities and differences

—Causes and effects

—Questions posed by the author and the answers given

—Steps in processes

—Opinions and the facts presented to back them up

UNDERSTANDING NONFICTION SELECTIONS

Genres, or Forms, of Nonfiction Writing

The following is a partial list of the genres of nonfiction writing. Notice the great variety of forms of nonfiction. Notice also that many of the types of nonfiction, such as briefs (law) and human interest stories (journalism), are related to particular professions.

Abstract	Consumer Report	Invitation	Proposal
Acceptance Speech	Contract	Itinerary	Protocol
Advertising Copy	Cookbook	Journal	Public Service
Advice Column	Course Description	Keynote Address	Announcement
Afterword	Court Decision	Lab Report	Radio Spot
Agenda	Credo	Law (Statute)	Rebuttal Speech,
Almanac	Critical Analysis	Learning Log	Debate
Analysis Essay	Curriculum	Lesson	Recipe
Annals	Demonstration	Letter of Complaint	Recommendation
Annotations	Deposition	Letter of Intent	Referendum Question
Annual Report	Diary	Letter to the Editor	Report
Appeal	Diatribe	Magazine Article	Research Report
Application Essay	Dictionary Entry	Manifesto	Resignation
Atlas	Directions	Manual	Restaurant Review
Autobiography	Docudrama	Marketing Plan	Résumé
Bibliography	Dream Analysis	Memoir	Roast
Billboard	Dream Diary	Memorandum	Sales Letter
Biography	Dunning Letter	Memorial Plaque	Self-Help Book/Column
Birth Announcement	Editorial	Menu	Schedule
Book Review	E-mail	Minutes	Science Journalism
Brief	Employment Review	Monument Inscription	Scientific Paper
Brochure	Encyclopedia Article	Movie Review	Sermon
Business Card	Epitaph	Music/Concert Review	Sign
Business Letter	Essay	Nature Guide	Slide Show
Business Proposal	Eulogy	News Story	Slogan
Bylaws	Explication	Nomination Speech	Specifications
Campaign Speech	Exposé	Obituary	Sports Story
Caption	Family History	Oral History	Storyboard
Catalogue Copy	Five-Paragraph Theme	Oral Report	Summary
Cause-and-Effect Essay	Field Guide	Packaging Copy	Summation
Character Sketch	Filmstrip	Paraphrase	Syllabus
Charter	Flyer	Party Platform	Technical Writing
Cheer	Foreword	Pep Talk	Test
Classification	Fund-Raising	Personal Essay	Textbook
Classified Ad	Letter/Solicitation	Persuasive Essay	Thank-You Note
College Entrance Essay	Graduation Speech	Petition	Theater Review
Column, Newspaper	Grant Application	Police/Accident Report	Toast
Comeback Speech	Guidebook	Political Advertisement	To Do List
Comedic Monologue	Headline	Political Cartoon	Training Manual, Video,
Commentary	History	Prediction	Tape, or Slide Show
Commercial	Homily	Preface	Travel Guide
Community Calendar	How-to Essay or Book	Presentation	Travelogue
Comparison-and-	(Guide)	Press Release	Treaty
Contrast Essay	Human Interest Story	Process Essay	Vows
Concordance	Informative Essay	Proclamation	Want Ad
Constitution	Instructions	Profile	Wedding
Constructive Speech,	Interview Questions	Program Notes	Announcement
Debate	Introduction	Prologue	Wish List

Your Turn

A   Review the selections by Annie Dillard on pages 2 and 3 and by John Donne on page 9. Answer any of the following questions that apply to either selection.

1   What is the title? What is the subject? Is the subject suggested by the title?

2   What is the thesis, or main idea, of the selection?

3   What is the primary purpose of the selection?

4   What modes of writing are used in the selection?

5   What is the genre of each selection?

6   What part of each selection is the introduction? What part is the conclusion?

7   Which parts of each selection have a chronological organization?

B   Find, in a newspaper or magazine, one example of each of the following. Identify, on a piece of paper, the title, genre, subject, thesis, and primary mode, purpose, and method of organization of each piece.

1   An editorial

2   A work dealing with a topic in popular science, medicine, or health

3   A "How-to" article

C   The best way for you to prepare for reading the nonfiction selections on the MCAS exam is to develop of habit of reading nonfiction works regularly. Begin now by reading at least four magazine or newspaper articles every week. In a notebook, keep a learning log about your reading. In your log, record the following information:

1   The title and author of each piece

2   The subject and purpose of each piece

3   Your reactions to or commentary on each piece. Possibilities include notes on what the piece taught you or, if the piece is persuasive, the reasons why you agree or disagree with the author.

4   A list of two or three words from each piece that you did not know before reading the piece or that you do not regularly use in your own speech and writing, along with the definitions of those words

LESSON 5.2 Understanding Persuasive Texts

As you saw in Lesson 5.1, some pieces of nonfiction writing are written to persuade. A letter to the editor of a newspaper urging eligible voters to get out and vote is an example of persuasive writing. So is the answer to a test question that asks the student to tell which novel has better stood the test of time, *A Tale of Two Cities* or *Adventures of Huckleberry Finn*. The first attempts to persuade the reader to to do something; the second attempts to persuade the reader to adopt a particular point of view. When reading a piece of persuasive writing, a reader should evaluate the thesis, or main point, and the supporting arguments being advanced by the writer. To do so, the reader must be able to

- distinguish between facts and opinions
- recognize logical fallacies
- recognize rhetorical devices

In today's world, in which examples of commercial and political persuasion abound—from television advertisements to sound bites from candidates on the evening news—knowing how to evaluate persuasive materials can be an extremely valuable skill. Mastering the elements of persuasion can also help you, throughout your life, to persuade others, such as college admissions people and potential employers.

Distinguishing Facts and Opinions

If you look at a newspaper, you will find that it contains many different kinds of stories. News stories present **facts**—statements that are true by definition or that can be proved by observation. **Editorials,** in contrast, present **opinions**—predictions or statements of value, belief, policy, or obligation that can be supported by facts but not proved. Consider these examples:

FACT: The president's official residence is the White House.

FACT: The White House is located on Pennsylvania Avenue, in Washington, D.C., across the street from Lafayette Park.

OPINION: The Congress and the president should do something to house the homeless people sleeping in the park across from the White House.

The first statement is true by definition. The expressions "the president's official residence" and "the White House" mean the same thing, and so the sentence has to be true. The second statement can easily be proved by observation. A person can go to Washington, D.C., take a taxi to the White House, and see if it is indeed located on Pennsylvania Avenue, across the street from Lafayette Park. An easier way to check that this is a fact, of course, would be to look up the White House on a map of Washington, D.C. The third statement does not express a fact. Instead, it expresses someone's opinion about what should be done. Try this exercise: Look through your textbooks, which are primarily books that present facts. How many statements of opinion can you find in them?

Proving Facts

As you just learned, a fact is a statement that is true by definition or that can be proved by observation. Sometimes, you can prove a statement of fact by making an observation yourself. Suppose, for example, that the label on a box of cereal says that the box contains 11 ounces of cereal. You could prove the statement

This box contains 11 ounces of cereal

by getting a large bowl, measuring its weight on a scale, pouring all of the cereal into the bowl, measuring the bowl full of cereal, and then subtracting the weight of the bowl from the weight of the bowl plus the cereal. In most cases, however, people do not prove the truth or falsehood of facts by making observations themselves. Instead, they depend on **reference works** or recognized **experts** to confirm or deny the facts. For example, the following is a statement of fact:

Light travels at approximately 186,000 miles per second.

You probably do not have the equipment to measure the speed of light yourself, but you can look up the speed in a reference work, such as a science book, that contains a record of an observation made by scientists. So, two ways of checking facts are to

- make observations on your own
- consult a reference work or a knowledgeable expert

Types of Opinions

There are many types of opinions. The types that you will encounter most frequently are as follows:

JUDGMENTS, OR STATEMENTS OF VALUE: Brussels sprouts taste horrible! Jewel is a great singer. Testing cosmetic products on animals is wrong.

STATEMENTS OF BELIEF: There is probably life on other planets. Eighteen-year-olds are mature enough to vote.

STATEMENTS OF POLICY: We should hold a canned food drive to raise money for the field trip. Hector should be elected student council president.

STATEMENTS OF OBLIGATION: You ought to send your grandmother a thank-you card. Ada should clean up her room once in a while.

PREDICTIONS: There will doubtless be a colony on Mars by the year 2050.

A **judgment,** or **statement of value,** tells how someone feels about something. A **statement of belief** tells something that a person thinks is true but that the person cannot absolutely prove to be true. A **statement of policy** tells what action someone thinks people should or should not take. A **statement of obligation,** which is really just another kind of statement of policy, tells what someone thinks people ought to think or do. A **prediction** tells what the writer thinks will happen in the future. All such statements are types of **opinions.**

Supporting Opinions

By definition, an opinion is a statement that cannot be proved with absolute certainty. Opinions differ from person to person, and there is even a proverb that says, "Everyone has a right to his or her own opinion." However, all opinions are not created equal. Suppose, for example, that a person holds the opinion that

Studying for tests is a waste of time.

It is not difficult to demonstrate that this is an unwise opinion. All one has to do is to perform an experiment. Try studying hard for one test and see what happens. Then try not studying for another test and see what happens. Obviously, the facts simply don't support this opinion. A **reasonable opinion** is one that is supported by the facts. Consider this example:

OPINION: Chandra's older brother is studying to become a pharmacy technician, and I think that's a really wise choice.

This opinion can be supported by facts such as these:

FACT: The American Association of Pharmacy Technicians estimates that the number of jobs for pharmacy technicians will grow from 81,000 in 1998 to 109,000 by the year 2004.

FACT: Many drugstore chains and many states are now requiring pharmacy technicians to have associate degrees and to be certified, but only 20,000 of the 81,000 pharmacy technicians now working have associate degrees and are certified.

Whenever you encounter a statement of opinion, you should ask yourself, "Is this opinion supported by the facts?" If it is supported by the facts, then it is a reasonable opinion, one worthy of being adopted by you. **If it is not supported by the facts, then it is an unreasonable opinion and should not be adopted.**

Often, when people have different opinions, they resort to arguing or shouting or other unproductive ways of dealing with their differences. It makes more sense, however, to look at the relevant facts to see which opinion is better supported. Consider, for example, how courts of law work. The defense attorneys may be of the opinion that their client is innocent and should be freed. The prosecuting attorneys may be of the opinion that the defendant is guilty and should go to jail. Instead of simply shouting opinions at one another, the attorneys go into court and present **evidence**—facts—to support the defendant's innocence or guilt. The jury and the judge weigh the evidence to see which opinion is better supported.

The following chart summarizes what you have learned about facts and opinions in this lesson.

Facts and Opinions

🦎 A fact is a statement that is true by definition (for example, "1 + 1 = 2" or "*Alma* means 'soul' in Spanish") or that can be, at least theoretically, proved by observation (for example, "Pluto is very cold.")

🦎 An opinion is a statement that is meaningful but that is not true by definition or absolutely provable by observation.

🦎 Types of opinions include judgments, predictions, and statements of policy, belief, or obligation.

🦎 An opinion is reasonable if it is supported by the available facts.

Your Turn

Part 1

A Tell whether each of the following expressions is a statement of fact or a statement of opinion.

1 The world's largest zoo is the San Diego Wild Animal Park.

2 The most fascinating animals in the San Diego Wild Animal Park are the Siberian tigers.

3 Julius Cæsar conquered Gaul, the area that is now France and Germany.

4 Julius Cæsar was a great military leader.

5 The tallest animal in the North American wilds is the moose.

6 Moose are really goofy looking.

7 Great Britain should return the Elgin Marbles to Greece.

8 The Elgin Marbles are beautiful sculptures that were taken from Greece by Lord Elgin.

9 The scientists at the Massachusetts Institute of Technology are building a robot named Cog.

10 By the year 2020, Cog should be able to hold a reasonable conversation in English, Spanish, German, or Japanese.

B Explain how you might prove or disprove each of the following statements of fact.

1 The average student in my school is five feet, seven inches tall.

2 The Metropolitan Museum houses several bronzes from Benin, Africa.

3 A quatrain is a verse form with four-line stanzas.

4 Europa, one of the moons of Jupiter, is covered with ice.

5 The Korean War ended in 1953.

C On your paper, write five opinions: a judgment, a statement of belief, a statement of policy, a statement of obligation, and a prediction.

D The following is a pie chart from a newspaper article about the 1998 United States Federal Budget. Based on the information provided in the chart, write five statements of fact. Then write two statements of opinion related to this information. For each statement of opinion, give at least one fact from the chart that supports the opinion.

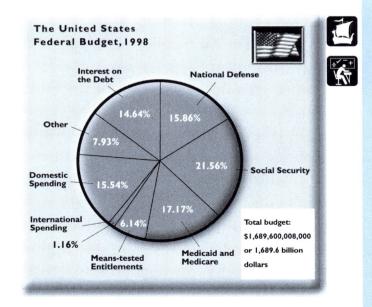

The United States Federal Budget, 1998

- Interest on the Debt 14.64%
- National Defense 15.86%
- Other 7.93%
- Domestic Spending 15.54%
- International Spending 1.16%
- Means-tested Entitlements 6.14%
- Medicaid and Medicare 17.17%
- Social Security 21.56%

Total budget: $1,689,600,008,000 or 1,689.6 billion dollars

Recognizing Logical Fallacies

In the lesson on making inferences, you read this logical argument:

All human beings are mortal.
Socrates is a human being.
Therefore, Socrates is mortal.

Now, consider this argument:

Socrates is a man.
Socrates is bald.
Therefore, all men are bald.

Is this a valid logical argument? You know from your own observation that it is not. The argument contains a logical fallacy. A logical **fallacy** is a failure in reasoning. A writer makes a fallacious argument when the conclusion is not **warranted,** or supported, by the facts. One example of a logical fallacy is the **false analogy.** An argument by analogy compares two things that are similar in a certain way and concludes that therefore they are also alike in other ways.

EXAMPLE: A surgeon who works at County Hospital wears a white uniform and is professionally trained to work with sharp knives. The surgeon can save your life by operating on you. A chef who works at County Hospital wears a white uniform and is professionally trained to work with sharp knives. Therefore, the chef can save your life by operating on you.

EXPLANATION: The similarity between the two workers does not necessarily equal similarity in capability.

Post hoc ergo propter hoc. This Latin phrase means "Following this, therefore because of this." It is a false argument that assumes that any event that follows another event must be the result of the event that preceded it.

EXAMPLE: After the Floyd family installed a larger mailbox, they started to receive more junk mail. The Floyds should go back to their old mailbox and stop the flood of junk mail coming into their house.

EXPLANATION: The Floyds' advisor is mixing up concurrence with causation. There is no evidence given to support the notion that the increase in junk mail is related to the size of the mailbox.

Affirming the antecedent and denying the consequent. An "if . . . then . . ." statement is made up of two parts—the antecedent, or "if" part, and the consequent, or "then" part. The statement holds that if the antecedent is true, then the consequent must be true. However, if the *consequent* is true, you can't conclude anything about the antecedent.

EXAMPLE: If you are on the Earth, then a rock thrown into the air must fall back down. Thus, if a rock thrown into the air falls back down, then you must be on the Earth.

EXPLANATION: The antecedent in the first statement is true, thus the consequent is true. However, the truth of the consequent (a rock thrown into the air falls back down) does not necessarily imply the truth of the antecedent (you must be on Earth). You might be on Earth, but you could also be on the moon or on any other body that has enough mass to produce the gravitational force required to overcome the upward acceleration of the rock.

Fallacy of Composition. If the individual members of a group possess a certain quality, it does not necessarily follow that the group as a whole shares that quality.

EXAMPLE: Every player on the soccer team is very talented. Therefore, the team is great!

EXPLANATION: A team's quality is made up of more that just the talent of its players. The members of the team might be fast, smart, and accurate, but they might not practice often or work well together. Therefore, they might lose to teams who practice more frequently or who are adept at working as a team.

Fallacy of Decomposition. It is not necessarily true that every member of a group possesses the qualities or characteristics of the group.

EXAMPLE: This is the worst soup I ever tasted. There are carrots in this soup. Therefore, carrots are the worst vegetable I ever tasted.

EXPLANATION: The problem might be the carrots, but delicious carrots could be part of soup that is bad because of other ingredients or improper preparation.

Non sequitur. This is a Latin phrase meaning "it does not follow." A *non sequitur* is a conclusion that simply does not follow from the facts presented.

EXAMPLE: *Dawson's Creek* is the best television show because all my friends like it.

EXPLANATION: The word *best* means "of higher quality than any other." The opinion of the writer's friends does not address the quality of other television shows and is not a complete survey of the opinions of all viewers. Therefore, the conclusion does not follow from the facts.

Ad hominem. This Latin phrase means "to the person." Someone making an *ad hominem* argument attempts to cast doubt on an opinion by attacking the person holding the opinion rather than the opinion itself. This kind of statement is a common characteristic of misleading propaganda. **Propaganda** is the process of spreading ideas that help one's own cause or discredit an opponent's cause.

EXAMPLE: My little brother is a dork. Don't pay any attention to what he thinks of our band.

EXPLANATION: The writer's evaluation of her brother's personality provides no objective evidence about the quality of the band. It is simply a personal attack, probably motivated by an emotional reaction to a comment that the brother has made.

False dichotomy. A false dichotomy, or **either . . . or argument,** falsely assumes that only two alternatives are possible.

EXAMPLE: You are either for our party, or you are against us.

UNDERSTANDING NONFICTION SELECTIONS

EXPLANATION: This statement does not allow for any degrees in the other person's opinion. The other person could support some of the party's platform and not other parts or could be completely neutral. This kind of all-or-nothing statement is a common characteristic of misleading propaganda.

The Fallacy of Omission. This fallacy occurs when important facts bearing on a particular issue are ignored. The worst instances of this fallacy occur when known but contradictory facts are purposefully withheld.

EXAMPLE: It's not my fault that I got a D in geometry. After all, I got a B on the midterm test, didn't I?

EXPLANATION: If the person speaking received a D, then there are facts that he or she left out, like his or her grades on the other work done for the class.

Note: A particularly dangerous version of this fallacy occurs when people refer to abstract principles to support an action but ignore the consequences of the application of those principles—the facts about what will or will not happen. To whip up support for his aggressive military campaigns against his neighbors, Hitler made speeches promoting dubious abstract principles related to Aryan supremacy and the destiny of the German people. What he omitted was any description of the concrete consequences—the carnage, for example—that would result from making war on his neighbors and turning group against group within his own country.

Overgeneralization. Inductive reasoning from particular facts to general conclusions is the primary means by which people gain knowledge of the world. However, induction based on too little evidence leads to the fallacy of overgeneralization.

EXAMPLE: Every bear I have seen has been brown; therefore, all bears are brown.

EXPLANATION: The maker of this statement has based a conclusion on insufficient personal observation and could have ascertained the existence of bears of other colors by consulting an expert source.

Indulgence in logical fallacies often leads to negative consequences. Logical fallacies are the stock-in-trade of those who spread racial and ethnic stereotypes, perpetrate consumer frauds, and stir up fanaticism. By developing an awareness of logical fallacies—by keeping a keen eye out for them in your daily life—you can keep from being duped and can become a force among your friends and acquaintances for reason and understanding.

Understanding Rhetorical Devices

According to one common definition, **rhetoric** is the art of persuasion, but a good argument can be made that almost all speech and writing, even when it is strictly informative, has persuasive elements. After all, the style, form, and tone of an *informative* scientific paper or encyclopedia article are adopted by the writer to *persuade* his or her readers that the information being presented can be trusted. So, in one sense, all writing and speech is rhetorical. This is one reason why the study of speech and composition, generally, is often referred to as rhetoric.

Rhetorical devices are special ways of using words to achieve an effect on an audience. Such manipulation of the audience is a type of persuasion. As opposed to figurative language, like metaphor or personification, rhetorical devices do not create their effect by making a novel comparison between a person or object and some other person or object ("She walks in beauty like the night"; "Nobody, not even the rain, has such small hands"). Instead, rhetorical devices make use of other aspects of language, such as grammar or sound, to create an effect on the reader or listener. Because an effective use of rhetoric can arouse powerful emotions in its audience, its use has come to be regarded with suspicion. Just as propaganda, which has also acquired a negative association, may be used legitimately to move people, so may rhetorical devices. It is when rhetorical techniques are used to mislead or falsify that they should be looked at askance. The chart to the right describes some common rhetorical devices used in persuasive speech and writing.

The Importance of Opinions

When students first learn that facts are statements that can be proved and that opinions are statements that cannot be proved absolutely, they often jump to the conclusion that facts are good and opinions are bad. In the opinion of the authors of this text, such a hasty conclusion is a mistake. Opinions, such as belief in the loyalty and value of a friend or pride in a job well done, are the essence of a healthy, happy, productive life. All the really important human activities—ethics, aesthetics, love, and politics, to name but a few—are

---

Rhetorical Devices

Antithesis. An antithesis is a strong contrast between two ideas. Examples: a. "I expected joy. I found despair." b. "cold hands, warm heart"

Loaded Words. Loaded words are ones with strong emotional content. Examples include epithets (disparaging nicknames) of all kinds and words that imply judgments, such as *stupid* or *wrong*.

Parallelism. Parallelism is the use of similar grammatical forms to give items equal weight, as in Lincoln's line "of the people, by the people, for the people."

Repetition. Repetition is the use, again, of any element, such as a sound, word, phrase, clause, or sentence. Example: "Rows of men marched away. Rows of men raised their rifles. Rows of men were mown down like winter wheat."

Rhetorical Question. A rhetorical question is one asked for effect but not meant to be answered because the answer is presumed to be clear. Example: "Are we not Americans? Will we not stand up against the enemies of freedom?"

---

matters of opinion. The point of this chapter is not that opinions, or the rhetorical devices used to support them, are bad but that they are more reasonable if the facts support them. In fact, that is what persuasion, as opposed to propaganda, is all about: providing good reasons—solid, incontestable facts—to support opinions.

Your Turn

Part 2

A   Review the article on the Etruscans on pages 21–23. Identify two facts and two opinions presented in the article. Is the article primarily informative or persuasive? Does it contain persuasive elements? Explain.

B   Identify, by name, the logical fallacy or fallacies in each of the following statements. (Some statements contain examples of more than one of the fallacies presented in the lesson.) Discuss with your classmates, in a small group, what is wrong with each argument.

1   Rock guitarists know all about amplifiers. Rick knows a lot about amplifiers. Therefore, he must be a rock guitarist.

2   In the decade after President Lyndon Johnson signed the 1964 Civil Rights Act, crime rates rose in every large city in America. Therefore, the Civil Rights Act must have caused an increase in the amount of crime.

3   The test scores at Woodlawn High School are the highest in the state of Massachusetts. Marc goes to Woodlawn High School, so he must be really smart.

4   There's no game after school today, so we should watch television.

5   We should buy that house. After all, wasn't that the most beautiful living room you ever saw?

6   Your friend said that alligators don't age, but I don't believe her because, in my opinion, she's an idiot, and have you seen the clothes that she wears? I bet she couldn't even spell the word *cool*.

7   You don't want Erica in your study group because she's not a "brain"; she's a "jock." I mean, she plays field hockey, doesn't she?

8   Ok, the way I see it, there are two choices for the prom theme: "Famous Couples" or "Somewhere Over the Rainbow."

9   Don't believe what you hear about spotted owls being endangered. My brother went hiking in Washington State, and he saw not one but two of them. How likely is that, huh?

10   Freud explained that the human brain was like a steam engine, and people's wishes or desires were like the steam inside the engine. Both build up over time. If the steam isn't released in some way, the engine explodes. If a person's wishes aren't acted upon, the person has a breakdown or becomes neurotic.

C   Work with a group of students to find examples in print advertisements and television commercials of the logical fallacies and rhetorical devices described in this lesson. Create a group report or a bulletin board display of the examples that you find, with labels and explanations.

LESSON 5.3
Understanding Informative Texts

Pick up a newspaper and scan its pages. Most of the writing that you will find there will be informative. Go to a magazine rack in a shop and flip through some of the popular offerings there. Again, informative writing will be the bulk of what you find. Informative writing is everywhere, in popular culture; in textbooks in school; in reports and memoranda in business and the professions. You will also encounter informative writing on the MCAS exam.

You can identify informative writing by one characteristic: Its primary purpose is to provide facts about some subject. A news story about a fire, a magazine article about what to look for when purchasing a new computer, a textbook chapter about the Civil War or astronomy—all exist to

provide information. Libraries and bookstores have many sections devoted entirely to informative titles on business, computers and computer programs, health and medicine, reference, science, nature, philosophy, art, music, self-help, gardening, cooking, and many other subjects. In addition, literally millions of pieces of informative writing, from news reports to scientific articles, are posted on the Internet each day. Often, people read informative works in order to teach themselves something essential, but equally often, people read such works simply because they are interested in the subject matter. The twentieth century has been called the **Information Age** because of contemporary people's tremendous need and appetite for information. Obviously, knowing how to read informative writing with understanding and discernment is an essential skill.

Types of Informative Essays

Of course, a comprehensive discussion of all informative writing is beyond the scope of this book, but a lot can be learned about informative writing in general by focusing on the narrower topic of the informative essay. An **essay** is a short, nonexhaustive treatment of a single subject. Book-length informative works are often simply collections of such essays or, indeed, longer, more complete versions of their shorter counterparts. The following are some of the major kinds of informative essays:

A **narrative essay** is one that tells a story about real events and people. Usually, a narrative essay focuses on one major event or series of events and is organized in chronological order, that is, in the order of the occurrence of the events. An essay about the Montgomery bus boycott, the event that really set the American Civil Rights Movement in motion, would be an example. When reading a narrative essay, ask yourself the following questions:

Questions to Ask About Narrative Nonfiction Writing

1. Who are the major characters involved?
2. What is the **setting,** or time and place, of the story?
3. What is the **sequence,** or order, of events in the story?
4. What issues or struggles, (**conflicts**) are involved? Are these resolved, and if so, how?
5. What is the significance, or importance, of the events being related?

A **process essay** describes the steps or stages in some activity. An essay that describes how a bill makes its way through Congress or what causes a volcano to erupt is an example of a process essay. One popular kind of process essay is the how-to essay, which describes how to do something, such as how to train a dog, how to do routine maintenance on a mountain bike,

how to write a press release in proper form, or how to choose an outfit for the prom. When reading a process or how-to essay, ask yourself these questions:

Questions to Ask About Process Writing

1. What process is the writer describing?
2. What are the steps, or stages, in the process?
3. In what sequence, or order, do the steps occur?
4. Has the writer left out any important steps?

A **classification essay** is one in which a writer presents a scheme for organizing a number of elements into classes, or groups. An essay in a field guide to a national park, for example, might break down the animals within the park into groups such as invertebrates, mammals, reptiles, birds, and fish, discussing each in turn. The section on the park's mammals might divide them into major predators and their prey. An article in a computer magazine about graphics software might divide the available programs into groups, such as drawing and painting programs, photo-editing programs, graphics cataloging and storage programs, programs for producing Web graphics, and so on. Classification is extremely useful because it helps to organize information, and organized information is easier to remember. When reading a classification essay, ask yourself these questions:

> ## Questions to Ask About Writing That Classifies
>
> 1. Into what groups, or **classes**, does the writer divide his or her subjects?
> 2. Upon what is the writer's system of classification based? Why did the writer choose to put an item into one class or group instead of another?

A **comparison-and-contrast essay** describes the similarities and differences between two or more subjects. For example, an article in the travel section of a newspaper might compare and contrast vacationing on two different islands in the Caribbean, or an article in a computer magazine might explain how the Internet works by comparing data moving on the Net to traffic moving on a highway. (One difference is that, on the Net, there is no penalty for going really fast!) When reading a comparison-and-contrast essay, ask yourself these questions:

> ## Questions to Ask About Writing That Compares and Contrasts
>
> 1. What subjects are being compared and/or contrasted?
> 2. What are their similarities?
> 3. What are their differences?

A **cause-and-effect essay** explains how one event or series of events (the **cause** or causes) brings about another event or series of events (the **effects**). An article in a magazine explaining the increase in the crow population nationwide as the result of an increase in the amount of garbage and roadkill available for these scavengers to eat would be an example of a cause-and-effect essay, as would a section in a textbook explaining how the Civil War resulted from tensions between the North and the South over such issues as slavery, export duties on cotton, import duties on manufactured goods, and so on. When discussing cause and effect, people often distinguish between necessary and sufficient causes. A **necessary cause** is one that has to exist for a particular effect to take place. A **sufficient cause** is even stronger. It is one that, by itself, is enough to bring about an effect. When reading a cause-and-effect essay, ask yourself these questions:

> ## Questions to Ask About Writing That Presents Causes and Effects
>
> 1. What cause or causes does the writer identify? What effects?
> 2. Has the writer correctly identified all the causes or effects?
> 3. Has he or she provided sufficient evidence to establish a causal relationship?
> 4. Are the causes identified by the writer necessary in order to bring about the effect or effects described? Are they sufficient, by themselves, to have brought about these effects?

An **analysis essay** is one in which a writer breaks down a subject into its parts and then shows how these parts are related to one another and to the whole. An in-depth essay in a Sunday newspaper magazine about how a movie was made, describing the work done by the producer, the director, the actors, the special effects people, the makeup people, and so on, might be an example of an analysis essay if it concentrated on the contributions of each to the final film. It might be a narrative essay if it simply told the story of the making of the movie from beginning to end. Often, chapters in textbooks are simply extended analysis essays. For example, a chapter on the digestive system in a biology textbook would be an analysis essay, describing the parts of the system—the mouth, the esophagus, the stomach, the liver, and so on—and how they work together. When reading an analysis essay, ask yourself these questions:

Questions to Ask About Analysis Essays

1. What is the whole subject being discussed?
2. What are the parts of the subject?
3. How are the parts related to one another?
4. What function does each part serve?
5. How are the parts related to the whole?

The **essay of definition** exists primarily to explain the meaning of a word or phrase. A teen magazine feature story called "What Is a Friend?" might be an example of an essay of definition, as might a feature in a business textbook called "What Does and Does Not Constitute a Contract?" A term

can be defined in many different ways, and often such essays make use of many of these. One way is simply to collect a lot of definitions from different people and compare and contrast them. Another way, the method used in dictionaries, is to write what is known as a **genus and differentia definition.** First, the thing to be defined is placed into some larger group (the genus). Then, the differences between it and other members of the group (the differentia) are presented. Here, for example, is a genus and differentia definition of friendship: "Friendship is a relationship between two people (genus) characterized by mutual admiration, affection, trust, loyalty and by a desire to communicate and to share activities (differentia)."

Other ways to define a term include giving a synonym (another word that has a similar meaning) for it; describing its appearance, parts, or functions; illustrating it; or giving examples of it. A particularly effective method for defining something is to present what is called an **operational definition,** one that turns identification of the thing being defined into a series of concrete steps or observations that can be carried out. Here, for example, is an operational definition of the term *friend*: "A friend is someone who, when you say, 'I've lost my car keys,' will answer, 'Can I help you look for them?'" Operational definitions are particularly important in science, engineering, law, medicine, and other professions that rely on precise observation or evidence. For example, a scientist might define the term *meter* as "the distance that light travels in one 299,792,458th of a second"!

When reading an essay of definition, ask yourself these questions:

Questions to Ask About Essays of Definition:

1. What term or terms are being defined?
2. What methods of definition are being used (synonyms, genus and differentia, examples, etc.)?
3. Are the definitions concrete and precise?
4. Are alternative definitions discussed?
5. Do you agree with the definitions presented?

Mixing It Up

Writers are creative people, and so they rarely produce work that rigidly follows any of the descriptions given in this lesson. Typically, writers mix up the forms of writing that we've been discussing, using within a single work elements from each form—a little narration, a little analysis, a couple of definitions, a comparison or two, and so on. Nonetheless, the advice given in this lesson stands. When you encounter such elements, ask the corresponding questions presented in this lesson, and you will be well on your way to understanding what the writer is saying.

Evaluating Informative Writing

People depend upon textbooks to provide them with factual information, and so the standards for informative writing in textbooks have to be very high. However, if you were to look back at a science or history textbook written in the early part of the twentieth century, you would probably be amused or appalled by some of what you would find there. The point is that opinion inevitably finds its way even into informative works such as textbooks or scientific papers. What today seems like fact might turn out, in the future, to have been merely mistaken conjecture, based upon unexamined biases or ignorance of facts later discovered. Therefore, whenever you read, you should do so with a critical mind. You should, to paraphrase the American poet Wallace Stevens, "read by your own light," constantly evaluating the material you are reading to determine whether it is accurate and reasonable. Ask yourself questions like these:

Questions to Ask About Informative Writing

1. Which part, if any, of this material is fact, true by definition or provable by observation, and which part is opinion or conjecture?
2. Is the author knowledgeable about this subject?
3. Are the author's sources reliable and up-to-date?
4. Is the author unbiased? Has he or she made a one-sided or partial presentation of the facts? Has he or she overlooked important facts or perspectives?
5. Do the general conclusions that the author draws follow from the facts presented? Does the author provide sufficient evidence to support his or her main idea, or thesis?

Your Turn

A Identify each of the following pieces of writing as an example of narrative nonfiction, process writing, classification, comparison and contrast, cause-and-effect writing, analysis, or definition. Once you have identified the type of each piece, find the corresponding questions about that type of writing in this lesson. Then, answer the questions about the piece, in writing, on your own paper.

1 A typical office computer network consists of the following parts: The center of the network is the **server,** a powerful computer with a great deal of storage space on which documents are stored. Attached to the server are **desktop computers,** which, as the name suggests, sit on the desktops of the workers. Usually, application programs, such as word processing programs and spreadsheet programs, are stored on the hard drives of these desktop computers. When an employee wants to work on a document, he or she connects to the server across the network, downloads the document to his or her computer, works on it, and then copies it back to the server for long-term storage.

The network itself, which connects the desktop computers and the server, is a system of cables, generally **Ethernet 10-Base T wiring.** In addition, most office networks make use of a device called a **hub** or **router,** which directs traffic on the network to and from the server and the desktop computers.

Finally, to ensure that the data stored on the server is safe, most office networks contain a **backup system,** such as a **tape drive.** Regularly, once a day or once a week, for example, the network administrator backs up, or makes copies of, all the data on the server, or all the data on all the computers on the network, using this backup system.

2 To create a woodcut, you use a block of wood with a smooth surface, a soft charcoal pencil, woodcutting tools, an ink roller, black ink, and paper. First, if the wood is not smooth, sand it down, using progressively finer pieces of sandpaper, until you have a very smooth surface indeed. Then, carefully clean away any dust created by the sanding. Next, draw your design as an outline on a piece of paper the same size as your wood block, using the soft charcoal pencil. Press this paper against the wood to transfer the design to the wood block. If necessary, after transferring the design to the wood, use a pencil to fill in details of the design.

You are now ready to begin the actual woodcut. Use your woodcutting tools to cut away all the places that you want to appear as white in the final work. Leave the places that you want to appear as black. When that is done, again clean the block. Next, use the roller to apply ink to the block. Finally, press the inked block onto a sheet of paper to transfer the design.

3   The weather phenomenon known as "El Niño" is a warming of waters in the Pacific Ocean. El Niño has produced wild weather all over the globe. As the waters of the eastern Pacific Ocean near the equator become warmer, heat and moisture from the ocean rise into the atmosphere, altering weather patterns in far-flung places. El Niño has brought drought and forest fires to Hawaii, Australia, Southeast Asia, and Central America. It has created typhoons in Indonesia and caused flooding and landslides in California and the Pacific Northwest. It produced a heat wave in western Canada and ice storms in New England and eastern Canada. El Niño blew frigid Arctic air into Texas and Georgia and fueled tornadoes in Florida, Alabama, and Tennessee. Although El Niño did bring pleasant weather to places like North Dakota, most of its effects have been extreme and destructive.

4 Cricket, one of the most popular sports in England, is played on an oval-shaped ground by two teams of eleven players each. One player, called the bowler, throws the ball to try to hit the wicket, a set of sticks standing at one end of the central part of the ground, called the pitch. The batsman tries to hit the ball with a flat-surfaced bat. If the batsman hits the ball, he may run to the other wicket at the opposite end of the pitch and exchange places with the batsman there. Fielders try to retire the batsman. Points, or runs, are scored in various ways, with as many as 300 or 400 runs occurring in a single match.

America's "national pastime" is similar to cricket. There are nine players on each baseball team. The game is played on a large field, with four bases arranged in a diamond shape. The pitcher tries to throw the ball over home base, and the batter tries to hit the ball with the bat. If he hits the ball, he runs to first base. Points, or runs, are scored by running counterclockwise to all the bases and back to home base without being put out by the fielders. It is unusual for either team to score more than 9 or 10 runs in a game.

B Choose any topic of interest to you that might be appropriate for an informative paragraph. Then, choose any two of the types of writing described in this lesson—narrative nonfiction, process writing, classification, comparison and contrast, cause-and-effect writing, analysis, or definition—and write two paragraphs about your topic, one for each of the two types.

C Work with other students in a small group, doing research in magazines in your school or public library. Find and photocopy one example of each of the types of informative writing described in this lesson—narrative nonfiction, process writing, classification, comparison and contrast, cause-and-effect writing, analysis, and definition. Assemble these examples into a booklet called "A Field Guide to Informative Writing." Label and define each type in your booklet.

LESSON 6.1 Analyzing Writing Prompts for Open-Response Questions

As you learned in Lesson 2.2, the MCAS exam contains a number of open-response questions, which require written responses. Each of these questions presents a set of directions for writing. Another name for a set of directions for writing is a **writing prompt**. To ensure success on the writing portions of the exam, you must learn how to **analyze**, or break apart and interpret, the writing prompt.

Identifying the Key Question

Consider the following sample writing prompt for an open-response question:

> What seems to be the writer's attitude toward the people and events he is describing? Cite details from the selection that reveal what the writer thinks about this episode from early American history.

This particular writing prompt consists of two sentences. The first is a question—the **key question** that the person taking the test is being asked to answer. The second sentence provides additional information about what should appear in the answer. The answer should contain details from the selection that support the answer to the key question. The key question may appear anywhere in the writing prompt—at the beginning, in the middle, or at the end. Often, but not always, the key question is signaled by a **question word** such as *who,*

what, where, when, why, or *how.* Make sure that your written response contains a one-sentence, general answer to this key question and also whatever specific details are required to back up your general answer.

Interpreting Action Words in Writing Prompts

A common mistake among test-takers is to write good responses that don't provide what was asked for by the writing prompt. Consider this example:

One Student's Response

Dwayne read the following prompt on a standardized exam:

> Based on information contained in the article, explain why scientists are planning a manned mission to Mars. Refer to specific details from the article in your response.

Dwayne wrote the following response to this prompt:

> In the nineteenth century, the astronomer Giovanni Schiaparelli observed what he thought were canals on Mars. Then, at the end of that century, a businessman named Percival Lowell, excited that there might be canal-building people on Mars, paid to have a large telescope

erected to study the planet. Unfortunately, the canals turned out not to exist, and unmanned missions to Mars in the latter part of the twentieth century found no evidence of life there. In 1996, however, scientists at NASA announced the discovery of a meteorite from Mars containing what may be fossil bacteria. Funding for a manned Mars mission remains in jeopardy, but many scientists believe that such a mission will take place within the decade.

Dwayne's response is an excellent summary of newsworthy events related to Mars, but it doesn't do what the prompt asked him to do. The prompt asks for the test-taker to "explain why scientists are planning a manned mission to Mars." **Therefore, this response, even though it is a well-written summary, would receive a low score.**

The moral of Dwayne's experience is that you must be careful, when taking the MCAS English exam, to ascertain what you are being asked to do and then to **do that and nothing else**. Don't write a comparison if you are being asked to describe causes and effects. Don't write a summary if you are being asked to explain the reasons for something. Be on the lookout, as you read writing prompts on the exam, for words like *analyze, assess, cite, compare, contrast, convey, critique, decide, describe, draw, evaluate, explain, express, generalize, illustrate, interpret, judge, list, paraphrase, point out, respond, review, show, state, summarize, support,* and *tell* that name the task or tasks that you are being asked to carry out. If you have any doubts about what any of these **action words** mean, stop now and look them up in the glossary starting on page 242 of this text.

Identifying the Parts of a Complete Response

You just saw an example of the importance of carrying out the task that the prompt requests of you. Sometimes, a prompt will ask you to carry out more than one task. Make sure, when you read the writing prompt, that you identify everything that must be included in your answer. Consider the following prompt:

> The author of this memoir tells about "a change of heart" that he experienced after witnessing the destruction of a mountain habitat by erosion due to logging. What change occurred in the author's opinions about clear-cutting of timberlands? Explain the reasons for this change, and summarize the actions that the author took because of the change.

This prompt asks the test-taker to do three separate things:

1. Tell what changed in the author's opinions about clear-cutting.
2. Explain why the author's opinions changed.
3. Summarize the actions that the author took because of the change.

A complete response to the prompt must do each of these things. A response that did only the first or only the first and the second would be incomplete and would receive a low score.

DEVELOPING WRITING SKILLS

Identifying Evidence That Must Be Cited

Often, a writing prompt will tell you what particular facts, or **evidence,** you should look for in the selection and include in your response. Consider this writing prompt:

You have decided to take a hiking trip through mountainous country in the winter. What preparations should you make for your trip? Support your response with facts from the selection.

A complete response to this writing prompt will contain facts from the selection, but what facts? Reading the prompt closely, you will see that the main question that you are being asked is "What preparations should a person make for a winter hiking trip in the mountains?" The answer must contain facts from the selection that are related to such preparations. A response that contained unrelated facts or that left out the relevant facts from the article would receive a low score. Make sure, when you read the prompts on the exam, to ask yourself what evidence you need to find in the selection to support your written answer to the key question.

The chart on the next page reviews the strategies that you should use when interpreting writing prompts. Look over the chart before doing the following exercises.

Your Turn

Read the writing prompts in Exercises A and B. Then answer the questions following each prompt.

A Edgar Allan Poe is known for producing chilling effects in his fiction. What is the mood of this story, and how is that mood created?

1 What are the key questions that the test-taker must answer? What question words signal these questions?

2 What parts must a complete answer to this question contain?

B The author of this essay says that the crash of Flight 2843 could have been avoided. Evaluate the actions that the pilot and his crew took when he realized that the plane was in trouble. Do you agree with the author? Why, or why not?

1 What is the key question that the test-taker must answer?

2 What action word identifies the task that the test-taker must carry out in order to answer the question? What does this action word mean?

3 What parts would have to be included in a complete answer to this question? What evidence would the test-taker look for in the selection to support his or her answer?

C Working with other students in a small group, study the open-response question prompts in the Language and Literature Pretest on pages 2–38 of this book (questions 6, 7, 16, 17, 24, 25, 32, 42, 43, 50). For each prompt, identify the key question that the response must answer, the question words and action words that appear in the prompt, and the parts that a complete answer to the question must contain.

Strategies for Interpreting Writing Prompts
for Open-Response Questions

When you come to the open-response question prompts on the exam, do the following:

Read the prompt over quickly to get the gist of it. Then read it over again, very carefully. Ask yourself, "What is the key question that I must answer in my written response?"

Look for question words such as *who, what, where, when, why,* and *how.* Often, you will find that the key question in the prompt is signaled by such a word and that one or more statements before or after the question provide additional information about what you are to do. (Example: "What is the nature of the conflict between the two brothers in the story?") Note, however, that not all questions contain such words.

Check to see whether the writing task you are being asked to do has more than one part. Make sure that your answer does each thing that the prompt requests that you do—that is, that it is a complete response to the prompt.

Look for action words like *analyze, cite, compare, contrast, convey, critique, decide, describe, draw, explain, express, generalize, illustrate, interpret, judge, list, paraphrase, point out, respond, review, show, state, summarize, support,* and *tell* that tell you what you are supposed to do.

Make a mental note of any specific kinds of evidence from the selection that you are requested to find. Make sure that you find such evidence in the selection and incorporate it into your answer.

tell interpret express summarize list paraphrase
support analyze convey show
critique state compare decide
point out describe explain
generalize review judge respond
draw contrast illustrate cite

DEVELOPING WRITING SKILLS

LESSON 6.2 Notetaking and Graphic Organizers for Writing

The great painters of the Renaissance, such as Michelangelo and da Vinci, used to make careful sketches of their subjects before they started to paint. These sketches are known, technically, as cartoons. In his books on learning to paint, the art instructor Jon Gnagy emphasized the importance of starting out with a good sketch before adding paint.

Just as making a sketch is a useful first step toward creating a painting, so it is useful to sketch out your ideas before you actually begin to write. When writing responses to the MCAS English open-response questions or composition prompts, you will not have time to make full-scale, formal outlines, but you can create quick outlines and organizers, jotting these in the margin or in the area for notes in your exam booklets. There are many ways to lay out your ideas visually as you begin to organize them. This lesson will present some of the techniques you can use to organize your writing.

Rough Outlines

A **rough outline** can be a very helpful way to give some structure to your ideas before you begin writing. This form can also be used to take notes from a source. When you make a rough outline, you jot down **main ideas** followed by **supporting details.** Recall that a main idea is any important point, and supporting details are facts, examples, and illustrations that demonstrate or elaborate upon the main idea. To create a rough outline for a piece of writing, jot down each

of the main points you want to make. Under each main idea, jot down some details that reinforce that point. Each of your main points, with its supporting details, can become a paragraph in your writing.

Look back at question 32 on page 26 of the Pretest. Here is one way to outline an answer to this question:

The Etruscans

Powerful empire
—From Arno River to Tiber River
—Fortified cities united to form govt.
—Developed elective form of govt.
—Conquered surrounding peoples

Commercial power
—As significant as Greek and
   Phoenician traders
—Reached all ports of Mediterranean
—Finely engineered roads
—Built wealth and spread influence to
   northern Europe and Africa

Well-developed culture
—Strong tradition of craftsmanship
—Advanced painting and sculpture
—Elaborate necropolises
—Tombs still stand today
—Unusual equality for women
—Strong influence on Roman culture

Comparison/Contrast Charts

A common kind of examination question is one that asks you to compare and contrast two subjects. When you **compare** two subjects, you point out their similarities. When you **contrast** two subjects, you point out their differences.

The simplest way to represent comparison or contrast information graphically is to prepare a **chart of similarities** or a **chart of differences.** Suppose you had been reading about the Iroquois Nations and needed to write a paragraph comparing their constitution to that of the United States. You might make a list of the similarities, as in the chart below, and then write a paragraph like the one that follows:

SIMILARITIES BETWEEN THE IROQUOIS AND UNITED STATES CONSTITUTIONS
—Two-house legislature —Elected representatives —Guarantees of certain rights —Confederation of independent states

The Constitution of the Iroquois Nations, created many hundreds of years ago, is similar to the United States Constitution. First, both constitutions call for a two-house legislature. Second, under both constitutions, the legislators are elected representatives of the people. Third, both documents guarantee certain rights, such as the freedom of religion and trial by jury. Fourth, both create a confederation of independent states. In the case of the Iroquois, the states that were joined together were the Mohawk, Oneida, Onondaga, Cayuga, and Seneca tribes. In the case of the early United States, the states were the thirteen original colonies.

A more complex kind of chart lists both similarities and differences. For example, you might want to compare television and the World Wide Web, which have some characteristics in common but which are also different in significant ways. As you think about how they are alike and how they are different, you could make a chart like the one below, which you could then use to compose a paragraph:

SIMILARITIES AND DIFFERENCES BETWEEN TELEVISION AND THE WORLD WIDE WEB
Similarities —Communications media —Used by millions of people —Receive text, pictures, sound, and video **Differences** —Text clear on Web but fuzzy on television —Web too slow, at present, for video, but video fine on television —Television a passive medium; Web an interactive medium —Web allows long-distance interaction with others; television doesn't

Television and the World Wide Web are alike in some ways but different in others. They are both communications media, and both are used by millions of people. Another similarity is that both can be used to receive text, pictures, sound, and video. On current televisions, however, text tends to be fuzzy and difficult to read, whereas text on computers, received via the World Wide Web, is generally clear and easy to read. While the Web is great for text, it is not yet a good medium for video. Full-length feature movies can easily be

DEVELOPING WRITING SKILLS

received and viewed on a television screen, but most Internet hookups are too slow, at present, for receiving full-length movies. Yet another difference between television and the World Wide Web is that the former is a passive medium, while the latter is interactive. In most cases, people simply watch on television whatever is broadcast to them. On the World Wide Web, however, people can often interact with what they see on the screen. For example, on the Web, people can play interactive computer games or chat with other people who are far away.

Making a chart of similarities and differences would be a good way to approach question 43 on the Pretest, which asks you to compare the attitudes of Franklin and Williams toward the treatment of Native Americans. A chart of differences would help you answer question

17, in which you are asked to contrast two attitudes toward death. You might also find comparison and contrast questions on the Composition portion of the exam. Remember, however, that the time available to answer questions on the Language and Literature and the Composition sessions of the exam is limited; you should practice jotting down your ideas with a few key words in such a way that you can clearly see the relationships among your ideas.

Venn Diagrams

Another way to represent comparison and contrast information graphically is to create a Venn diagram. To make a Venn diagram, you draw circles for each of your subjects in such a way that the two circles overlap. Each circle is labeled with the name of one of the subjects. To complete the chart, you list the similarities (the things that the two subjects have in common) in the space

VENN DIAGRAM FOR COMPARISON AND CONTRAST

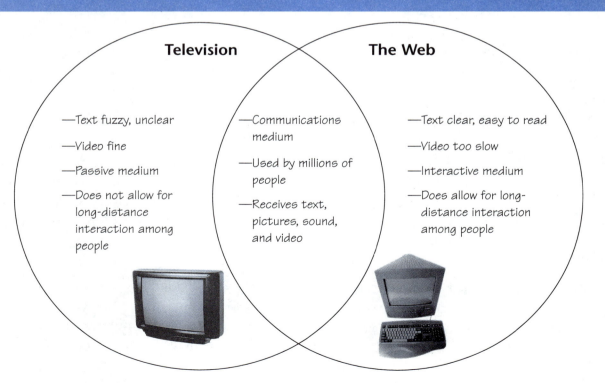

Television

—Text fuzzy, unclear

—Video fine

—Passive medium

—Does not allow for long-distance interaction among people

—Communications medium

—Used by millions of people

—Receives text, pictures, sound, and video

The Web

—Text clear, easy to read

—Video too slow

—Interactive medium

—Does allow for long-distance interaction among people

where the two circles overlap. Then you list the differences for each subject in the space specific to that subject. The example on the preceding page shows how the information about television and the World Wide Web might be diagrammed.

Pro-and-Con Charts

A writing prompt on the MCAS English exam might call for you to create a **persuasive** response. Persuasive writing is writing in which you attempt to convince your readers to adopt some belief or to take some action. Suppose that your school district is considering a proposal to hold school year-round. You might write a letter to the school board or to your local newspaper supporting this idea or opposing it. Your letter would be a piece of persuasive writing.

One way to represent information for persuasive writing is to produce a **pro-and-con chart.** A **pro** is simply an argument or reason in favor of some idea. A **con** is an argument or reason against it. Suppose that you wanted to discuss the benefits and disadvantages of exploring Mars. You could set up a chart like the one below, listing the pros and cons, and then use the items in your list as points in your paragraph:

MARS EXPLORATION: PRO AND CON	
Pro	**Con**
—Can lead to commercial spinoffs	—Expensive
—Satisfies curiosity	—Uses resources that could be allocated to solving other problems
—Prepares way for colonization	

In recent years, a debate has raged in the United States over support of NASA's Mars exploration program. Some people believe that the program is too costly and that it uses up technical and scientific resources that could better be used to address problems here on Earth, such as pollution and disease. The Mars program offers many benefits, however. First, the research that goes into the program can lead to important commercial spinoffs. For example, the robot rover created to wander about the surface of Mars collecting samples might be adapted to create a robot vacuum cleaner. Second, the Mars program satisfies the human desire to know more about the universe. The Mars exploration program will help us to answer interesting questions, such as whether life ever existed on Mars and, if so, what that life was like. Third, by exploring Mars, we can lay the groundwork for future colonization and mining of the planet, possibilities that could ease overpopulation and the depletion of resources here on Earth.

You might be asked to read a selection and then take a stand on the issue presented. A pro-and-con chart could help you to evaluate the reasons for and against the idea. Question 50 on the Pretest asks you to write your opinion about whether experimentation with cloning should be encouraged. You could read through the article and jot down the pros and cons in a chart like the one on this page, which would help you organize the arguments for and against cloning. Then you could choose your position and write your paragraph.

Cause-and-Effect Charts

Discussions of causes and effects appear in all kinds of writing. For example, a newspaper report about a hurricane might discuss how it was caused by the collision of a cold front and a warm front and how it affected people and property. You may be called upon to write about causes and effects. To represent cause-and-effect relationships graphically, you can create a **cause-and-effect chart.** Observing these relationships will give your writing greater clarity.

> ### CAUSE AND EFFECT:
> ### WEALTH OF THE UNITED STATES
>
> **Causes**
> —Abundant natural resources
> —Strong work ethic
> —Free market economy
> —Universal education
>
> ↓
>
> **Effect**
> —United States one of the wealthiest countries in the world

 What made the United States one of the wealthiest countries in the history of the world? This is a complex question with many answers. One answer is that the country is blessed with an abundance of natural resources—water, lumber, iron, and oil being among the most important. Another is that it was settled by pioneers with a strong work ethic—people who believed that by working hard, they could get ahead, prosper, and make better lives for themselves and their families. Yet another answer is the free market economy of the United States, which encourages competition and invention.

A question might ask you to show how an influential person made an impact on the world. A cause-and-effect chart could help you to see the effects of his or her actions on the world.

Sensory Detail Charts

Descriptive writing is writing that presents a portrait of a subject in words. One way to represent information given in descriptive writing is to prepare a **sensory detail chart.** Such a chart uses a list of the five senses as headings. Under each heading, you list particular details that you perceive with each of your **senses**—sight, hearing, touch, smell, and taste. If you spent a day at the beach, you might make a chart like the one below to record stimuli received by each of your senses. You could then develop your chart into a paragraph like the one that follows.

> ### SENSORY DETAIL CHART: THE BEACH
>
> **Sight**
> —Hundreds of people
> —White sand, green sea, blue sky
> —Colorful beach towels and umbrellas
>
> **Sound**
> —Sea gulls cawing
> —Waves lapping
> —Children laughing
> —Radios playing top forty hits
>
> **Touch**
> —Warm rays of the sun
>
> **Smell**
> —Hot dogs and suntan oil
>
> **Taste**
> —Hot dogs

DEVELOPING WRITING SKILLS

On the last day of the season, hundreds of people crowded the beach. On the horizon, the emerald sea blended into the blue sky. The warm rays of the sun shone upon a second sea of colorful beach towels and umbrellas. Sea gulls cawed overhead, and the waves gently lapped the shore. The air was filled with the sounds of children laughing and splashing in the surf and radios playing top forty hits. Wafting over the crowd was the smell of hot dogs and suntan oil.

Question 18 on the Posttest asks you to imagine that you are present at the eruption of a volcano and to write an account of what you see and how you feel. Making a sensory detail chart could help you to engage all of your senses and write a vivid description.

Analysis Charts

To write an analysis of a subject, you will find it useful to create an **analysis chart,** which lists the parts of the subject in one column and descriptions of those parts in the other column. Here are two paragraphs based on information from an analysis chart for John D. Rockefeller, Sr.

 At the beginning of this century, the wealthiest person in America was John D. Rockefeller, Sr., who built and controlled the Standard Oil Company. At one point, his income amounted to what, in today's dollars, would be a billion dollars a year. A tall, extremely thin, well-dressed man, often seen sporting a top hat and tails or fancy golfing attire, he was known for his very conservative political and religious views. A disease called alopecia caused him to lose all of his facial hair, giving him a somewhat elflike appearance.

In his personal life, Rockefeller was frugal to the point of miserliness. He avoided cards and theater, shunning them as vices, and preferred home life to socializing with other wealthy people. Although he could be a stern businessman, merciless to his competitors, Rockefeller became one of the largest donors to charity in all of history.

CHARACTER ANALYSIS: ROCKEFELLER	
Appearance	Tall, thin No facial hair Elflike
Dress	Well-dressed Top hat, tails Golfing attire
Occupation	Founder, Standard Oil Became world's wealthiest man Became world's foremost philanthropist
Interests	Family, business, religion, golf, medicine
Habits/Personality	Frugal, conservative Avoided cards, theater Stern in business but charitable

"The Story of an Hour" and "The Death of Iván Illych" in the Pretest present literary characters. As you read these kinds of stories, you might use a chart like the one above to jot down the character's actions and statements made about him or her that reveal what he or she is like.

DEVELOPING WRITING SKILLS

Word Webs, or Cluster Charts

An excellent graphic organizer for exploring ideas before you commit them to paper is the word web, or cluster chart. To create such a chart, you write the main subject in the middle of a piece of paper and circle it. Then, outside the circle, you write related main ideas and circle these. Then, next to each idea, you write related specific details and circle those. You can indicate a connection between any two ideas by drawing a line. Have a look at the word web below. A paragraph based on this word web follows.

A freshman at a university would do well to take a wide variety of course-work, sampling all that the university has to offer before deciding upon an area in which to major. Most universities offer courses in three broad areas—the sciences, the humanities, and the professions. The sciences include physics, chemistry, computer science, astronomy, geology, biology, and anthropology. The humanities include English, languages, fine arts, theater, philosophy, and music. The professions, often represented by separate schools within the university, include business, journalism, medicine, and law.

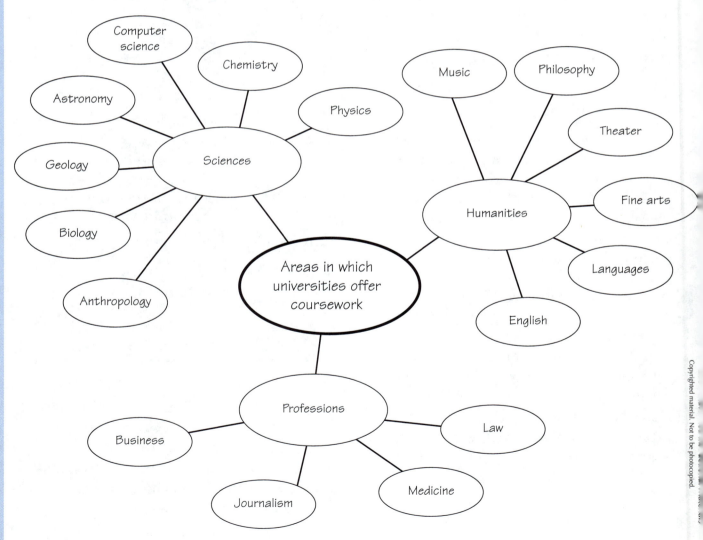

Your Turn

1 Choose one of the open-response questions from the Pretest on pages 2–38. Review the selection on which the question is based. Then, write a brief rough outline for an acceptable written response to the question.

2 Choose two similar commercial products that would be interesting to other high-school students. Possibilities include the following:

—Two brands of running shoes
—Two personal computers
—Two computer games
—Two new music CDs

Do some research on these products by visiting stores or by checking out the products at company sites on the World Wide Web. Create a Venn diagram showing the products' similarities and differences.

3 Based on the information in the chart that you created for Exercise 2, write a product review. In your review, compare and contrast the two products. Then state which product you would recommend to your friends.

4 Choose a career in which you are interested and do some research on it in the library or on the World Wide Web. A good source of information on careers is *The Occupational Outlook Handbook*, which is updated yearly by the U.S. Department of Labor. Most libraries have recent copies of this handbook, and it is available online at http://www.bls.gov/ocohome.htm. Prepare a chart of the pros and cons for a person entering the career that you chose.

5 Find a copy of a national or big-city daily newspaper, such as *USA Today*, the *Miami Herald*, the *Boston Globe*, or the *New York Times*. Study the articles in a single edition of the paper. Find at least five examples of cause-and-effect relationships described in the paper. Choose two of these and create cause-and-effect charts describing the relationships.

6 Create a sensory detail chart to describe one of the following scenes:

—A carnival
—An ape house in a zoo
—A museum
—A school cafeteria at lunchtime
—A skateboarding park
—A concert
—A football, baseball, basketball, or soccer game
—An amusement park

7 Write a descriptive paragraph based on the information in the chart you created for Exercise 6.

8 Create a word web for an essay about extracurricular activities at your school. Try to fill an entire page with information that might be used to develop the essay. Follow the model word web given on the preceding page.

LESSON 6.3 *Writing Answers to Open-Response Questions*

The open-response questions on the MCAS English test require you to answer in writing. For this type of question, you must compose your own response, in contrast to multiple-choice questions, for which you simply choose one of the given answers. This lesson will teach you the steps to take when answering open-response questions. You will learn how to develop a complete and coherent paragraph-length response.

Using Proper Paragraph Form

When you write answers to open-response questions, it is important that you use standard **paragraph form.** A **paragraph** is a group of logically connected sentences on a single topic. It should include the following parts:

TOPIC SENTENCE: The topic sentence should introduce the subject of the paragraph and state its main idea.

SUPPORTING SENTENCES: The paragraph should contain a minimum of two or three sentences that develop and support the main idea.

TRANSITIONS: The paragraph should contain words and phrases that connect its ideas. See the chart on page 157 for a list of transitions that are useful for connecting ideas.

CLINCHER SENTENCE: The clincher sentence should bring the paragraph to a satisfying conclusion. This sentence can serve any of a number of functions. It can:

—restate the main idea in different words

—sum up the ideas presented in the rest of the paragraph

—draw a conclusion from the information in the rest of the paragraph

—call upon the reader to adopt some belief or to take some action

Nonnarrative paragraphs commonly have a topic sentence, supporting sentences, and transitions. Paragraphs often lack a clincher sentence.

Reread the selection from *Pilgrim at Tinker Creek* on pages 2 and 3 of the Pretest. Then consider the following open-response writing prompt: "How are the plants described in the excerpt 'flying in the teeth of it all'? Use details and information from the excerpt to support your answer."

One Student's Response

Irene wrote the following paragraph in response to this prompt:

The plants that Annie Dillard writes about in the excerpt from <u>Pilgrim at Tinker Creek</u> are remarkable because they manage to survive despite harsh conditions; Dillard calls their ability to flourish in difficult growing conditions "flying in the teeth of it all." First, she describes a tree limb knocked down by a storm. A month after being stranded on a dry rock, this limb sprouts new leaves, even though no part of it rests in the water. Second, Dillard writes about an ailanthus tree that is growing on a garage rooftop. The tree has grown to fifteen feet, even though it is rooted in dust and roofing cinders, and not in soil. Third and, as Dillard says, "most spectacular," is the desert plant that looks like a dead chunk of loose wood. A specimen of this plant survives in an enclosed glass case in a museum without soil or water for seven years. The plant puts out sprouts and roots every year in anticipation of a rainy season that never arrives. In conclusion, Dillard calls this ability to survive "flying in the teeth of it all," because such survival goes beyond what logic tells us living things need to thrive.

Steps to Answering Open-Response Questions

Step 1: Read the Question Carefully.

Before you can write a good answer, you must understand exactly what the question is asking. In Lesson 6.1, you learned how to analyze the question, or writing prompt, so you will know just what is required. As you read the writing prompt, identify the key question; pay particular attention to question words like *who, what, where, when, why,* and *how;* and note action words that tell you what to do, like *describe, explain, compare,* and *contrast.* See Appendix A for definitions of terms often found in writing prompts.

Step 2: Look for the Answer in Your Notes or in the Selection.

From your reading of the selection or selections, you may remember the answer to the key question, but check back over the selection to make sure that your answer is correct. Notes you may have taken in the margin may also be helpful in pinpointing the answer. For example, the writing prompt about the Dillard selection asks about the plants the author describes. As you were reading the selection, you may have made some notes in the margin about each plant. Your answer might include these details.

Step 3: Write a Complete Sentence Stating Your Answer.

Organize your thoughts and try to summarize the essence of your answer in one sentence. This general answer to the key question will be your topic sentence. Jot the sentence down on your note paper. In the sample response on this page, Irene's topic sentence is the first sentence of her paragraph.

DEVELOPING WRITING SKILLS

Step 4: Back Up Your Answer With Supporting Details.

Look over the selection for details that support your answer. A single sentence might be sufficient to answer the question, but supporting details will strengthen your answer. Irene backed up her answer with details from the selection about three plants that illustrate the author's concept of "flying in the teeth of it all." Jot down the supporting details to create a rough outline. Irene's rough outline might have looked something like this:

—Plants survive harsh conditions
   —Stranded limb sprouts new leaves
   —Tree grows on roof
   —Plant lives in glass case

Step 5: Write Your Paragraph.

First, write your topic sentence in the space provided. Make sure that the first line of the paragraph is indented.

Second, using the supporting details from your outline, write several sentences to support your topic sentence. As you write, vary the length, complexity, type, and organization of your sentences.

Third, use transitions from the chart on the next page to connect your ideas. Notice how Irene has used each of the details in her rough outline to create a supporting sentence in her paragraph. She has used the words *First*, *Second*, and *Third* to express the transitions between her sentences.

Fourth, write a clincher sentence to sum up your paragraph or to restate your main idea. Irene pulls together her paragraph with a clincher sentence that restates the main idea of her response. She introduces this sentence with the transition *In conclusion*.

Step 6: Check and Correct Your Writing.

Read over your answer carefully to make sure that it makes sense, that all words are spelled correctly, that you have answered every part of the question, and that you have written complete sentences. Look for errors in paragraph form, spelling, grammar, usage, punctuation, and capitalization. (For more information on correcting errors, see Lessons 6.4 and 6.5.) Make any necessary corrections. If you have first written your answer on scrap paper, now write it correctly in the space provided.

Strategies

- 📖 Write a topic sentence that states a general answer to the question.

- 📖 Develop the paragraph with sentences that provide evidence supporting your main idea.

- 📖 As you write, vary the type and length of your sentences to make the writing interesting.

- 📖 Use transitions to connect your ideas.

- 📖 Always proofread your finished answer before moving on to the next portion of the exam.

Using Transitions to Connect Ideas

A **transition** is a word or a phrase that relates two parts of a piece of writing. Within paragraphs, transitions are used to connect sentences and, sometimes, parts of sentences. When you write for the MCAS English exam, be sure to use transitions to show how your ideas are connected to one another. The following are some transitions that you will find useful:

1. **Transitions to show chronological order, or order in time**
   first, second, finally, next, then, afterward, later, before, eventually, in the future, in the past, recently

2. **Transitions to show spatial order**
   beside, in the middle, next to, to the right, on top, in front, behind, beneath

3. **Transitions to show degree order**
   more, less, most, least, most important, least important, more importantly

4. **Transitions to show comparison and contrast**
   likewise, similarly, in contrast, a different kind, unlike this, another difference

5. **Transitions to show cause-and-effect order**
   one cause, another effect, as a result, consequently, therefore

6. **Transitions for classification**
   another group, the first type, one kind, other sorts, other types, other kinds

7. **Transitions to introduce examples**
   for example, one example, one kind, one type, one sort, for instance

8. **Transitions to introduce a contradiction**
   nonetheless, however, in spite of this, otherwise, instead, on the contrary

9. **Transitions to introduce a conclusion, summary, or generalization**
   in conclusion, therefore, as a result, in summary, in general

Examples of Use of Transitions:

First, heat the water. **Then,** add the cocoa.
One kind of familiar marsupial is the opossum. **Another** kind is the kangaroo.
It was a rainy day. **Nonetheless,** people thronged the streets to view the Macy's Thanksgiving Day Parade.

DEVELOPING WRITING SKILLS

Presenting Evidence: Quotations, Paraphrases, and Summaries

Generally speaking, a response that you write to an open-response question on the exam will consist of

- a general answer to the question, followed by
- evidence from the selection or selections to back up your answer

Providing evidence from the selection or selections in your response is crucial. You can provide this evidence in one of three ways:

1. Quotation. You can quote words, groups of words, or whole sentences from the selection.

2. Paraphrase. You can restate material from the selection in your own words, using roughly the same number of words as were used to state that material in the selection.

3. Summary. You can restate material from the selection in your own words, condensing it into fewer words than were used in the selection.

When you quote from a selection, you pick up material **verbatim,** or word-for-word, as the author stated it, and you place that material in **quotation marks** (" . . . "). When you paraphrase or summarize material from a selection, no quotation marks are needed.

Note that a common mistake that students make on standardized tests of reading and writing is to respond to questions by retelling the selection. In particular, students often make this mistake when writing about stories or nonfiction narratives. Do not simply retell the story. Think about what the writing prompt is asking you. Answer the key question. Then look back over the selection for specific evidence to support your answer. Present this evidence in your answer, using quotation, paraphrase, summary, or, best of all, some combination of the three.

Study the sample student response on the next page. Notice that the response uses a combination of quotation, paraphrase, and summary to present supporting evidence.

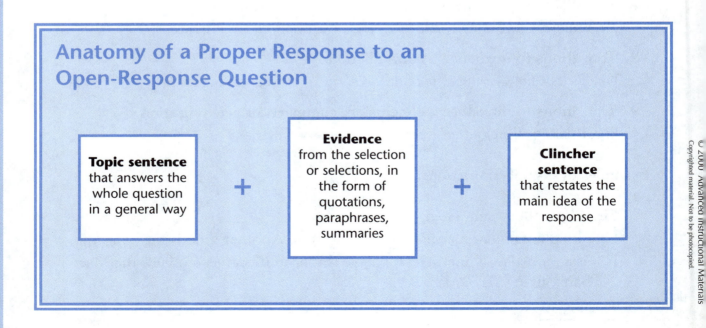

Anatomy of a Proper Response to an Open-Response Question

Topic sentence that answers the whole question in a general way

+

Evidence from the selection or selections, in the form of quotations, paraphrases, summaries

+

Clincher sentence that restates the main idea of the response

Sample Student Response
Using Quotation, Paraphrase, and Summary

Question:

What is the central conflict in "The Story of an Hour"? Use details from the selection to describe the conflict and tell whether it is an internal or an external conflict.

Response:

The topic sentence provides a general answer to the question.

To provide background for discussing the central struggle, the writer summarizes the basic plot situation in sentences 3 and 4.

In the sentences that follow, the writer uses a combination of quotation from the story and paraphrase of events to explain the central conflict.

Throughout the paragraph, the writer uses transitions, such as *at the beginning, at first, then, once,* and *in short* to connect ideas.

The writer concludes with a clincher sentence that restates her main idea—what the central conflict is—in different words.

In Kate Chopin's short story "The Story of an Hour," the central conflict is an internal struggle that takes place within the main character. Mrs. Mallard feels conflict between what society expects and her own desire for independence. At the beginning of the story, Mrs. Mallard learns of her husband's death, reacts with sudden grief, and then, exhausted, retires to her own room. It is within this room, alone, that Mrs. Mallard experiences the central struggle. At first, she looks blankly out a window. Then, she begins to recognize "something coming to her . . . too subtle and elusive to name." Once she starts to recognize the thought that is coming to her, she tries, by an act of will, to suppress it, but she is unable to. The thought that she is trying to suppress is that her husband's death has set her free. There will be no man to impose his will on her, and the "years to come" will "belong to her absolutely." Alone in her room, Mrs. Mallard struggles between the socially proper response to her husband's death, which would be grief, and her growing recognition that she feels joy at the prospect of a life on her own terms. Ironically, having resolved this conflict in favor of the "self-assertion which she suddenly recognized as the strongest impulse of her being," Mrs. Mallard then learns that her husband is still alive, and she drops dead of a heart attack. The other characters in the story seem to think that Mrs. Mallard has been struggling with grief and has died from excessive joy, but the reader knows what the real conflict is. In short, Mrs. Mallard has struggled to accept her own desire for freedom and won that struggle, only to lose her freedom moments later.

DEVELOPING WRITING SKILLS

When quoting from a selection, follow these guidelines:

Incorporating Quotations into Your Writing

1. Use quotation marks around direct quotations but not around paraphrases.

2. When quoting fewer than three lines from the selection, run the quotation into your paragraph, as in the sample response on the preceding page. When quoting more than three lines, set the quotation off from the left and right margins, single-space the quotation, and do not use quotation marks, as in this example:

   > The mood of the protagonist changes dramatically halfway through the story. At first she is not even aware, herself, of what is happening to her. She just knows that she is beginning to feel something different:

   > > There was something coming to her and she was waiting for it, fearfully. What was it? She did not know: it was too subtle and elusive to name. But she felt it, creeping out of the sky, reaching toward her through the sounds, the scents, the color that filled the air.

   > The change coming over her seems to be related to the spring scene outside her window. Spring, of course, is a traditional symbol of rebirth and awakening, and it is just such a rebirth that she is starting to feel.

3. When quoting more than one line from a poem, use a slash mark (/) with spaces on either side to separate the lines. Capitalize the quotation exactly as in the source.

   > The speaker of "A Birthday" has also experienced a rebirth, but of a different kind. She says that she is overjoyed "Because the birthday of [her] life / Is come."

4. Make sure that quotations fit grammatically into your sentences. If you need to change a verb or a pronoun to make it agree, as in the above example, place the changed, nonverbatim material in brackets [ ].

5. Enclose quotations within quotations in single quotation marks (' ').

   > The protagonist slowly comes to recognize that she feels happy about the news of Mr. Mallard's death. She repeats "over and over under her breath: 'free, free, free!' " Obviously, her mood is not, at this point in the story, one of sorrow over her husband's demise.

(continued)

DEVELOPING WRITING SKILLS

6. Conventionally, stories are written in the past tense, as in "Once upon a time, there was a young man who set out to seek his fortune." When writing about the events that occur in a literary work, however, you should use the present tense, as below.

> In the story, a young man leaves home to seek his fortune.

When quoting, you might have to change the tenses of verbs to make them work grammatically in your sentences. Again, any changes that you make within a quotation should be placed in brackets:

> Mrs. Mallard notices that there is a "delicious breath of rain" in the air and that "sparrows [are] twittering in the eaves."

7. Sometimes, you may wish to leave out some of the words within a quotation. Use ellipsis dots (. . .) to indicate any words that are missing.

> Mrs. Mallard notices "countless sparrows . . . twittering in the eaves."

8. Use a period and ellipsis dots (. . . .) when omitting a sentence or more from a quotation, but be sure that complete sentences precede and follow the ellipsis dots.

> Mrs. Mallard looks forward to her life on her own. The narrator says that "Her fancy was running riot along those days ahead of her. . . . It was only yesterday she had thought with a shudder that life might be long."

9. Always use a comma to set off **speaker's tags** such as *he says* or *she replies*.

> Josephine asks Mrs. Mallard to open the door. Mrs. Mallard replies, "Go away. I am not making myself ill."

10. A colon may be used to introduce a quotation in a formal way, especially after phrases such as *Here are* or *the following*.

> Mrs. Mallard is truthful when she says the following to her sister: "I am not making myself ill." In fact, Mrs. Mallard is "drinking in a very elixir of life through that open window."

11. Periods and commas at the ends of quotations always go within the quotation marks. Other punctuation marks, such as colons, semicolons, question marks, and exclamation points, go outside the quotation marks, except when they are part of the quotation.

> Why does Mrs. Mallard tell her sister to "Go away"?

> Josephine asks, "What are you doing, Louise?" and her sister replies, "Go away."

Your Turn

A   Reread the sample paragraph in the box labeled "One Student's Response" on page 155, and review the teaching for this lesson. On a separate piece of paper, answer these questions about the paragraph:

1   What is the topic sentence of the paragraph?

2   How many supporting sentences does this paragraph contain?

3   What transitions are used to connect ideas in the paragraph?

4   What is the clincher sentence of the paragraph?

B   Read the following paragraph. Underline the topic sentence once. Underline the clincher sentence twice. Circle the transitions, and number the supporting sentences.

Throughout history, new ideas have often been met with skepticism, resistance, and even fear. For example, many people vehemently rejected the idea that the Earth is round, and there are those today who still believe that the Earth is flat. Similarly, Galileo faced hostility and imprisonment in the 1600s when he promoted Copernicus's idea that the sun, not the Earth, is the

Galileo

center of the solar system. Only a little more than a hundred years ago, many people doubted that a heavier-than-air machine would ever fly. As recently as the 1970s, many people thought that the idea of home computers was completely impractical. Maybe you will someday have an idea that seems crazy to the world but will eventually be proved true, or perhaps you will help to make some "impossible" invention a reality.

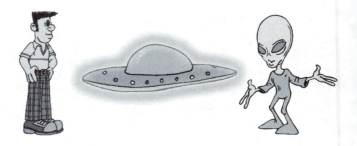

C   Choose a transition from the list on page 157 to connect the ideas in each of the following sentences.

1   As twilight approached, we began to worry about the hikers who had fallen behind. _____, they staggered into camp, weary but safe.

2   Rainfall this summer has been much lower than normal. _____, the ground is hard and dry, lawns are turning brown, and flowers are withering.

3 Green, leafy vegetables are a good source of iron. _____, a cup of cooked spinach provides about 4 mg of iron.

4 Isaac Newton was a poor student at first, but then he got motivated to learn and went on to become a great scientist. _____, Albert Einstein had trouble in school when he was young, but he became one of the most remarkable geniuses of the twentieth century.

5 Louie jammed his finger in the fourth quarter. _____, he kept on playing and sank the winning basket at the buzzer.

D Write a sentence that could follow, logically, each of the following sentences. Introduce your sentence with a transition from the list on page 157. Use a different transition for each sentence. Write your answers on a separate piece of paper.

EXAMPLE: Shanaz isn't afraid of heights.

ANSWER: Shanaz isn't afraid of heights. On the contrary, she enjoys activities like rock climbing and parasailing.

1 The weatherman has predicted a severe ice storm with possible power outages.

2 The policemen rushed to the scene of the burglary.

3 Melvin has a gloomy disposition and is always complaining.

4 Jeff locked himself out of the house in the rain.

5 One way to become famous is by creating a brilliant invention.

E Write topic sentences for paragraphs about the following subjects:

—A job you would like to have

—An actor or actress

—Gardening

—Dinosaurs

—Homework

—The ideal vacation spot

F Choose two topic sentences that you wrote for Exercise E, and develop these into complete paragraphs. Make sure that each paragraph has a topic sentence, several sentences related to the topic sentence, transitions to connect the ideas, and a clincher sentence.

DEVELOPING WRITING SKILLS

G Read the following selections. Then rewrite the sentences that follow, correcting the errors.

By the rude bridge that arched the flood,
　　Their flag to April's breeze unfurled,
Here, once the embattled farmers stood,
　　And fired the shot heard round the
　　　world.

"Come back!" the boy called to his friend. Jimmy could not hear him, however. The river was raging, high and wild, and its sound drowned out all else. Jimmy was already halfway across the narrow foot-bridge, and there was nothing to be done. Mike watched as the bridge collapsed. Minutes later, Jimmy washed up on the bank a hundred yards downstream, safe but wet.

1 The first stanza is made musical by its rhymes and by alliteration, the repetition of the initial *f* sound in words and phrases like the following "the flood," "their flag," "unfurled," "the farmers," and "fired".

2 Concord Bridge crosses over the Concord River near Lexington, Massachusetts. It was "Here, once the embattled farmers stood, and fired the shot heard round the world.

3 The boy says "Come back"! but Jimmy cannot hear him.

4 "Jimmy fell into the river but did not drown."

5 The setting plays a crucial role in the scene. The river "was raging, and its sound drowned out all else." Because the river is so loud, Jimmy couldn't hear his friend calling.

H Write one paragraph of your own, illustrating each rule from the chart on pages 160 and 161.

LESSON
6.4
Evaluating and Proofreading Your Response

Your answers to the open-response questions on the MCAS English exam will be graded primarily on content—how well you have fulfilled the requirements of the task. Your responses will be evaluated on how well you understand the reading and the elements of literature. You will not be given a specific grade for **mechanics**—grammar, spelling, capitalization, and punctuation. Nevertheless, using good mechanics will improve the overall quality of your writing. The power of an idea is weakened if faulty mechanics cause the reader to falter, whereas using good form and grammar will make your ideas come across clearly. Therefore, it is very important to **proofread** your writing—to read it through, check for errors, and mark corrections. The list below tells you what to look for as you check your work.

Proofreading Checklist

Manuscript Form	☑ Every paragraph is indented.
	☑ Ample margins have been left on either side.
	☑ The writing is legible.
Grammar and Usage	☑ Each verb agrees with its subject.
	☑ Each pronoun has a clear antecedent and agrees with it.
	☑ Commonly confused pronouns, such as *I/me* and *who/whom*, are used correctly.
	☑ Commonly confused words, such as *to/too/two*, *among/between*, and *effect/affect*, are used correctly.
	☑ There are no sentence fragments or run-ons.
	☑ There are no double negatives.
Spelling	☑ All words, including names, are spelled correctly.
Capitalization and Punctuation	☑ Every sentence begins with a capital letter.
	☑ All proper nouns and proper adjectives, including the names of people and places, begin with capital letters.
	☑ Every sentence ends with an end mark—a period (.), exclamation mark (!), or question mark (?).
	☑ Commas and other punctuation marks are used correctly.
	☑ All direct quotations are enclosed in quotation marks.

DEVELOPING WRITING SKILLS

When marking corrections in your writing, use the standard **proofreading symbols,** marks that indicate corrections that need to be made. In this way it will be clear to the reader what you intend to say. Your answers will be graded according to the corrected version, as long as the corrections can be clearly understood by the evaluator.

Study the chart below to learn the proof-reading symbols. Most of the symbols have obvious meanings, and with just a little practice, you will find them very easy and convenient to use. As you proofread, keep in mind that attention to these details will improve your writing and your scores and make you a more effective communicator.

Proofreading Symbols

Symbol and Example	Meaning of Symbol
∧ bicycle built $_\wedge^{for}$ two	Insert (add) something that is missing.
⌐ Paris in the ~~the~~ spring	Delete (cut) these letters or words.
— ^{extreme} ~~estreme~~ skiing	Replace this letter or word.
∼ the glass delicate slippers	Transpose (switch) the order.
↶ give to the needy gifts	Move this word to where the arrow points.
⌒ chair person	Close up this space.
⌍ truely	Delete this letter and close up the space.
≡ five portuguese sailors	Capitalize this letter.
/ a lantern and a Sleeping bag	Lowercase this letter.
¶ waves. "Help me!" she cried.	Begin a new paragraph
⊙ All's well that ends well⊙	Put a period here.
⌄ parrots macaws, and toucans	Put a comma here.
⌄ childrens toys	Put an apostrophe here.
⦂ There are three good reasons⦂	Put a colon here.
# the grand opening	Put a space here.

This lesson gives you the basics of proofreading. You will not have much time to correct open-response answers, but knowing what to look for will help you to make key corrections quickly, enhancing the presentation of your work. In addition, proofreading skills will help you write clear responses in the Composition sessions, for which you will be writing a full-length essay. Responses for the Composition sessions (see Unit 7) *will* be graded for, among other things, mechanics. Lesson 6.5, "Conventions of English," explains each of these items in greater detail.

Your Turn

A   Rewrite the following sentences, making the corrections indicated by the proofreading symbols.

1   # chewing gym (gum) was invented by pure accident in the 1870s when a man tried to make rubber of out chicle, the sap of a mexican tree.

2   The mans rubber experiment failed, but he and his son started chewing prices of the chicle, realized its potential, and went into the chewinggum business.

B Use the proofreading symbols to make corrections in the following sentences as indicated.

1 Hazardous waists are the Dangerous sub stances that are leftover form places like factories power hospitals, and plants.

Begin a new paragraph with the word "Hazardous."

Replace the word "waists" with the word "wastes."

Lowercase the "D" in the word "Dangerous."

Close up the space between "sub" and "stances."

Put a space between "left" and "over" in "leftover."

Switch the letters "o" and "r" in the word "form" to make "from."

Insert a comma after "factories."

Move the word "power" and put it before the word "plants."

2 some scientist's have found away make fake lightening that turns hazardous wastes into a glassy material has that pratical uses

Capitalize the "s" in "some."

Delete the apostrophe in "scientist's" and close up the space.

Put a space between "a" and "way" in "away."

Insert the word "to" before "make."

Delete the letter "e" from "lightening" and close up the space.

Switch the order of the words "has" and "that."

Insert the letter "c" between "a" and "t" in "practical."

Put a period after "uses."

C Use proofreading symbols to correct the following paragraph.

A close reeding of Gary Levitt's essay, "How to Become a Martian, reveals that the evidince for life on Mars is mixed according to Levitt, the chanels observed by Giovanni Schiaparelli back in 1877 turned out not to be canals, as Percival Lowell and others thought they were. Further more, the so-called "Mars face" turned out to be a natural formation it was a volcano, not "a monumental, carved portrait." Despite these setbacks to arguements for existance of life on Mars, some resent evidence sugests that life once existed their. Scientists now no that in the past, "Mars had a much thcker atmosfere and lots of running water" Of course, water and an atmosfere are crucial to life. In addition, in 1996 NASA scientists announces the discovery on Earth of a meteorite that may contain fossil bacteria. That lived on Mars billions of years ago. In sumary while there probablee isn't no life on Mars today, their may well have been life on Mars in the distant past and if humans ever colonise the planut, their will be life their in the future.

LESSON 6.5 *Conventions of English*

Conventions are agreed-upon rules for writing. There are conventions governing manuscript form, spelling, grammar, capitalization, and punctuation. If you follow these standards, your writing will come across as intelligent and coherent. This lesson will outline some of the basic conventions of English and give you practice in following these rules.

Manuscript Form

If you were producing a typewritten or word-processed paper, you would have to observe certain rules regarding the elements of **manuscript form,** such as margins, paragraph format, and line spacing. For the open-response questions, you will be writing your answers in a blank space. Leave margins on either side of your paragraphs, and try to leave enough space above each written line for neatly written additions or corrections. For the Composition sessions, you will be given lined paper, so the margins and line spacing are already established for you. Since your answers will be handwritten, your main concern regarding form will be to make sure that your handwriting is neat and legible. Use the standard proofreading symbols. Do not scratch out an unwanted word; draw a line through it instead. Also remember to indent every paragraph so that the arrangement of your ideas is clear.

Keep in mind that no matter how good your ideas are, you will not get credit for them if the evaluator cannot decipher your handwriting. You may be accustomed to using a keyboard for most of your writing, but try to make your handwriting legible so that your penmanship will not interfere with the communication of your ideas.

Grammar and Usage

Grammar is the study of the structure of a language—how words are put together to form phrases, clauses, and sentences. Following the rules of English grammar will help you to produce good writing. **Usage** is the way in which people use language. Only **standard usage,** according to the agreed-upon rules, is acceptable in formal writing.

As you proofread, check your writing for errors in grammar and usage. Especially keep in mind the following points:

- Make sure that each verb **agrees** with, or matches, its subject in number. Both should be singular or both plural.

  WRONG   The girl with six brothers are very athletic.

  RIGHT   The girl with six brothers is very athletic.

  (Think, "The girl . . . is")

DEVELOPING WRITING SKILLS

- An **antecedent** is the noun that a pronoun refers to or replaces. Every pronoun should have a clear antecedent and agree with it.

  WRONG   A tight end with the Panthers broke their leg.

  RIGHT   A tight end with the Panthers broke his leg.

  (Think, "A tight end . . . broke his leg")

- Be careful not to mix up commonly confused pronouns.

  WRONG   Mom gave Al and I the third degree when we arrived late.

  RIGHT   Mom gave Al and me the third degree when we arrived late.

  (Think, "Mom gave . . . me")

- Be aware of commonly confused words and make sure that you use these words correctly.

  WRONG   The equipment was divided evenly between the four teams.

  RIGHT   The equipment was divided evenly among the four teams.

- A **fragment** is a group of words that lacks some essential part of a sentence and does not express a complete thought. Check your writing for fragments and turn them into complete sentences.

  WRONG   The Vietnam Veterans Memorial in Washington, D.C.

  RIGHT   The Vietnam Veterans Memorial in Washington, D.C., honors Americans who died in the Vietnam War.

- A **run-on** is two or more sentences joined without a word to connect them or a punctuation mark to separate them.

  WRONG   The owner of the goose cut her open to get the gold she turned out to be an ordinary goose inside.

  RIGHT   The owner of the goose cut her open to get the gold, but she turned out to be an ordinary goose inside.

- A **double negative** is a sentence with two negative words such as *aren't*, *doesn't*, *haven't*, *no*, *not*, *none*, and *never*.

  WRONG   Sammy doesn't have no money.

  RIGHT   Sammy doesn't have any money. Sammy has no money.

- Make sure not to confuse words that are similar in spelling but different in meaning, such as *affect/effect*, *desert/dessert*, *loose/lose*, and *weather/whether*.

  WRONG   General Washington lead his army to victory at the Battle of Yorktown.

  RIGHT   General Washington led his army to victory at the Battle of Yorktown.

Spelling

One of the best things you can do to improve your spelling is to read a lot. The more often you see a word in print, the more likely you will be to remember how to spell it. You should also keep a list in your journal of the words that you misspell. Use a dictionary to find correct spellings as well as definitions.

Although English has many exceptions to its spelling rules, the majority of words *do* follow the rules. Therefore, when uncertain about the spelling of a word, you can think about a similar word that you know how to spell and take a clue from it. Appendix C in this book contains a list of commonly misspelled words. Try to learn at least ten of these words every week in preparation for the exam. One good way to practice is to have someone else read each word to you as you write it down. Check your answers. Then, write each word that you spelled incorrectly over and over until you can remember the correct spelling.

Capitalization and Punctuation

Punctuation is the use of periods, commas, question marks, and other marks to help make meaning clear. Punctuation does for writing what pauses and changes in pitch do for speech. Consider the words below:

Jill is a great friend who cares about you

These words can take on very different meanings depending on how you say them; so, too, changing the punctuation can completely change the meaning:

Jill is a great friend who cares about you.
Jill is a great friend. Who cares about you?

It is important to punctuate your writing carefully so the meaning will be clear. Every sentence should end with an **end mark**—either a period, an exclamation mark, or a question mark. Make sure that commas, which represent slight pauses or interruptions, are correctly placed. Quotation marks should enclose quotations and titles of such short works as essays and stories. The names of longer works, such as novels, should be italicized or underlined.

Also remember to capitalize the first word of every sentence. All proper nouns (Liza, Iowa, Brooklyn Bridge) and proper adjectives (Shakespearean, Spanish, Tibetan) should be capitalized as well.

Your Turn

A Fill in the blanks with the correct present tense form of the verb in parentheses.

1 Every year, the philanthropist _____ ten scholarships to promising students. (give)

2 Each of the four sisters _____ a different musical instrument. (play)

3 The Inuit people of the Arctic _____ igloos that keep them warm even when the temperature drops to −100° F. (build)

DEVELOPING WRITING SKILLS

B Circle the correct word in parentheses in each sentence below.

1 Just between you and (I, me), Gilbert is really clumsy on the dance floor.

2 (Their, There) are more than 250,000 species of beetles.

3 After doing her aerobics workout, Sally always (lays, lies) down for fifteen minutes.

C Use proofreading marks to correct the commonly confused words in the sentences below.

1 We drove threw nineteen states on our trip to Washington.

2 Seeing all the children at the orphanage effected her deeply.

3 The Atacama Dessert in Chile is one of the driest in the world.

D Rewrite each sentence below on the lines provided, eliminating sentence fragments, run-ons, and double negatives.

1 In 1906, Fanny Workman reached the summit of Pinnacle Peak in the Himalayas. She was wearing a skirt and didn't carry no oxygen.

_____

_____

_____

_____

_____

2 In 1921, Charles Lindbergh became the first person. To fly solo across the Atlantic Ocean.

_____

_____

_____

_____

_____

Charles Lindbergh

3 The duck-billed platypus and the spiny anteater are the only mammals that lay eggs they are called monotremes.

_____

_____

_____

_____

_____

Ornithorhynchus anatinus

E Use the proofreading symbols to mark corrections in grammar and usage in the following passage. Also indicate that a new paragraph should begin with the sentence, "Almost every source of energy. . . ."

Energy is the ability too do work. One of the first forms of energy harnessed by humans were fire, fueled by would from trees. Over the centuries, people have found many other ways. To harness energy to do work. Flowing water turn waterwheels that grinds grain or cut lumber. The wind powers sailing ships and windmills, which can convert wind energy in to electricity. Coal, gas, and oil can be burned as fuel four heating or for powering engines. The son's energy can be captured to provide heat or produce electricity. In this century, people has even discovered how to split atoms to release atomic, or nuclear, energy. Almost every source of energy that people have tapped have sum disadvantages. If fire gets out off control they can be dangerous. Fossil fuels like coal and oil causes pollution furthermore, they will not last forever. Solar energy doesn't cause no pollution, but when it is cloudy or dark, solar energy is not reliable. The wind can also be undependable. And their are serious dangers involved in using nuclear power.

F Use proofreading symbols to correct each misspelled word below. If a word is spelled correctly, put a check mark next to the word.

1 approximately

2 caracter

3 committment

4 hypocricy

5 necessary

6 occassion

7 recieve

8 relevent

9 rhythm

10 wierd

G Use proofreading symbols to make corrections to the misspelled words in the passage below.

In 1939, a sientist flying over the region of Nazca in southern Peru spoted some huge drawings etched on the dessert floor. Eventualy, hundreds of these spectaculer drawings, some up to 1000 feat in size, were discoverd. Their are geometric figures, birds, and animals, including killer wales, a monky, and a spider.

Allthough no one is absolutely certan who made the Nazca lines, it is believed that they were drawn by the ancient Nazca Indians, a pre-Inca sivilization. Apparantly they brushed away the surface soil to reveal the lighter colored soil beneeth. Fortunatly, the drawings have been prezerved for nearly two thousend years owing to a compleet lack of rain in the regeon.

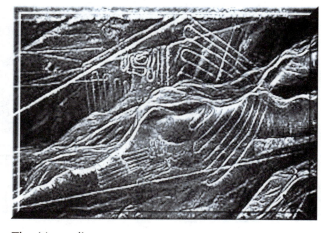

The Nazca lines

Vareous explainations of the purpose of these incredible drawings have been offered. Some reserchers think they serve as an astronomical calender. Others beleive they are linked to mountin worship. Some say the lines were made to be seen by the gods and to plead for there assistence. One fancifull idea is that the lines were drawn by aleins as part of an extraterrestrial landing stripe! In any case, the Nazca lines are beatiful works of art and represent a high level of cultural acheivement.

Similar markings on an island off the coast of Peru

H Insert correct punctuation (including end marks, commas, apostrophes, and quotation marks) into each sentence below.

1 When did the Battle of Bunker Hill take place

2 Some of the major Impressionist painters were Monet Renoir Degas and Manet.

3   Alan thinks its highly unlikely that man will ever live on the moon

4   Mark Twain once commented When I was a boy of fourteen, my father was so ignorant I could hardly stand to have the old man around. But when I got to be twenty-one, I was astonished at how much he had learned in seven years.

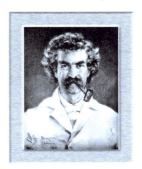

Mark Twain

I   Use the proofreading symbols to mark corrections in capitalization and punctuation in the passage below.

what do the tasmanian devil the opossum, and the kangaroo have in common All are marsupials a kind of mammal who'se babies grow inside a

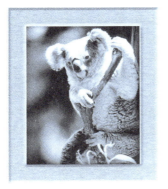

special pouch for several months after birth Almost all marsupial's are found in australia and on nearby Islands. the only marsupial, Found in north or south america is the opossum. which can hang from a branch by it's tail. The largest marsupial is the red Kangaroo, which can grow as tall as seven feet. the koala weighs, less than a paper clip at birth It takes refuge in the mothers pouch for the first six or seven month's, then begins to eat the leaves of eucalyptus trees the only item in its diet The Tasmanian devil resembles a small, hairy pig. it has powerful jaws and a reputation for ferocity

J   Use proofreading symbols to mark corrections in spelling, grammar, usage, capitalization, and punctuation in the following passage. Indicate that one new paragraph begins with the sentence "The first stage . . ." and that another begins with the sentence "The building of Stonehenge. . . ."

DEVELOPING WRITING SKILLS

A misterious monument from the stone Age raises out the grasslands of Salisbury Plane in southeastern england. No one really know why Stonehenge was built or by who. One medieval writer sugested that Merlin the Magician raised the boulders of the monument by majic. People use to beleive. That it was a temple for Druids, ancient Celtic priests. But carbon dateing show that Stonehenge was finished more then three thousands years ago, long befor the rise of the Druidic religeon. The bilding took place in three stages over a period of nearly too thousand years, so the monument could not of been built by just one cultural group. The first stage of construction begun about 3100 B.C. and included the diging of a circuler ditch and a ring of fifty-six wholes. About a thousand years later, massive pillars of stone was brought by land and see from Wales, 280 miles a way, and

erected at the center the of original circle. Some of these stones are now laying on there sides, but some remain standing. During the third phase, thirty upright stones wieghing as much as fifty tuns each was placed in an outer circle other huge stones were then lifted up and placed ontop of the uprights. The building of Stonehenge was a marvel of tecnology. Skilled engineers must of directed the carving and raising of the stones. Their is evidence that the builders were aquainted with astronomy; they used astro nomical calculations to align the stones with heavenly bodies. They may even have been abel to predict eclipses of the son and moon. By the posision of these celestial bodys in relation to the stones of the monument

LESSON 7.1 — *Understanding the MCAS Composition Exam*

In the MCAS English Composition sessions, you will write an essay-length response to a question about literature. In this unit, you will learn the skills you need to pass this part of the exam with flying colors. This lesson describes the Composition sessions, explains the writing task, analyzes the writing process, and discusses how the composition will be scored. Lesson 7.2 reviews the parts of a five-paragraph essay and takes you step by step through the process of producing an essay for the exam.

Organization of the Exam

The Composition portion of the MCAS English exam will be administered in two sessions separated by a break. In the first session, you will be given the writing prompt, space in which to organize your answer, and pages on which to write a draft of your composition. You will have forty-five minutes to read the writing prompt, generate your ideas, plan your essay, and write your draft answer. A **draft** is a first, rough effort in which you usually concentrate on what you are saying—not on style or on details of spelling, grammar, usage, and mechanics. At the end of the first session, you will have a short break.

In the second session, after the break, you will revise your draft and write a final version of your composition. A dictionary will be available to you to help you with

vocabulary and spelling. No other tools will be permitted. You will have another forty-five minutes to revise your draft and write your final essay. Because this is a timed test, it is important that you budget your time and use it to its full advantage.

Types of Writing Assignment

In the Composition portion of the MCAS exam, you will find one of two possible types of writing assignment. For the first type, you will be given a literary passage in the test materials. You will be asked to read and respond to a writing prompt about this literary selection. You will not need to recall details from any particular previous reading to complete this type of assignment. You will, however, be expected to apply your knowledge of literary elements and techniques to the literary passage. The prompt for the Composition on the Pretest is an example of this type of assignment.

The second kind of writing assignment will ask you to respond to a question about literature by writing an essay based on some work or works of literature that you have read previously. You will read the writing prompt. Then you will choose from among works you have read in or out of class a work that will best lend itself to the assignment. It is a good idea to prepare for the Composition exam by reading and taking notes on a couple of works.

Understanding the Writing Prompt

The writing prompt will describe the task or tasks that you must complete in creating your essay. Read the prompt and make sure that you understand all the assigned tasks. Pay attention to question words, such as *who*, *what*, *when*, *why*, and *how*. Also note action words in the prompt, such as *describe*, *explain*, *illustrate*, and *compare* (see Appendix A on page 242 of this book for definitions of terms that commonly appear in writing prompts.) When you understand the assignment in the writing prompt, read the literary selection, if any, noting any details that will help you to complete the assigned task. Then you are ready to begin the writing process.

Sample Writing Prompts

Prompts That Include a Reading Selection

PROMPT 1

Read the passage from the novel *Jane Eyre*, by Charlotte Brontë. When you have finished reading, respond to the writing assignment that follows.

They went, shutting the door, and locking it behind them.

The red room was a square chamber, very seldom slept in, I might say never, indeed, unless when a chance influx of visitors at Gateshead Hall rendered it necessary to turn to account all the accommodation it contained: yet it was one of the largest and stateliest chambers in the mansion. A bed supported on massive pillars of mahogany, hung with curtains of deep red damask, stood out like a tabernacle in the center; the two large windows, with their blinds always drawn down, were half shrouded in festoons and falls of similar drapery; the carpet was red; the table at the foot of the bed was covered with a crimson cloth; the walls were a soft fawn color with a blush of pink in it; the wardrobe, the toilet table, the chairs were of darkly polished old mahogany. Out of these deep surrounding shades rose high, and glared white, the piled-up mattresses and pillows of the bed, spread with a snowy Marseilles counterpane. Scarcely less prominent was an ample cushioned easy chair near the head of the bed, also white, with a footstool before it; and looking, as I thought, like a pale throne.

This room was chill, because it seldom had a fire; it was silent, because remote from the nursery and kitchen; solemn, because it was known to be so seldom entered. The housemaid alone came here on Saturdays, to wipe from the mirrors and the furniture a week's quiet dust: and Mrs. Reed herself, at far intervals, visited it to review the contents of a certain secret drawer in the wardrobe, where were stored divers parchments, her jewel casket, and a miniature of her deceased husband; and in those last words lies the secret of the red room—the spell which kept it so lonely in spite of its grandeur.

Mr. Reed had been dead nine years: it was in this chamber he breathed his last; here he lay in state; hence his coffin was borne by the undertaker's men; and, since that day, a sense of dreary consecration had guarded it from frequent intrusion.

My seat, to which Bessie and the bitter Miss Abbot had left me riveted, was a low ottoman near the marble chimney piece; the bed rose before me; to my right hand there was the high, dark wardrobe, with subdued, broken reflections varying the gloss of its panels; to my left were the muffled windows; a great looking glass between them repeated the vacant majesty of the bed and room. I was not quite sure whether they had locked the door; and when I dared moved, I got up and went to see. Alas! yes: no jail was ever more secure. 🍎

Writing Assignment: Setting is very important in *Jane Eyre*. Write an essay in which you analyze the author's description of the setting in this passage. You may want to pay particular attention to the author's use of such elements and techniques as mood, tone, imagery, metaphor, personification, and foreshadowing.

Prompt 2

Read the passage from *Three Lives*, by Gertrude Stein. When you have finished reading, respond to the writing assignment that follows.

Anna followed Mrs. Lehntman into the other room in a stiff silence, and when there she did not, as invited, take a chair.

As always with Anna when a thing had to come it came very short and sharp. She found it hard to breathe just now, and every word came with a jerk.

"Mrs. Lehntman, it ain't true what Julia said about your taking that Lily's boy to keep. I told Julia when she told me she was crazy to talk so."

Anna's real excitements stopped her breath, and made her words come sharp and with a jerk. Mrs. Lehntman's feelings spread her breath, and made her words come slow, but more pleasant and more easy even than before.

"Why Anna," she began, "don't you see Lily couldn't keep her boy for she is working at the Bishops' now, and he is such a cute dear little chap, and you know how fond I am of little fellers, and I thought it would be nice for Julia and for Willie to have a little brother. You know Julia always loves to play with babies, and I have to be away so much, and Willie he is running in the streets every minute all the time, and you see a baby would be sort of nice company for Julia, and you know you are always saying Anna, Julia should not be on the streets so much and the baby will be so good to keep her in."

Anna was every minute paler with indignation and with heat.

"Mrs. Lehntman, I don't see what business it is for you to take another baby for your own, when you can't do what's right by Julia and Willie you got here already. There's Julia, nobody tells her a thing when I ain't here, and who is going to tell her now how to do things for that baby? She ain't got no sense what's the right way to do with children, and you out all the time, and you ain't got no time for your own neither, and now you want to be takin' up with strangers. I know you was careless, Mrs. Lehntman, but I didn't think that you could do this so. No, Mrs. Lehntman, it ain't your duty to take

© 2000 Amsco School Publications, Inc.
Copyrighted material. Not to be photocopied.

up with no others, when you got two children of your own, that got to get along just any way they can, and you know you ain't got any too much money all the time, and you are all so careless here and spend it all the time, and Julia and Willie growin' big. It ain't right, Mrs. Lehntman, to do so."

This was as bad as it could be. Anna had never spoken her mind so to her friend before. Now it was too harsh for Mrs. Lehntman to allow herself to really hear. If she really took the meaning in these words she could never ask Anna to come into her house again, and she liked Anna very well, and was used to depend on her savings and her strength. And then too Mrs. Lehntman could not really take in harsh ideas. She was too well diffused to catch the feel of any sharp firm edge.

Now she managed to understand all this in a way that made it easy for her to say, "Why, Anna, I think you feel too bad about seeing what the children are doing every minute in the day. Julia and Willie are real good, and they play with all the nicest children in the square. If you had some, all your own, Anna, you'd see it don't do no harm to let them do a little as they like, and Julia likes this baby so, and sweet dear little boy, it would be so kind of bad to send him to a 'sylum now, you know it would Anna, when you like children so yourself, and are so good to my Willie all the time. No indeed Anna, it's easy enough to say I should send this poor, cute little boy to a 'sylum when I could keep him here so nice, but you know Anna, you wouldn't like to do it yourself, now you really know you wouldn't, Anna, though you talk to me so hard.—My, it's hot to-day, what you doin' with that ice tea in there Julia, when Miss Annie is waiting all this time for her drink?" 🍎

Writing Assignment: This passage describes an interaction between two characters. Based on the information in the passage, write an essay in which you explain the nature of the interaction between these characters. Use evidence from the passage to support your analysis.

Prompts That Ask for a Response Based on Other Reading

PROMPT 3

According to critic Northrup Frye, the purpose of literature is to "educate the imagination" to train us to see "what is possible." Think about what this statement means to you. Then write an essay in which you relate this statement to a work of literature that you have read in or out of class.

PROMPT 4

A common theme in literature is the individual's struggle with society. Write an essay in which you discuss how this theme is presented in a work of literature that you have read in or out of class.

Understanding the Writing Process

A **process** is any activity that involves a series of stages or steps that takes place over time. The **writing process** is usually divided into the following parts:

Prewriting. In this stage of the writing process, you determine what kind of piece you need to write; identify your audience; decide on a purpose for your writing; come up with a thesis statement, or main idea; gather ideas and information to include in your piece; and organize your ideas.

Drafting. In this stage of the process, you put your ideas down on paper in rough form, creating what is known as a **rough draft.** At this stage you usually concentrate on what you are saying, not on how you are saying it or on details of spelling, grammar, usage, and mechanics.

Evaluation. In this important stage of the writing process, you go back over your rough draft to identify its strengths and weaknesses. As you look over the work, you ask yourself questions like these:

Is the writing **focused**? That is, have I stated a main idea, elaborated on that idea, and included only details that are relevant, or related to that idea?

Is the writing well **organized**? Does the piece have a clear beginning, middle, and end? Are the ideas presented in a logical order? Have I used transitions to show the relationships among the ideas throughout the piece?

Is the thesis well **supported**? Is the information that I have provided clear, accurate, vivid, concrete, precise, relevant, and sufficient to support the thesis?

Is the writing **appropriate** to my audience? Does the language that I have used suit the topic, audience, and situation? Is it too formal or too informal? Is the tone, or attitude, expressed by the writing appropriate? Is the writing at the proper level of simplicity or complexity for the audience?

Does the writing accomplish the **purpose** that I set out to accomplish? If my purpose is to explain, is the explanation complete, clear, and accurate? Have I avoided expressions of unsubstantiated opinion? If the purpose is to persuade, have I provided sufficient reasons to convince my readers?

Is the writing **interesting** and engaging? Have I used vivid, concrete language? Have I varied the structure and lengths of my sentences?

Revision. Good writing involves rewriting. In this stage of the process, you use the information that you have gathered during evaluation to rewrite your draft. You will be able to improve its focus and organization and make other changes, as necessary, to increase the interest and corrections of your essay. There are three ways to revise, and most writers make use of all three. You can add parts, delete parts, and change parts. For example, you might add a transition to clarify the relationship between two sentences, you might delete an irrelevant or unnecessary word or phrase, and you might change a vague verb like *moved* to a vivid, concrete verb like *hobbled* or *skated*. Often, writers revise their work many, many times before producing the finished version, which is called the **final draft.**

Proofreading. The final draft is not really final, because two steps remain. After you have written out the final version, you need to check it carefully for errors in paragraph indention, spelling, grammar, usage, capitalization, and punctuation. After correcting these errors, you may need to make a clean final copy.

Publishing. The last stage in the process is the point of it all. In this stage, you share your work with others. You can do this through formal publishing—in a student newspaper, for example—or through informal sharing, as when you read aloud in class something you've written.

The Writing Process for Timed Tests

On a timed test like the MCAS Composition exam, you will follow a slightly different process from the one outlined above. The following chart outlines the major differences.

1. For the MCAS, you will have time to write only one rough draft and one finished composition.
2. Because you will not be able to write multiple drafts, prewriting becomes very important. You need to make sure that you plan your essay carefully by making a rough outline or a graphic organizer before you begin writing.

3. As you draft, you need to be careful that you are remaining on your topic, that you are following the organizational pattern that you decided on during your prewriting, and that you are using transitions to connect your ideas.
4. You need to budget your time. In the first session, you have forty-five minutes to read the literary text, if any; plan your answer; and write your first draft. By the end of the first session, you should be close to finishing your first draft. Most of the second session should be devoted to revising your draft and producing your final composition.
5. Because this is a handwritten composition, you will have to be very neat. Of course, you are not being graded on your handwriting skills, but it is important that the evaluator be able to read your writing and your corrections.

Scoring the Composition

The essay that you create for the MCAS Composition exam will be scored in two areas: focus and development and use of standard English conventions.

Evaluators consider the following when scoring the **focus and development** of your composition: clarity of focus, organization, use of logically related ideas, use of supporting details, and effectiveness of language.

Focus refers to how clearly the essay presents and maintains a main idea. An essay is well focused when it deals with a single topic; presents a main idea, or thesis, related to that topic; and contains only material related to the main idea (does not contain unrelated or extraneous information).

Organization refers to the structure, or plan of development, of the essay and to the logical relationship of its parts. An essay is well organized when it has a clear beginning, middle, and end; when its sentences and paragraphs follow logically from one another; and when the relationships among ideas in the essay are indicated by transitions. (Transitions are words and phrases used to connect ideas. See the list of transitions on page 157.)

Support refers to the number and quality of the details used to elaborate upon the main idea of the essay. In a well-written essay, the main idea is thoroughly supported with illustrations, facts, examples, or other details that are concrete, vivid, credible, and related to the main idea. In evaluating how well you have supported your main idea, the readers of the essay will consider both content and expression. If you have stated your details using precise, engaging, concrete language, an appropriate tone, and varied sentences, your score will be higher.

When scoring your essay for use of standard English **conventions,** evaluators will look for an essay that follows the rules that govern spelling, sentence variation, grammar, usage, punctuation, and capitalization. A good response to an MCAS writing prompt will observe the conventions for formal writing. See Lesson 6.5 for a discussion of conventions.

Your Turn

A Based on what you have learned in this lesson, answer these questions about the Composition portion of the MCAS English exam.

1 What kind of writing will you do for the Composition portion of the exam? What will you produce?

2 How long will you have to complete the writing assignment?

3 Why is planning what you are going to write especially important on the MCAS Composition exam?

4 How is the composition scored? What qualities of your essay will the evaluators consider when scoring it?

B Answer these questions based on the sample writing prompts on pages 178 through 180.

1 What should be the subject (the main topic the essay is about) of Writing Prompt 1? of Writing Prompt 2?

2 What might be an appropriate thesis statement for Writing Prompt 2?

3 What work of literature might you choose to create your response to Writing Prompt 3?

4 Suppose that you were going to write an essay in response to Writing Prompt 4. The essay will contain three body paragraphs, each dealing with one subtopic related to the main topic. What might be the subtopics of your body paragraphs?

WRITING AN ESSAY FOR THE COMPOSITION SESSIONS

LESSON 7.2 Creating Your MCAS Essay, Step by Step

In the previous lesson, you learned about the writing process and about how this process must be modified for the MCAS Composition exam or for any other writing test that does not allow time for creating multiple drafts. In this lesson you will learn about the structure of an essay and you will follow one student as she creates an essay in response to an MCAS Composition exam–style prompt.

The Structure of an Essay

 As you learned in Unit 5 of this book, there are many types of essays. To name a few, there are narrative essays that tell about real-life events; personal essays in which people share their experiences and reflections; persuasive essays that convince others to take an action or to adopt a point of view; and informative essays that define, analyze, compare and contrast, classify, or describe processes. Despite their astonishing variety, most essays have three elements in common:

1. Essays are relatively short. For the Composition portion of the exam, you will have two lined pages on which to write a response. Your essay will probably be no more than five paragraphs long.

2. Essays present and elaborate on a single main idea, or thesis.

3. Essays have a clear beginning, middle, and end.

The Five-Paragraph Theme

The safest approach to the Composition portion of the exam is for you to write a **five-paragraph theme.** This is an essay that consists of a one-paragraph introduction, three body paragraphs, and a one-paragraph conclusion.

Paragraph 1. The **introduction** grabs the attention of your audience and presents your thesis statement, or main idea.

Paragraphs 2–4. Each **body paragraph** presents a major supporting idea related to your thesis statement. This idea is expressed in a topic sentence. Supporting sentences within the body paragraph elaborate on the topic sentence, presenting additional information or details.

Paragraph 5. The **conclusion** sums up your essay and gives the reader what critic Frank Kermode has called "the sense of an ending."

Throughout the five-paragraph theme, transitions should be used to connect ideas. **Transitions** are words and phrases that relate paragraphs, sentences, and parts of sentences to one another. For a list of transitions that you can use to express various kinds of relationships among ideas, see the chart on page 157.

The chart on the next page shows the parts of a five-paragraph theme. On the following page is a graphic organizer that can be used for planning such an essay.

The Structure of a Five-Paragraph Essay

The Parts of the Essay and What They Should Include	Suggestions for Writing Each Section of the Essay
INTRODUCTION —Introductory material to grab the reader's attention —Thesis statement	**Follow one of these strategies:** —Begin with a quotation or proverb —Begin with an anecdote —Begin with a startling or interesting fact —Begin by posing a question Note: Make sure that your introduction states the main idea, or thesis, of the essay.
EACH BODY PARAGRAPH —Main supporting idea (topic sentence) —Details related to main supporting idea Note: A five-paragraph essay should contain three body paragraphs	**Do the following for each paragraph:** —Use transitions at the beginning of and within the paragraph —Include a topic sentence that states a single main idea related to the thesis of the essay
CONCLUSION —Any material that will wrap up the essay and give your reader a satisfying sense of closure	**Follow one or more of these strategies:** —Restate your thesis in other words or as a question —Summarize the main ideas from your body paragraphs —Draw a conclusion based upon the information that you have presented in the rest of the essay —Relate your topic to your reader, telling why it is important to his or her life —Suggest that your reader take some action related to the topic

WRITING AN ESSAY FOR THE COMPOSITION SESSIONS

Graphic Organizer for Planning Essays

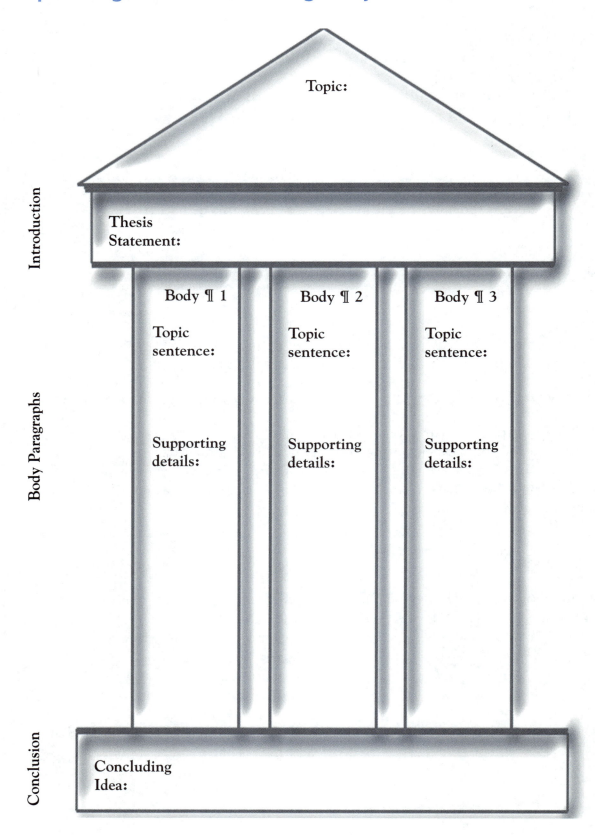

Topic:

Introduction

Thesis Statement:

Body Paragraphs

Body ¶ 1

Topic sentence:

Supporting details:

Body ¶ 2

Topic sentence:

Supporting details:

Body ¶ 3

Topic sentence:

Supporting details:

Conclusion

Concluding Idea:

Writing the Introduction

There are many ways to introduce an essay. Whichever way you choose, however, you need to make sure that your introduction includes your thesis statement, which is the main idea that the rest of the essay will elaborate upon, or support. Imagine that you are going to write an essay about the benefits of taking part in a drama club production. Here are some possible ways to introduce the essay:

1. Begin with a quotation or proverb.

My grandmother used to say, "Many hands make light work." I learned the truth of this statement by taking part in a play given by my school's Drama Club. Few activities are as complicated as producing a play; however, when everyone pulls together and does his or her job—the director, the actors, the stage manager, the costumers, the makeup artists, the technical crew, and the house crew—the difficult job of mounting a production becomes, if not easy, at least doable. Learning the value of teamwork is just one of many valuable lessons that can be gained from taking part in a theatrical production.

2. Begin with an anecdote, or very brief story.

A few weeks ago, I had to give a speech in my English class. Most of my classmates were scared to death about getting up in front of the rest of the students to speak. I was not afraid, however, because I had learned how to overcome stage fright by taking part in a production given by the Drama Club. This is only one of the many benefits of taking part in a school play.

3. Begin with a startling or interesting fact.

In one nineteenth-century production of Shakespeare's tragedy Macbeth, a sword flew out of the hands of one of the characters and stuck into one of the seats in the audience. While nothing this dramatic happens to most students who take part in a school play, nearly everyone who has done so comes away from the experience with lots of lessons learned and lots of stories to tell.

4. Begin with an analogy to something else. (An **analogy** is a comparison presented to make a point.)

Coaches often make the claim that participating in sports builds character and teaches the value of teamwork. If you really want to build character, however, I would recommend joining the Drama Club. There you can build character in more ways than one, and you can also learn how a team—what theater people call an ensemble—can pull together to create something magical. Building character, learning about teamwork, and just having a great deal of fun are three benefits of Drama Club membership.

5. Begin by posing a question.

How often does a high-school student get a chance to demonstrate bravery? As everyone knows, high-school students are obsessed with how they look in front of their peers. For that reason, it takes a lot of courage to stand in front of one's classmates as an actor in a play. Proving that one is capable of overcoming the fear of looking foolish is one of many positive results of taking part in a school play.

Writing the Body Paragraphs

Each of the body paragraphs in your essay should present a single main idea that supports the thesis statement. The sentence in the paragraph that states this main idea is called the **topic sentence**. The rest of the sentences in a body paragraph present details to support the topic sentence. Here is an example of a rough outline for a body paragraph that supports the thesis statement "Taking part in a school play has many benefits":

Benefit 1: Teaches responsibility
—Must learn lines and movements on time because director and other actors depend on this
—Must not miss rehearsals or show up late
—Must remember to bring materials to rehearsals, such as script, director's notes, and rehearsal schedule

When writing body paragraphs, make sure to use transitions like those shown on page 157 to show how your ideas are connected. You may use transitions both at the beginnings of paragraphs and within them. Notice how transitions are used in the following paragraph to connect the ideas:

One important lesson that acting in a play teaches is responsibility. For example, an actor must learn his or her lines and movements on time because the director and the other actors depend on this. In addition, out of courtesy to others working on the production, an actor must not miss rehearsals or show up late. Furthermore, an actor has to remember to bring important materials to rehearsals, such as his or her script, notes given by the director during the previous rehearsal, and his or her copy of the rehearsal schedule. An actor soon learns that responsibility means not letting others down.

Writing the Conclusion

Suppose that you were watching a movie on television, one that you really loved, and that ten minutes before the end of it, the power in your home went out. In essays, as in movies, giving the reader a good experience depends a great deal on bringing the work to a satisfactory close.

Usually, the conclusion will be a single paragraph. Often, its beginning will be signaled by a transition such as "In conclusion," "In summary," or "As the preceding paragraphs show."

One way to develop a conclusion is to restate your thesis in different words and then summarize the supporting ideas presented in the essay. For instance, suppose that your thesis statement is this:

Few experiences in life teach one as much as one learns from participating in a school play.

If this is your thesis statement, you might begin your conclusion by restating your thesis as a question, like this:

What are the positive consequences of taking part in a school play? As this essay has shown, . . .

The chart on page 185 includes additional ideas for writing your conclusions.

The Writing of an MCAS Essay

In this section we will follow one tenth-grader through the steps of developing and writing an essay in response to Prompt 3 on page 180. The prompt reads as follows:

> According to critic Northrup Frye, the purpose of literature is to "educate the imagination" to train us to see "what is possible." Think about what this statement means to you. Then write an essay in which you relate this statement to a work of literature that you have read in or out of class.

Session 1: Prewriting

After receiving her test materials, Gabi read the prompt carefully. She read the critic's statement and figured out what it meant by restating it to herself. Gabi jotted on her scratch paper,

Literature uses imaginary people and events to teach us something about real life through the experiences of literary characters.

She knew that this prompt called for her to write about a literary work that she had read. She had prepared in advance for this kind of prompt by studying and taking notes on three works of literature that she could call on for this type of response. Thinking about these works, Gabi decided that the short story "The Devil and Daniel Webster" would make a good subject for an essay about how imagination reveals truth about life.

Then Gabi brainstormed quickly on paper, creating a word web to generate ideas. (See Gabi's word web below.)

Based upon her word web, Gabi came up with three major ideas to use in the body paragraphs of her essay. Then she wrote a rough outline of her essay, again on her scrap paper. Her outline appears on the next page.

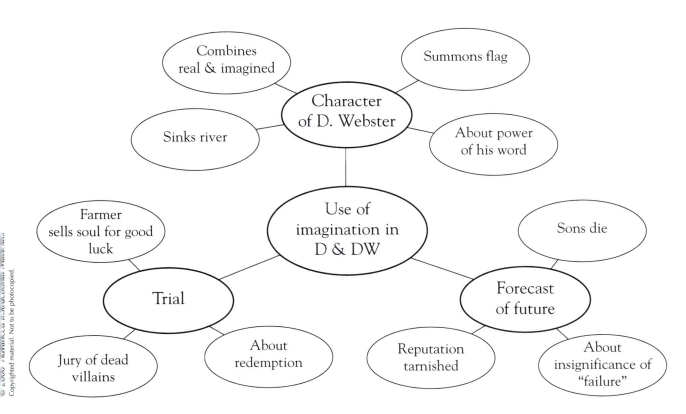

Lesson 7.2—Creating Your MCAS Essay, Step by Step   189

WRITING AN ESSAY FOR THE COMPOSITION SESSIONS

Introduction

—Grab reader's attention w/ interesting examples: 12th century Japan? android?

—Thesis: Literature allows us to go outside our own experience by way of imagination and so expand our notions of the way that life might be.

Body ¶ 1

Topic Sentence: Combines real and imaginary

—Webster historic figure

—Given supernatural abilities

—Placed in imaginary situation (trial)

Clincher sentence: See the possibility of words as power

Body ¶ 2

Topic Sentence: Imagination reveals theme of redemption

—Why farmer sold soul

—Humanity in hearts of dead villains

Clincher sentence: See the possibility of redemption for every person

Body ¶ 3

Topic Sentence: Very powerful truth about the poss. when devil forecasts W's future

—Sons die, reputation tarnished

—W. not dismayed; loved children, spoke sincerely

Clincher sentence: Dashed hopes not failure if intent and effort were good

Conclusion

—Words can conquer death and evil

—Even worst people capable of redemption

—Life judged by how it was lived, not if all prospered

Notice that Gabi planned her essay very carefully on her scrap paper before she began writing. Her plan includes an introduction that grabs the reader's attention and states the thesis; three body paragraphs, each of which presents a single related topic and supporting details; and a conclusion that summarizes her ideas.

Gabi wrote a quick, rough outline because there was no time available for making a complete, formal outline of the kind that one might make for an essay assigned as homework.

Session 1: Drafting

After completing her rough outline, Gabi could simply draft her essay, from the beginning to the end, using information from the outline. Of course, during the drafting, additional ideas might occur to her, and she could incorporate these.

Gabi made a quick draft, being careful, as she proceeded, to indent her paragraphs, write neatly, use transitions, vary the length and structure of her sentences, and incorporate details from her outline. If she wanted to use a word that she didn't know how to spell correctly, she marked her draft to remind herself to look it up in the dictionary during revision.

Gabi checked her watch. She was close to finishing her draft, and the first session was about to end. Gabi knew she should be just about finished with her draft by the end of Session 1, so she was happy to see that she was on schedule. She hurried to finish her draft before the break.

Session 2: Evaluating, Revising, and Proofreading

Gabi came back from the break prepared to revise her draft in Session 2. She read her draft over carefully. First, she made a revision pass, checking her content, focus, organization, and expression. She drew a line through one sentence that she decided was irrelevant. She added some concrete details and changed a couple of words to make them more precise. She drew a line around a sentence that seemed out of place and an arrow showing the place to which the sentence should be moved.

Next, she proofread her completed essay carefully, looking for errors and correcting any that she found. She checked her manuscript form, making sure that all the paragraphs were indented. She read through the work to make sure that each sentence had a verb, that the verb agreed with its subject, that she had included no run-on sentences or sentence fragments, and that all words were spelled correctly. She also checked her capitalization, making sure that she had capitalized proper nouns, and she checked her punctuation throughout, being particularly careful to make sure that every sentence began with a capital letter and ended in an end mark.

Session 2: The Finished Essay

Gabi completed her revision and was ready to write out her finished essay. She had twenty-five minutes, enough time to write out her essay neatly, incorporating all her revisions into her finished response. After writing out her finished copy, she proofread it, looking for any errors. Gabi felt confident that she had done her best. Her final essay follows.

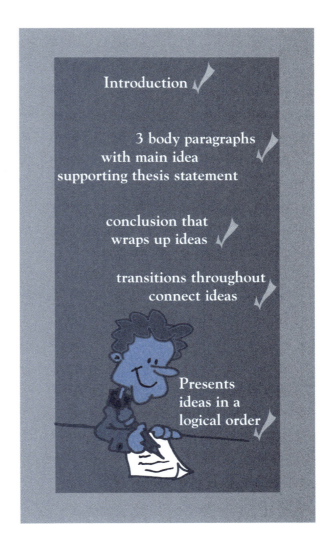

Introduction ✓

3 body paragraphs with main idea supporting thesis statement ✓

conclusion that wraps up ideas ✓

transitions throughout connect ideas ✓

Presents ideas in a logical order ✓

Gabi's Five-Paragraph Essay

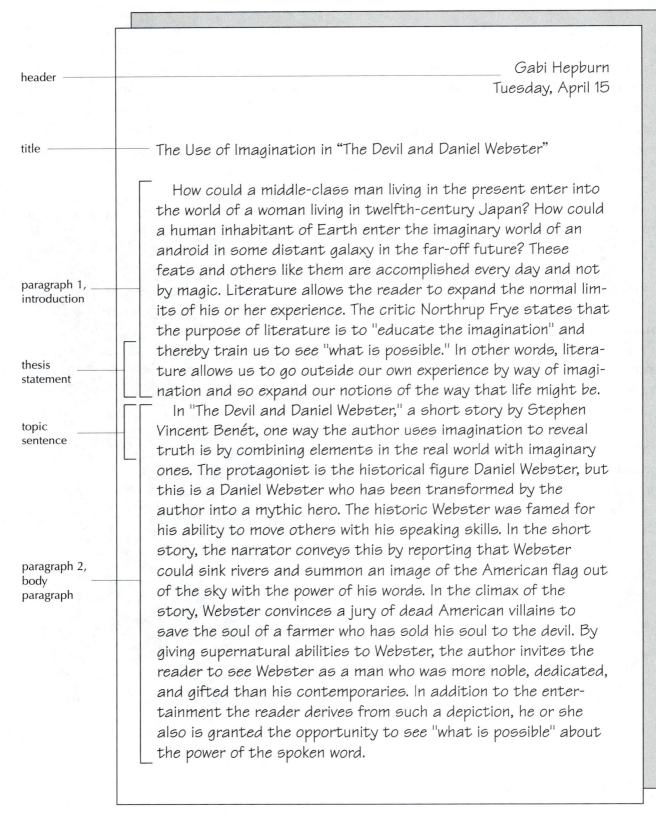

header

title

paragraph 1, introduction

thesis statement

topic sentence

paragraph 2, body paragraph

Gabi Hepburn
Tuesday, April 15

The Use of Imagination in "The Devil and Daniel Webster"

How could a middle-class man living in the present enter into the world of a woman living in twelfth-century Japan? How could a human inhabitant of Earth enter the imaginary world of an android in some distant galaxy in the far-off future? These feats and others like them are accomplished every day and not by magic. Literature allows the reader to expand the normal limits of his or her experience. The critic Northrup Frye states that the purpose of literature is to "educate the imagination" and thereby train us to see "what is possible." In other words, literature allows us to go outside our own experience by way of imagination and so expand our notions of the way that life might be.

In "The Devil and Daniel Webster," a short story by Stephen Vincent Benét, one way the author uses imagination to reveal truth is by combining elements in the real world with imaginary ones. The protagonist is the historical figure Daniel Webster, but this is a Daniel Webster who has been transformed by the author into a mythic hero. The historic Webster was famed for his ability to move others with his speaking skills. In the short story, the narrator conveys this by reporting that Webster could sink rivers and summon an image of the American flag out of the sky with the power of his words. In the climax of the story, Webster convinces a jury of dead American villains to save the soul of a farmer who has sold his soul to the devil. By giving supernatural abilities to Webster, the author invites the reader to see Webster as a man who was more noble, dedicated, and gifted than his contemporaries. In addition to the entertainment the reader derives from such a depiction, he or she also is granted the opportunity to see "what is possible" about the power of the spoken word.

paragraph 3, body paragraph

Another way Benét uses imagination to show the reader what is possible in human experience is the way he treats the theme of redemption in this story. The farmer whom Webster defends has been plagued by bad luck, and despite years of effort and virtue, is sinking further into ruin and misery. In a moment of despair, he agrees to sell his soul to the devil in exchange for prosperity. The devil in this story and his infernal bargain are imaginary creations. The author uses these creations to communicate experience: The story symbolically demonstrates how good human beings worn out by ill-fortune might be tempted to actions that destroy their integrity. Furthermore, when Webster appeals to the jury of dead villains, the author is showing that sincere emotions eloquently expressed can awaken the humanity in the heart of even the most hardened person. The author reveals what is possible: Not only the weak, but also the worst among us, are capable of redemption.

paragraph 4, body paragraph

A third, and very powerful, way that this story reveals what is possible in human experience through the use of imagination occurs when the devil forecasts Webster's future after the trial. The devil is angry that Webster defeated him and wants to have the last laugh. The historic events of Webster's later life are accurate: His sons die in war, and his reputation is tarnished. It is how the literary character Webster reacts to this forecast that allows the reader to learn what is possible. Webster shakes off the label of failure that the devil applies to his life with the assurance that as long as he speaks sincerely and loves his children, failure is not possible. The author reveals what is possible: Aspirations that end in seeming failure are redeemed by the integrity with which they are pursued.

paragraph 5, conclusion

In conclusion, Stephen Vincent Benét has created in this short story a work of literature that uses imagination to reveal the possible. By combining real and imagined events and characters, the author leads the reader to see: that words are so powerful they can conquer death and evil; that even the worst human being may be redeemed; and that a life should be judged not by whether its efforts succeeded but by how well it was lived.

Lesson 7.2—Creating Your MCAS Essay, Step by Step   193

Your Turn

A   Study the sample essay presented on pages 192 and 193. Then answer the following questions about it.

1   What is the subject of the essay?

2   What is the main idea of the essay? Where is this main idea stated?

3   What method has the writer used to grab the reader's attention in the introduction?

4   What is the topic sentence for the third paragraph?

5   What is the topic sentence for the fourth paragraph?

6   What strategies does the writer use to conclude her essay?

7   What are four transitions used in the essay?

8   What details are presented to support the topic sentence in paragraph 2?

9   What is the clincher sentence of paragraph 4?

B   Get one piece of blank paper and two sheets of lined paper. Choose one of the prompts given in the chart on pages 178–180 and create a draft of an essay in response to it. Allow yourself a full hour to plan your draft on the blank paper and to write it on the lined paper. Make sure that your plan for the draft essay includes a rough outline or a graphic organizer that details the parts of the essay.

C   Repeat Exercise B, but with a different prompt. If you chose a prompt that contains a reading selection last time, choose one that does not contain a reading selection this time. If you chose a prompt that does not contain a reading selection last time, choose one that does this time. For this essay, allow yourself only forty-five minutes, the time actually allowed for Session 1.

D   Now take the draft you wrote for Exercise C and revise it. Check your content, focus, organization, and expression. Proofread your essay and look up any words you are unsure of in a dictionary. Mark all your changes and corrections. Then write out a finished version of your essay on two sheets of lined paper. Proofread this version, neatly marking any corrections. Take forty-five minutes for your revision and rewrite, the actual time you will have for Session 2 of the exam.

E   Reflect on your writing process for Exercises B, C, and D. Then answer the following questions:

1   Which was the easier assignment for you, the prompt with or the prompt without the reading selection? Why?

2   What do you think are the major strengths of your finished essay? the major weaknesses?

3   What skills do you think you need further practice on before you take the actual exam?

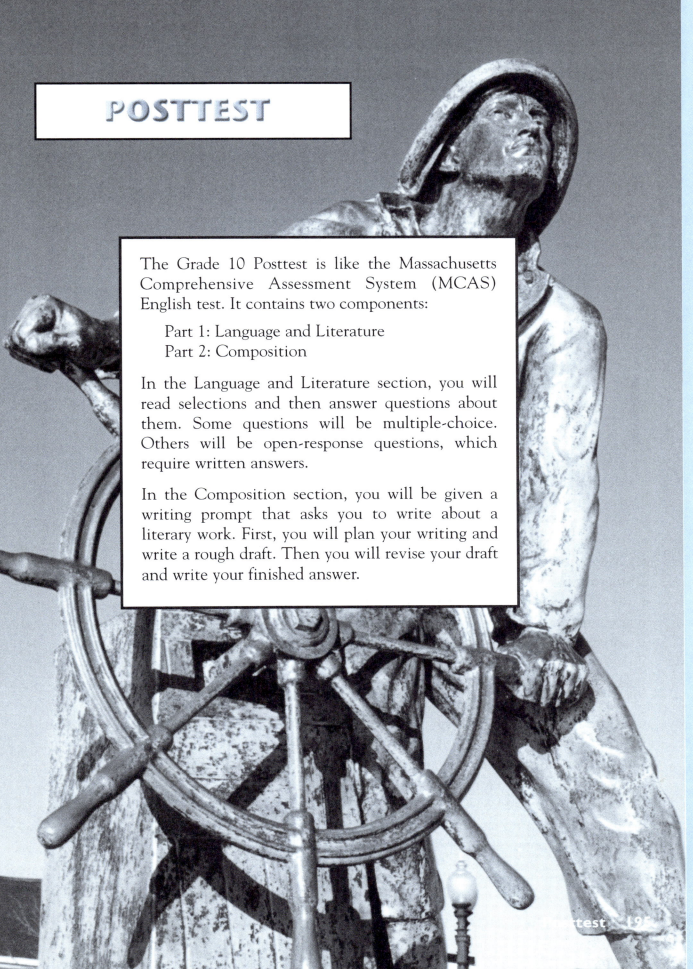

POSTTEST

The Grade 10 Posttest is like the Massachusetts Comprehensive Assessment System (MCAS) English test. It contains two components:

Part 1: Language and Literature
Part 2: Composition

In the Language and Literature section, you will read selections and then answer questions about them. Some questions will be multiple-choice. Others will be open-response questions, which require written answers.

In the Composition section, you will be given a writing prompt that asks you to write about a literary work. First, you will plan your writing and write a rough draft. Then you will revise your draft and write your finished answer.

Mrs. Packletide

Reading Selection #1, Session 1

DIRECTIONS

Read the following humorous account of one woman's tiger hunt. Then answer the questions that follow.

Mrs. Packletide's Tiger
by Saki (H. H. Munro)

It was Mrs. Packletide's pleasure and intention that she should shoot a tiger. Not that the lust to kill had suddenly descended on her, or that she felt she would leave India safer and more wholesome than she had found it, with one fraction less of wild beast per million of inhabitants. The compelling motive for her sudden deviation towards the footsteps of Nimrod[1] was the fact that Loona Bimberton had recently been carried eleven miles in an aeroplane by an Algerian aviator and talked of nothing else; only a personally procured tiger-skin and a heavy harvest of Press photographs could successfully counter that sort of thing. Mrs. Packletide had already arranged in her mind the lunch she would give at her house in Curzon Street, ostensibly in Loona Bimberton's honor, with a tiger-skin rug occupying most of the foreground and all of the conversation. She had also already designed in her mind the tiger-claw brooch that she was going to give Loona Bimberton

on her next birthday. In a world that is supposed to be chiefly swayed by hunger and by love, Mrs. Packletide was an exception; her movements and motives were largely governed by dislike of Loona Bimberton.

Circumstances proved propitious. Mrs. Packletide had offered a thousand rupees for the opportunity of shooting a tiger without over-much risk or exertion, and it so happened that a neighboring village could boast of being the favored rendezvous of an animal of respectable antecedents, which had been driven by the increasing infirmities of age to abandon game-killing and confine its appetite to the smaller domestic animals. The prospect of earning the thousand rupees had stimulated the sporting and commercial instinct of the villagers; children were posted night and day on the outskirts of the local jungle to head the tiger back in the unlikely event of his attempting to roam away to fresh hunting-grounds, and the cheaper kinds of goats were left about with elaborate carelessness to keep him satisfied with his

---
[1] Nimrod. Biblical hunter

Loona Bimberton

present quarters. The one great anxiety was lest he should die of old age before the date appointed for the memsahib's shoot. Mothers carrying their babies home through the jungle after the day's work in the fields hushed their singing lest they might curtail the restful sleep of the venerable herd-robber.

The great night duly arrived, moonlit and cloudless. A platform had been constructed in a comfortable and conveniently placed tree, and thereon crouched Mrs. Packletide and her paid companion, Miss Mebbin. A goat, gifted with a particularly persistent bleat, such as even a partially deaf tiger might be reasonably expected to hear on a still night, was tethered at the correct distance. With an accurately sighted rifle and a thumb-nail pack of patience cards,[2] the sportswoman awaited the coming of the quarry.

"I suppose we are in some danger?" said Miss Mebbin.

---

[2] **thumb-nail pack of patience cards.** Small pack of cards for playing solitaire

She was not actually nervous about the wild beast, but she had a morbid dread of performing an atom more service than she had been paid for.

"Nonsense," said Mrs. Packletide; "It's a very old tiger. It couldn't spring up here even if it wanted to."

"If it's an old tiger I think you ought to get it cheaper. A thousand rupees is a lot of money."

Louisa Mebbin adopted a protective elder-sister attitude towards money in general, irrespective of nationality or denomination. Her energetic intervention had saved many a ruble from dissipating itself in tips in some Moscow hotel, and francs and centimes clung to her instinctively under circumstances which would have driven them headlong from less sympathetic hands. Her speculations as to the market depreciation of tiger remnants were cut short by the appearance on the scene of the animal itself. As soon as it caught sight of the tethered goat, it lay flat on the earth, seemingly less from a desire to take advantage of all available cover than for the purpose of snatching a short rest before commencing the grand attack.

"I believe it's ill," said Louisa Mebbin, loudly in Hindustani, for the benefit of the village headman, who was in ambush in a neighboring tree.

"Hush!" said Mrs. Packletide, and at that moment the tiger commenced ambling towards his victim.

"Now, now!" urged Miss Mebbin with some excitement, "if he doesn't touch the goat we needn't pay for it." (The bait was extra.)

The rifle flashed out with a loud report, and the great tawny beast sprang to one side and then rolled over in the stillness of death. In a moment, a crowd of excited natives had swarmed on to the scene, and their shouting speedily carried the glad news to the village, where a thumping of tom-toms[3] took up the chorus of triumph. And their triumph and rejoicing found a ready echo in the heart of Mrs. Packletide; already that luncheon-party in Curzon Street seemed immeasurably nearer.

It was Louisa Mebbin who drew attention to the fact that the goat was in death-throes from a mortal bullet-wound, while no trace of the rifle's deadly work could be found on the tiger. Evidently the wrong animal had been hit, and the beast of prey had succumbed to heart failure caused by the sudden report of the rifle, accelerated by senile decay. Mrs. Packletide was pardonably annoyed at the discovery; but at any rate, she was the possessor of a dead tiger, and the villagers, anxious for their thousand rupees, gladly connived at the fiction that she had shot the beast. And Miss Mebbin was a paid companion. Therefore did Mrs. Packletide face the cameras with a light heart, and her pictured fame reached from the pages of the *Texas Weekly Snapshot* to the illustrated Monday supplement of the *Novoe Vremya*. As for Loona Bimberton, she refused to look at an illustrated paper for weeks, and her letter of thanks for the gift of a tiger-claw brooch was a model of repressed emotions. The luncheon-party she declined; there are limits beyond which repressed emotions become dangerous.

From Curzon Street the tiger-skin rug traveled down to the Manor House, and was duly inspected and admired by the

Louisa Mebbin

county,[4] and it seemed a fitting and appropriate thing when Mrs. Packletide went to the County Costume Ball in the character of Diana.[5] She refused to fall in, however, with Clovis's tempting suggestion of a primeval dance party, at which everyone should wear the skins of beasts they had recently slain. "I should be in rather a Baby Bunting[6] condition," confessed Clovis, "with a miserable rabbit-skin or two to wrap up in, but then," he added, with a rather malicious glance at Diana's proportions, "my figure is quite as good as that Russian dancing boy's."

"How amused everyone would be if they knew what really happened," said Louisa Mebbin a few days after the ball.

"What do you mean?" asked Mrs. Packletide quickly.

"How you shot the goat and frightened the tiger to death," said Miss Mebbin, with her disagreeably pleasant laugh.

---

[3] **tom-toms.** Hand drums

[4] **county.** Neighbors in the country
[5] **Diana.** Roman goddess of the hunt
[6] **Baby Bunting.** Nursery rhyme character who is dressed in a rabbit skin.

"No one would believe it, said Mrs. Packletide, her face changing color as rapidly as though it were going through a book of patterns before post-time.[7]

"Loona Bimberton would," said Miss Mebbin. Mrs. Packletide's face settled on an unbecoming shade of greenish white.

"You surely wouldn't give me away?" she asked.

"I've seen a week-end cottage near Dorking that I should rather like to buy," said Miss Mebbin with seeming irrelevance. "Six hundred and eighty, freehold. Quite a bargain, only I don't happen to have the money."

Louisa Mebbin's pretty week-end cottage, christened by her "Les Fauves,"[8] and gay in summer-time with its garden borders of tiger-lilies, is the wonder and admiration of her friends.

"It is a marvel how Louisa manages to do it," is the general verdict.

Mrs. Packletide indulges in no more big-game shooting.

"The incidental expenses are so heavy," she confides to inquiring friends. 🍎

---

[7] **going through a book of patterns before post-time.** Displaying the colors worn by jockeys and horses in a racing form before the start of a race

[8] **"Les Fauves."** In French, "The Wild Beasts"

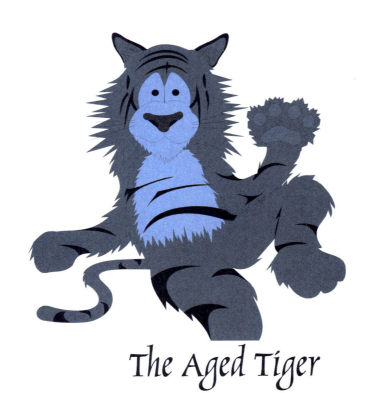

The Aged Tiger

POSTTEST

1   What motivates the villagers to help Mrs. Packletide shoot the tiger?

   A   fear that the tiger will kill an inhabitant of the village

   B   the prospect of earning money

   C   the desire to help Mrs. Packletide upstage Loona Bimberton

   D   the thrill of the hunt

2   What is Louisa Mebbin's relationship to Mrs. Packletide?

   A   sister

   B   friend

   C   employee

   D   co-worker

3   What causes the death of the tiger?

   A   harassment by the villagers

   B   fatigue from lack of sleep

   C   heart failure brought on by the noise of the rifle shot

   D   gunshot

4   The story says that circumstances were propitious for hunting the tiger. Which of the following is the closest synonym to *propitious*?

   A   favorable

   B   adverse

   C   unremarkable

   D   complicated

5   The author says that Loona Bimberton's thank-you letter for the tiger-claw broach is "a model of repressed emotions." What is most likely the tone of the letter?

   A   the epitome of graciousness

   B   indifference

   C   sincere appreciation

   D   hostility veiled by civility

Open-Response Questions, Session 1

6 How does the reader know what the tiger is like? How does evidence from the story (for example, the narrator's descriptions of the tiger and the portrayal of the villagers' actions) show that the tiger is not really dangerous?

7 Characterization is the use of literary techniques to create a character. A writer creates characters by describing them directly; by portraying their behavior, thoughts, and words; and by telling what other characters say about them. How does Saki use these techniques to portray the character of Mrs. Packletide?

_____

_____

_____

_____

_____

_____

_____

_____

_____

_____

_____

_____

_____

_____

_____

_____

_____

_____

_____

DIRECTIONS

Read the following report from a newspaper edited by Benjamin Franklin. Then answer the questions that follow.

A Witch Trial at Mount Holly

from the *Pennsylvania Gazette*, Oct. 22, 1730

Saturday last, at Mount-Holly, about eight miles from this place, near three hundred People were gathered together to see an Experiment or two tried on some Persons accused of Witchcraft. It seems the Accused had been charged with making their Neighbours' Sheep dance in an uncommon manner, and with causing Hogs to speak and sing Psalms, etc., to the great Terror and Amazement of the king's good and peaceable Subjects in this Province; and the Accusers being very positive that if the Accused were weighed in scales against a Bible, the Bible would prove too heavy for them; or that, if they were bound and put into the river they would swim;[1] the said Accused, desirous to make Innocence appear, voluntarily offered to undergo the said Trials if two of the most violent of their Accusers would be tried with them. Accordingly, the time and place was agreed on and advertised about the Country. The Accusers were one Man and one Woman; and the Accused the same. The Parties being met and the People got together, a grand Consultation was held, before they proceeded to Trial, in which it was agreed to use the scales first; and a Committee of Men were appointed to search the Men, and a Committee of Women to search the Women, to see if they had any thing of weight about them, particularly pins. After the scrutiny was over, a huge great Bible belonging to the Justice of the Place was provided, and a lane through the Populace was made from the Justice's house to the scales, which were fixed on a Gallows erected for that Purpose opposite to the house, that the Justice's wife and the rest of the Ladies might see the

---

[1] **Swim.** Float

POSTTEST

Trial without coming amongst the Mob, and after the manner of Moorfields, a large ring was also made. Then came out of the house a grave, tall Man carrying the Holy Writ before the supposed Wizard etc., (as solemnly as the Sword-bearer of London before the Lord Mayor). The Wizard was first put in the scale, and over him was read a Chapter out of the Books of Moses, and then the Bible was put in the other scale, (which, being kept down before, was immediately let go); but, to the great surprise of the spectators, flesh and bones came down plump, and outweighed that great good Book by abundance. After the same manner the others were served, and their Lumps of Mortality[2] severally were too heavy for Moses and all the Prophets and Apostles. This being over, the Accusers and the rest of the Mob, not satisfied with this Experiment, would have the Trial by Water. Accordingly a most solemn Procession was made to the Millpond, where both Accused and Accusers being stripped (saving only to the Women their shifts), were bound hand and foot and severally placed in the water, lengthways, from the side of a barge or flat, having for security only a rope about the middle of each, which was held by some in the flat. The accused man, being thin and spare, with some difficulty began to sink at last; but the rest, every one of them, swam very light upon the water. A Sailor in the flat jump'd out upon the back of the Man accused thinking to drive him down to the bottom; but the Person bound, without any help, came up some time before the other. The woman Accuser being told that she did not sink, would be duck'd a second time; when she swam again as light as before. Upon which she declared that she believed the Accused had bewitched her to make her so light, and that she would be duck'd again a Hundred Times but she would duck the Devil out of her. The Accused Man, being surprised at his own swimming, was not so confident of his Innocence as before, but said, "If I am a Witch, it is more than I know." The more thinking part of the spectators were of opinion that if any Person so bound and placed in the water (unless they were mere skin and bones) would swim, till their breath was gone, and their lungs fill'd with water. But it being the general Belief of the Populace that the Women's shifts and the garters with which they were bound help'd to support them, it is said they are to be tried again the next warm weather, naked.

---

[2] **Lumps of Mortality.** That is, their physical bodies

8 Which of the following does NOT accurately describe the people's reaction to the supposed acts of witchcraft?

    A amusement

    B hysteria

    C amazement

    D dread

9 What did the crowd do when the accused were weighed on the scales and found to be weightier that the Bible?

    A They decided that the accused were innocent after all.

    B They realized that the test they had devised was ridiculous.

    C They proposed that the accused be subjected to a trial by fire.

    D They proceeded with the trial by water as planned.

10 In which sense is the word *spare* used in the selection?
"The accused man, being thin and spare, with some difficulty began to sink at last."

    A *verb* to show mercy

    B *verb* to free from

    C *adjective* lean

    D *adjective* extra

11 How did the woman accuser explain the fact that she floated?

    A She said that she was guilty.

    B She said that she was innocent.

    C She said that her clothes made her buoyant.

    D She said that the accused had bewitched her.

12 Which of the following is NOT true?

    A The accused were anxious to be tried so they could be proved innocent.

    B A path was made through the crowd to the gallows so the higher-class women could watch the proceedings without mingling with the crowd.

    C The people believed that an innocent person would float and a guilty one would sink.

    D After being ducked, the accused man began to doubt his innocence.

POSTTEST

Open-Response Question, Session 1

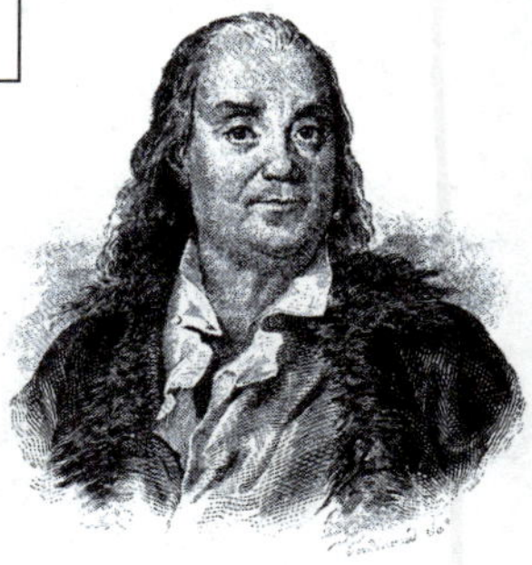

13 What seems to be the writer's attitude toward the people and events he is describing? Cite details from the selection that reveal what the writer thinks about this episode from early American history.

POSTTEST

DIRECTIONS

Read the following article about a first-century catastrophe. Then answer the questions that follow.

Pompeii: the Time Machine

by Robin Shulka

In A.D. 79, during the reign of the Roman emperor Titus, Pompeii was one of the most prosperous cities of Italy. Located just south of Naples, it was a busy, bustling seaport town, built in a rough circle about two miles in circumference and surrounded by a great wall with eight gates.

The inhabitants of Pompeii were very comfortable by the standards of the day. Taking advantage of their location on the southeastern Italian coast, the Pompeians were able to carry on a flourishing trade with Rome, 125 miles to the north, and with various cities in the Mediterranean. Pompeii was known far and wide for its wines, oil, bread, millstones, fish sauces, perfumes, and cloth.

Within the city, the wealthy, urbane Pompeians had built two theaters, a large amphitheater, a gymnasium for the training of its youth, many public fountains and baths, temples, and a forum. Pompeians could entertain themselves at the theater, watch gladiatorial combats, bathe in luxury, and purchase goods from the shops of artisans, bakers, and wine merchants. Outside the city walls, on the green slopes of Mount Vesuvius, the Pompeians grazed their goats and grew figs and olives.

Sixteen years before, in A.D. 63, the city had been shaken by an earthquake, but the citizens had quickly set about the task of rebuilding and had returned to their happy day-to-day lives. Then, suddenly, in August of A.D. 79, Vesuvius began to rumble, filling the sky with a light rain of ash. The Pompeians must have been dismayed by this, but not so dismayed as to leave their homes. This proved to be a fatal mistake, for the volcano suddenly erupted, throwing a column of hot gas and ash at very high speed tens of thousands of feet into the sky. As much as a cubic mile of material was blown from the volcano at temperatures as high as 700° Fahrenheit. A deadly rain of superheated ash and stone traveling at over seventy miles an hour, far faster than a person can run, fell upon the city, burying it and killing thousands of people. From fifteen to twenty feet of tephra—ash, pumice, and other materials from the crater of the volcano—fell upon Pompeii, preserving it for all time as a record of the Roman way of life.

In 1748, the buried city of Pompeii was discovered, and shortly after that, archaeological excavations began. Today, most of the ancient city has been unearthed. The ash has been cleared away, and beneath the ash, almost perfectly preserved, are the homes, shops, public facilities, streets, walls, and other parts of this ancient Roman city. Walking down the streets of Pompeii today is an eerie experience, like being transported back two thousand years via a time machine. One can sit on a seat in an ancient Roman theater, look at the mosaics on the floors of private homes, see in shops the jars where wine was stored, look into the baths, admire the statues and frescoes on the walls—all as one might have done over two thousand years ago.

Not only the buildings and the streets but also the very people and animals of ancient Pompeii have been preserved. By pouring plaster into the spaces left after the bodies of the buried Pompeians decayed, archaeologists have created casts of these bodies, allowing us, today, to gaze on the faces of these ancient Romans, to see the very folds of their clothing and straps of their sandals.

Today, thousands of tourists visit Pompeii every year to walk down the streets of this ancient city and to view the plaster casts of these ancient Romans. Many tourists also take the trip up the slopes of Vesuvius to gaze into the caldera—the boiling mouth—of the volcano.

Pompeii offers a unique opportunity to look into the past and see it as it actually was. It also offers a warning about the power of nature, a warning that modern people seem not to have heeded. There have been more than thirty eruptions of Vesuvius since A.D. 79, the most recent in 1944. An eruption in 1631 killed around 3,500 people. Today, Vesuvius remains an active volcano. Another eruption of the magnitude of the one in A.D. 79 would destroy an area of about four square miles around the volcano. There are nearly a million people living now in the area that would be immediately affected by another eruption. 🍎

14 The destruction of Pompeii occurred

    A about two hundred years ago

    B almost two thousand years ago

    C about two decades ago

    D over five thousand years ago

15 Pompeii was

    A buried under ashes and later dug up in well-preserved condition

    B sunk beneath the ocean and later raised in well-preserved condition

    C leveled by an earthquake but later pieced together by archaeologists

    D destroyed by a fire and later rebuilt

16 Viewing the ruins of Pompeii gives a modern visitor an opportunity to see what life was like in an ancient

    A Roman city

    B underground city

    C Chinese village

    D necropolis

17 The article mentions plaster casts made of

    A buildings from Pompeii

    B bread, figs, olives, and other foodstuffs from Pompeii

    C the bodies of people and animals who died at Pompeii

    D all of the above

POSTTEST

Open-Response Question, Session 1

18   Imagine that you are an inhabitant of Pompeii when Mt. Vesuvius erupts. Write a brief account of what you see and how you feel when the eruption occurs.

_____

_____

_____

_____

_____

_____

_____

_____

_____

_____

_____

_____

_____

_____

_____

_____

_____

STOP

DIRECTIONS

In this poem, William Butler Yeats adopts the voice of a young Irish man in World War I. Read the poem and answer the questions that follow.

An Irish Airman Foresees His Death
by William Butler Yeats

I know that I shall meet my fate
Somewhere among the clouds above;
Those that I fight I do not hate
Those that I guard I do not love;
5   My country is Kiltartan Cross,
My countrymen Kiltartan's poor,
No likely end could bring them loss
Or leave them happier than before.
Nor law, nor duty bade me fight,
10 Nor public man, nor cheering crowds,
A lonely impulse of delight
Drove to this tumult in the clouds;
I balanced all, brought all to mind,
The years to come seemed waste of breath,
15 A waste of breath the years behind
In balance with this life, this death.

IRELAND

Multiple-Choice Questions, Session 2

19 What is the occupation of the speaker of this poem?
   A He is a fighter pilot.
   B He is delivering the mail by air.
   C He is one of Kiltartan's poor.
   D He is a commercial pilot.

20 What is the significance of the phrase "I shall meet my fate"?
   A It is an apostrophe, in which the speaker addresses Death.
   B It is a simile meaning "I shall do my duty."
   C It is a symbol for the "Grim Reaper."
   D It is a metaphor meaning "I shall die."

21 What likely outcome of the war does the speaker foresee for his countrymen?
   A They will experience further loss.
   B They will gain their independence.
   C They will experience greater happiness.
   D They will neither gain nor lose.

22 This poem is an example of
   A a limerick
   B rhymed, metered verse
   C free verse
   D an epic

Open-Response Question, Session 2

23   The speaker of this poem lists various motivations that might inspire someone to join the fighting. What motivation has led the speaker to join the war? What motivations did NOT influence the speaker to join the war?

_____

_____

_____

_____

_____

_____

_____

_____

_____

_____

_____

_____

_____

_____

_____

_____

_____

_____

DIRECTIONS

Read "A Brief History of Everything."
Then answer the questions that follow.

A Brief History of Everything
by Robin Lamb

Author's Note: In the 1960s, a new literary form emerged, called sometimes "flash fiction" and sometimes simply "the short short story." The trick of the genre is to tell a story very, very briefly, in less than 350 words. When I first learned of the form, I thought it would be a challenge to use it to tell the story of everything, from the very beginning. So, here's a bit of flash fiction that begins with the biggest flash of them all, the Big Bang:

At first there was the void. Then? (one can't say *then*, exactly, because time did not yet exist) a bubble appeared in the undifferentiated vacuum. This was no ordinary bubble. It was a singularity, an infinitely small speck containing all that was to be.

The bubble exploded. In the instants that followed, time and space sorted themselves out, and the four fundamental forces were born—the weak atomic force, the strong atomic force, electromagnetism, and gravity.

The baby universe blew up like a balloon. As it cooled, elementary particles formed—photons, quarks, neutrinos, electrons, then protons and neutrons, then nuclei, then atoms of hydrogen and helium. The atoms condensed under the influence of gravity to form superclusters containing galaxies, and within these, stars.

Some stars lived out their lives, forging in their bellies the heavier elements—carbon, nitrogen, oxygen, iron, gold, and so on through the periodic table. Some of these stars went supernova, scattering their precious progeny into space, where they were swept up into planets and moons.

Far out on one arm of a spiral galaxy called the Milky Way, in the system of the star Sol, meteors pelted the molten surface of the newly formed Earth, which spewed forth gases—methane, ammonia, carbon dioxide, water vapor—an atmosphere. Clouds burst into rains, filling the hollow places below, over millions of years, with warm oceans.

Life appeared—bacteria, plankton, ammonites, trilobites, dragonflies, coelacanths, velociraptors, ferns and flowers, hippos and whales, lemurs and gibbons, women and men. A few billion people had babies, and some of these took up speech, then art, then agriculture, then writing and founding civilizations—Indus Valley folk, Mesopotamians, Persians, Greeks, Romans, Mayans, Inca, Great Zimbabweans, Mongols, Manchurians, Guptas, the British, Spanish, Portuguese, Americans—leading, eventually, to Gail Grimke, who kissed me under the Wilson Avenue el and said, "You ain't seen nothin' yet."

I was fifteen at the time of this last, most important event in the history of the universe. 🍎

POSTTEST

24   "A Brief History of the Universe" is an example of the genre known as

   A   the novella

   B   flash fiction

   C   lyric poetry

   D   epic poetry

25   Using the shortest of narrative genres to tell the entire history of the universe is an example of the literary technique known as

   A   satire

   B   irony

   C   metaphor

   D   personification

26   The last event described in "A Brief History of the Universe" is the only one in the piece that

   A   happens after the big bang

   B   is personal

   C   might be discussed in a science textbook

   D   involves people

27   The humor of "A Brief History of Everything" derives from the fact that

   A   something comes out of nothing

   B   ancient empires led by people who thought themselves incredibly powerful are now simply footnotes in history

   C   the speaker treats his being kissed as an event important enough to be placed in a 350-word history of the entire universe

   D   it is about history

Open-Response Questions, Session 2

28   What is flash fiction? Use information from the selection to support your answer.

_____

_____

_____

_____

_____

_____

_____

_____

_____

_____

_____

_____

_____

_____

_____

_____

_____

_____

_____

29 What do you believe to be the message, or theme, of "A Brief History of the Universe"? Explain, using details from the selection to support your answer.

_____

_____

_____

_____

_____

_____

_____

_____

_____

_____

_____

_____

_____

_____

_____

_____

_____

_____

_____

_____

_____

GO
ON

DIRECTIONS

Read the following newspaper article about current trends in the world economy. Then answer the questions that follow.

Economic Report Card Shows Continued Inequity

by Elizabeth Brinkman

NEW YORK—The human rights organization Global Watch, Inc., today released its annual "World Economic Report Card," a 158-page report on the state of the world's economy. According to the annual report card, which ranks economies around the world by assigning letter grades corresponding to quality of life, differences between the richest and poorest nations of the Earth continue to be dramatic.

Topping the Global Watch ranking for quality of life, with a grade of A+, was Sweden, with an annual gross national product (GNP) of $27,010 per person and an average life expectancy at birth of 78.3 years. At the bottom of the list was Afghanistan, with an annual GNP per person of $175 dollars and an average life expectancy of only 42.5 years. Gross national product is a measure of the total worth of goods and services produced in a country in a year's time.

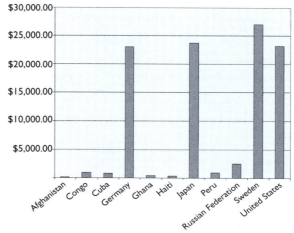

Gross National Product Per Capita

Afghanistan, Congo, Cuba, Germany, Ghana, Haiti, Japan, Peru, Russian Federation, Sweden, United States

The United States continued to do extremely well in the Global Watch rankings, placing third among the world's countries with a grade of A, a per capita (per person) GNP of $23,240, an average life expectancy of 75.9 years, and an

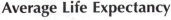

Average Life Expectancy

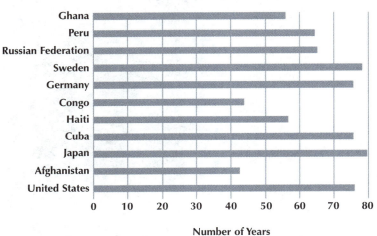

Ghana
Peru
Russian Federation
Sweden
Germany
Congo
Haiti
Cuba
Japan
Afghanistan
United States

0 10 20 30 40 50 60 70 80

Number of Years

average birth rate, per female citizen, of 2.1 children. However, the United States lagged behind both Sweden and Japan in life expectancy and GNP per capita.

For the third straight year, Japan led the list in life expectancy. A Japanese child born today can expect to live 79.5 years, the report said.

Also for the third straight year, income and life expectancy fell in the Russian Federation. The economic woes of the newly independent Russian state are underscored by its extremely low annual GNP of $2,510 per capita, less than one tenth of the per capita GNP of Sweden. "What this means," said Global Watch director Myron Fieldman, "is that the Russian Federation is producing only $2,510 worth of goods and services per person in a year's time, as opposed to $23,240 worth in the United States. Obviously, the average Russian citizen is far worse off than the average American."

The low Russian per capita GNP could be a source of political instability. "If people in Russia continue to be hungry and unemployed, and if the developed countries

don't do something, then I worry that Russia might be ripe for takeover by Communists or by Fascists. It really could happen," Mr. Fieldman said.

Most troubling in the new Economic Report Card, however, are the continued dramatic differences between the wealthiest and poorest nations of the Earth. Twenty-eight percent of the people of the world control 80 percent of the wealth. Among the wealthiest are citizens of industrial nations, such as Sweden, Japan, the United States, and Germany, and of oil-rich nations, such as Kuwait and Saudi Arabia. Among the poorest are African countries such as Congo, Chad, Ethiopia, and Ghana; Caribbean and Latin American countries, such as Peru, Ecuador, Cuba, and Haiti; Southeast Asian countries, such as Java and New Guinea; and newly independent former members of the Soviet Union, such as Afghanistan, Albania, Romania, and Bulgaria.

According to the report, 1.5 billion people in the world—roughly a fifth of the global population—live in extreme poverty, on less than $370 per person per year.

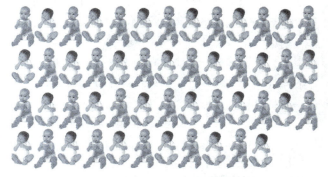

50 CHILDREN
WERE BORN INTO POVERTY
WHILE YOU READ THIS ARTICLE

Worldwide, 50 children are born into poverty every minute. Nearly 800 million people—20 percent of the population of the developing world—suffer from hunger or malnutrition. Most of these people—62 percent of the hungry people of the world—live in Asia.

On a positive note, the overall life expectancy in the developing countries has risen since 1960 by more than a third, from 46 to 62 years. In many parts of the world, however, life expectancy continues to be quite low. Average life expectancy in Congo, for example, is only 44 years and in Ghana, only 56.

Fertility rates are also decreasing, on average. The total fertility rate for women in developing countries dropped from 5.7 children per woman in 1970 to about 3.5 per woman this year. However, in some places, rates continue to be high. The average woman in Afghanistan gives birth to an astonishing 6.9 children in her lifetime. In Congo, the number is 6.3. In Ghana, it is 6.0. In contrast, women in developed countries continue to give birth to fewer children. Average birth rates per woman in Japan and Germany, for example, are 1.5 and 1.3, respectively, while the U. S. has an average birth rate per woman of 2.1, slightly above the rate of zero population growth (ZPG). Overall, the world's population is expected to double, to over 10 billion, in the next thirty years.

Among other positive notes in the report is an overall increase in democracy worldwide. Two-thirds of the people of the world now live in countries with democratic or representative governments. In addition, global crime rates have decreased, and access to health services has increased. 🍎

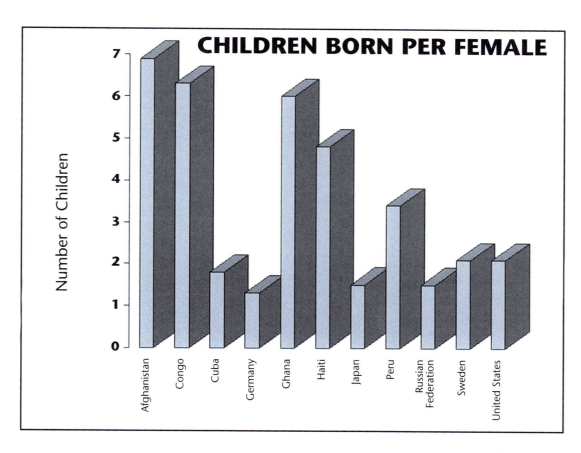

Multiple-Choice Questions, Session 2

30   According to the Global Watch Economic Report Card, the country with the highest overall quality of life is

   A the United States

   B Germany

   C Japan

   D Sweden

31   According to the article, 28 percent of the world's people control _____ percent of the world's wealth.

   A 20

   B 50

   C 80

   D 100

32   On average, the number of children born to each woman in Afghanistan is

   A 1.5

   B 2.1

   C 5.4

   D 6.9

33   The difference between the Gross National Product per person in the United States and Afghanistan is $_____ per year.

   A 450

   B 2,510

   C 23,065

   D 27,010

34   _____ of the global population lives in extreme poverty

   A One tenth

   B One fifth

   C One third

   D Half

Open-Response Question, Session 2

35   According to the article, what are some positive trends in the world's economy and in the welfare of its people?

_____

_____

_____

_____

_____

_____

_____

_____

_____

_____

_____

_____

_____

_____

_____

_____

_____

_____

POSTTEST

Reading Selection #1, Session 3

DIRECTIONS

Read the following selection from *Lake Wobegon Days*, in which Garrison Keillor describes the mythical town of Lake Wobegon, settled by emigrants from Norway. Then answer the questions that follow.

from
Lake Wobegon Days
by Garrison Keillor

hat's special about this town; it's pretty much like a lot of towns, isn't it? There is a perfectly good answer to that question, it only takes a moment to think of it.

For one thing, the Statue of the Unknown Norwegian. If other towns have one, we don't know about it. Sculpted by a man named O'Connell or O'Connor in 1896, the granite youth stands in a small plot at a jog in the road where a surveyor knocked off for lunch years ago and looks down Main Street to the lake. A proud figure, his back is erect, his feet are on the ground on account of no money remained for a pedestal, and his eyes—well, his eyes are a matter of question. Probably the artist meant him to exude confidence in the New World, but his eyes are set a little deep so that dark shadows appear in the late afternoon and by sunset he looks worried.

His confident smile turns into a forced grin. In the morning, he is stepping forward, his right hand extended in greeting, but as the day wears on, he hesitates, and finally he appears to be about to turn back. The right hand seems to say, Wait here. I think I forgot something.

Nevertheless, he is a landmark and an asset, so it was a shame when the tornado of 1947 did damage to him. That tornado skipped in from the northeast; it blew away one house except for a dresser mirror that wasn't so much as cracked—amazing; it's in the historical society now, and people still bring their relatives to look at it. It also picked up a brand-new Chevy pickup and set it down a quarter of a mile away. *On a road. In the right-hand lane.* In town, it took the roof off the Lutheran church, where nobody was, and missed the Bijou, which was packed for *Shame*, starring Cliff DeCarlo. And it blew a stalk of quackgrass about six inches into the Unknown Norwegian, in an unusual place, a part of the body where you've been told to insert nothing bigger than your finger in a washcloth.

Bud, our municipal employee, pulled it out, of course, but the root was imbedded in the granite, so it keeps growing out. Bud has considered using a pre-emergent herbicide on him but is afraid it will leave a stain on the side of his head, so, when he mows, simply reaches up to the Unknown's right ear and snips off the blade with his fingernails. It's not so noticeable, really; you have to look for it to see it.

The plaque that would've been on the pedestal the town couldn't afford was bolted to a brick and set in the ground until Bud dug it out because it was dinging up his mower blade. Now in the historical society museum in the basement of the town hall, it sits next to the Lake Wobegon runestone, which proves that Viking explorers were here in 1381. Unearthed by a Professor Oftedahl or Ostenwald around 1921 alongside Country Road 2, where the professor, motoring from Chicago to Seattle, had stopped to bury garbage, the small black stone is covered with Viking runic characters which read (translated by him): "8 of [us] stopped & stayed awhile to visit & have [coffee] & a short nap. Sorry [you] weren't here. Well, that's about [it] for now."

Every Columbus Day, the runestone is carried up to the school and put on a card-table in the lunchroom for the children to see, so they can know their true heritage. It saddens Norwegians that America still honors this Italian, who arrived late in the New World and by accident, who wasn't even interested in New Worlds but only in spices. Out on a spin in search of curry powder and hot peppers—a man on a voyage to the grocery—he stumbled onto the land of heroic Vikings and proceeded to get the credit for it. And then to name it *America* after Amerigo Vespucci, an Italian who never saw the New World but only sat in Italy and drew incredibly inaccurate maps of it.[1] By rights, it should be called Erica, after Eric the Red,[2] who did the work five hundred years earlier. The United States of Erica. Erica the Beautiful. The Erican League. 🍎

---

[1] **Amerigo Vespucci . . . of it.** In fact, the Italian explorer Amerigo Vespucci did make several voyages to the New World. America was named by a German geographer, Martin Waldseemüller.
[2] **Eric the Red.** Norse explorer (circa 950–1000) who discovered Greenland. His son, Leif Ericson, discovered and wintered in Vinland, on the North American continent.

Multiple-Choice Questions, Session 3

36   How did the tornado of 1947 damage the statue of the Unknown Norwegian?

   A   It drove the root of a weed into the statue's ear.
   B   It picked up the statue and set it down in a jog in the road.
   C   It broke the plaque on the brick.
   D   It picked it up and set it down in the right-hand lane of a road a quarter of a mile away.

37   What is unusual about the "runestone" unearthed alongside County Road 2?

   A   It proves that Viking explorers were in Lake Wobegon.
   B   It is now in the Historical Society Museum.
   C   The Vikings carved it to say that they stopped for coffee and a short nap.
   D   It is put on display on Columbus Day.

38   How do shadows affect the impression made by the statue of the Unknown Norwegian?

   A   They make his eyes look blue.
   B   By sunset, they make him look worried.
   C   They make him look as though he were floating rather than standing on a pedestal.
   D   By noon, they make him look tired.

39   The artist meant the statue "to exude confidence in the New World," What does **exude** mean?

   A   leave unsaid
   B   give off or radiate
   C   weaken or wear away
   D   inhibit or hold back

40   What happens FIRST?

   A   Columbus arrives in the New World.
   B   America is named after Amerigo Vespucci.
   C   The statue of the Unknown Norwegian is built.
   D   Eric the Red arrives in the New World.

Open-Response Question, Session 3

41   The word *woebegone* means "looking sorrowful, mournful, or wretched."
     Use details from the selection to show why *Lake Wobegon* is an
     appropriate name for this town.

_____

_____

_____

_____

_____

_____

_____

_____

_____

_____

_____

_____

_____

_____

_____

_____

_____

DIRECTIONS

Read the following articles and the speeches by two Native American leaders. Then answer the questions that follow.

Chief Joseph:
"I Shall Fight No More Forever"

Chief Joseph was the leader of the Nez Percé Indians who lived in the Oregon Territory before white settlers moved in and claimed the land. Joseph was his English name. His Indian name was *Hin-mah-too-yah-lat-kekt*, which meant "Thunder Rolling Down the Mountains."

In the 1850s, the United States government entered into a treaty with Chief Joseph's people, granting the Nez Percé rights to a large territory stretching from Oregon into Idaho. However, in the 1860s, gold fever gripped the West, and hundreds of white settlers rushed onto Nez Percé land, hoping to strike it rich. In the 1870s, the U.S. government reversed itself. Breaking the treaty, the government sent troops under the command of General Oliver Otis Howard to force Joseph and his people, who lived in the Wallowa Valley of Oregon, to move to a small reservation in Idaho.

Chief Joseph wished to remain in the Wallowa Valley, where he was born, but

when General Howard of the United States Army threatened to attack him, Joseph reluctantly agreed to move his people onto the Idaho reservation. Before he could do so, however, a small group of Nez Percé made an attack on some white settlers. Knowing that the United States Army would retaliate, Chief Joseph decided to flee with his people to Canada.

Joseph and about seven hundred of his people left their homeland and headed north, pursued by two thousand United States troops. In the months that followed, the small band of Nez Percé traveled over fourteen hundred miles, attempting to dodge the pursuing soldiers. Vastly outnumbered, the Nez Percé nonetheless managed to survive four major battles and many smaller skirmishes with the U.S. troops. By October of 1877, with winter setting in, food scarce, and many of his people dead or lost, Chief Joseph was forced to surrender. When he surrendered, Chief Joseph delivered the following speech:

"Tell General Howard I know his heart. What he told me before, I bear in my heart. I am tired of fighting. Our chiefs are killed. Looking Glass is dead. Toohoolhoolzote is dead. It is the young men who say yes and no. He who led on the young men is dead. It is cold and we have no blankets. The little children are freezing to death. My people, some of them, have run away to the hills and have no blankets, no food; no one knows where they are—perhaps freezing to death. I want to have time to look for my children and see how many I can find. Maybe I shall find them among the dead. Hear me, my chiefs. I am tired; my heart is sick and sad. From where the sun now stands, I will fight no more forever." 🍎

Chief Ten Bears:
"Where the Wind Blew Free"

In the mid-1800s, the Comanche Indians of Texas fought a long and fierce war to retain control of their homeland, which had in the past included much of Texas, Oklahoma, Colorado, and New Mexico. A treaty signed with the United States government in 1865 failed to end the fighting. In 1867, a meeting was held between the Comanche and representatives of the U.S. government to negotiate a new agreement. At this meeting, known as the Medicine Lodge Council, Comanche Chief Ten Bears spoke, in part, as follows:

"There are things which you have said to me which I do not like. They were not sweet like sugar, but bitter like gourds. You said that you wanted to put us upon a reservation, to build us houses and to make us medicine lodges. I do not want them.

"I was born upon the prairie, where the wind blew free, and there was nothing to break the light of the sun. I was born where there were no enclosures, and where everything drew a free breath. I want to die there, and not within walls. I know every stream and every wood between the Rio Grande and Arkansas. I have hunted and lived over that country. I lived like my fathers before me, and like them, I lived happily.

"When I was at Washington, the Great Father [President Andrew Johnson] told me that all the Comanche land was ours, and that no one should hinder us living upon it. So why do you ask us to leave the rivers and the sun and the wind, and live in houses? Do not ask us to give up the buffalo for the sheep. The young men have heard talk of this, and it has made them sad and angry. Do not speak of it more. I love to carry out the talk I get from the Great Father. When I get goods and presents, I and my people feel glad since it shows that he holds us in his eye. If the Texans had kept out of my country, there might have been peace. But that which you now say we must live on is too small.

"The Texans have taken away the places where the grass grew the thickest and the timber was the best. Had we kept that, we might have done the thing you ask. But it is too late. The white man has the country which we loved, and we only wish to wander on the prairie until we die." 🍎

42 Why did hundreds of white settlers move onto Nez Percé land in the 1860s?

    A They wanted to conquer the Nez Percé.

    B They were looking for gold.

    C The government gave the land to the settlers.

    D They wanted the rich land for growing crops.

43 Which of the following statements is true?

    A When the U.S. Army threatened to attack Chief Joseph, he mobilized his people to fight.

    B The Nez Percé vastly outnumbered the U.S. troops.

    C A small group of Nez Percé attacked some white settlers.

    D The U.S. government honored the treaty giving the Nez Percé a large territory in the Northwest.

44 All of the following were reasons why Chief Joseph eventually surrendered EXCEPT

    A The weather was brutally hot and dry.

    B Many of the Nez Percé leaders had died.

    C Food was becoming scarce.

    D Chief Joseph's heart was sad, and he was tired of fighting.

45 What does Chief Joseph say about the young men of his people?

    A The young men are sad and angry because they have to herd sheep.

    B The young men want to go on fighting.

    C The young men now make the decisions.

    D The young men are dead.

46   In his speech, Chief Ten Bears contrasts the Comanche homeland with the reservation where the government wants his people to live. The two columns below list words and phrases from his speech that refer to the reservation (Column 1) and to the Comanche homeland (Column 2). Tell whether the descriptions are in the correct columns.

Column 1	Column 2
Reservation	**Comanche Homeland**
• houses	• prairie
• medicine lodges	• wind blew free
• enclosures	• nothing to break the light of the sun
• walls	• no enclosures
• herding sheep	• everything drew a free breath
• too small	• streams, woods
	• the people lived happily
	• rivers, sun, wind
	• hunting buffalo
	• the grass grew the thickest and the timber was the best
	• the country which we loved

A   All the items in both columns are correct.

B   All the items in Column 1 are correct, but not all those in Column 2.

C   All the items in Column 2 are correct, but not all those in Column 1.

D   There are errors both in Column 1 and in Column 2.

47 Which of the following is true of BOTH Chief Joseph's people and Chief Ten Bears's people?

    A They lived in the northwestern area of the United States.

    B The U.S. government made agreements with them that were later broken.

    C To escape from the U.S. army, they fled north.

    D They fought a long and fierce war to keep their homeland.

48 Why does Chief Ten Bears reject the U.S. government's offer?

    A It was bitter, like gourds.

    B He wanted to live in a warmer climate.

    C He and his people wanted to follow their traditional way of life.

    D President Andrew Johnson did not keep his promises.

49 Which statement does NOT reflect how Chief Ten Bears' people felt?

    A They were grateful that the U.S. government offered to build houses and medicine lodges for them.

    B They hated the idea of being shepherds.

    C They were sad and angry that the Texans had taken away the best of their land.

    D They were happiest when they were free to roam the prairie.

POSTTEST

Open-Response Question, Session 3

50   Use details from both articles and both speeches to describe the lives of the Nez Percé and the Comanche peoples after the white settlers moved into their lands.

_____

_____

_____

_____

_____

_____

_____

_____

_____

_____

_____

_____

_____

_____

_____

_____

_____

_____

_____

STOP ⬤

Composition

DIRECTIONS

You may use a dictionary during the Composition portion of the exam.

Session 1: You will have forty-five minutes for this session. During this session, you should

- plan what you are going to write (make notes, or make an outline or web)
- write a first draft on the pages provided

If you have not finished your rough draft by the end of Session 1, you should be close to finishing. Most of your time during Session 2 should be spent revising your draft and producing your final composition.

Session 2: You will have another forty-five minutes for this session. During this time, make changes that improve your composition, and write your final composition on the pages that follow in this book. When you correct your draft, remember what the person who scores your test will be looking for in your composition (see below).

Scoring Guidelines

Your composition will be given two scores. The first score will be for your ideas and how well you organize and explain them. The second score will be for spelling, grammar, punctuation, and capitalization.

Session 1

PLANNING PAGE

You may use the space below to plan your composition. You might wish to make notes, an outline, or a word web. Write the first draft of your composition on the next two pages. You will have about forty-five minutes for this session.

> **Writing Prompt:** According to the Victorian poet and literary critic Matthew Arnold, literature is "at bottom a criticism of life." Write an essay in which you explain what it means to you for literature to be a criticism of life. First, state whether you agree or disagree with Arnold's view of literature. Then select a work of literature that you have read, either in or outside the classroom, that you believe best supports your opinion. Refer to specific literary elements (e.g., plot, setting, characterization, tone, theme) to show how the work you have chosen supports your opinion about Arnold's statement. Be sure to identify the title and author of the work of literature you have chosen.

_____

_____

_____

_____

_____

_____

_____

_____

_____

_____

_____

_____

_____

_____

_____

_____

_____

_____

_____

_____

_____

_____

_____

GO ON

_____

_____

_____

_____

_____

_____

_____

_____

_____

_____

_____

_____

_____

_____

_____

_____

_____

_____

_____

_____

_____

STOP ⬣

Session 2

In this session, you have another forty-five minutes to change and correct the draft of the composition you wrote in Session 1 and to write the final copy of your composition. Use proofreading marks to make corrections to your draft. Keep in mind the guidelines that the evaluator will use to score your test (see page 235). Write your final composition on the lines below and on the following pages.

_____

_____

_____

_____

_____

_____

_____

_____

_____

_____

_____

_____

_____

_____

_____

_____

_____

GO ON

_____

_____

_____

_____

_____

_____

_____

_____

_____

_____

_____

_____

_____

_____

_____

_____

_____

_____

_____

_____

_____

STOP

Appendix A: Terms Used in Writing Prompts

analyze, v. To break something into its parts, describe the parts, and show how the parts are related to each other and to the whole

argument, n. Writing or speech that puts forward reasons in support of an opinion or factual proposition

assess, v. To determine the value of something

assessment, n. A judgment. See *judgment*.

categorize, v. To put items into categories; to classify them

cause, n. That which produces an effect, result, or consequence

chart, n. Any of a number of different kinds of informative graphic materials, such as a table, illustration, or graph

cite, v. To refer to or mention as an example or proof

coherent, adj. Said of a piece of writing in which the ideas are logically connected and in a sensible order. To make a piece of writing coherent, one organizes the ideas and uses transitions to connect them.

compare, v. To show the similarities between two or more subjects

contrast, v. To explain the differences between two or more subjects

conventions, n. Agreed-upon rules in writing or speech, including the rules for spelling, grammar, usage, punctuation, capitalization, and manuscript form

convey, v. Literally, to carry; figuratively, to show or illustrate to someone else

criterion, n. A standard, rule, test, or benchmark on which a decision or judgment is based. For example, one might choose a college based on the criterion of cost or based on the criterion of size. Plural: *criteria*.

critique, v. To perform a critical analysis of a work or an idea

describe, v. To tell about something in detail, to give a detailed verbal account of something

effect, n. The result or consequence of something. For example, the images and events in a horror story might have the effect of creating suspense.

evaluate, v. To judge the merits and demerits of something

evidence, n. Facts given in support of an opinion or argument. In essays about literary works, evidence takes the form of information from the literary works, including quotations, paraphrases, summaries, and descriptions of literary elements and techniques.

excerpt, n. A part of a longer work. For example, one might select a single anecdote, or very short story told to make a point, from an autobiography or biography. Such a selection would be an *excerpt*.

explain, v. To tell why or how something is the way it is

express, v. To make a statement that reveals thoughts or feelings

expression, n. A statement or part of a statement

generalization, n. A broad statement, one that implies but does not itself mention specific instances or particulars

graph, n. A drawing that shows relationships between or among variables, such as a bar graph, line graph, or pie chart

graphic, n. Any item, such as a graph, map, or diagram, that presents information visually

illustrate, v. To give an example

inference, n. A conclusion that can be drawn from a set of facts

interpret, n. To explain or describe the meaning or significance of something, such as a painting or a poem

interpretation, n. An explanation of the meaning or significance of a work of art, based upon careful study of the work and attention to its details and techniques; the act of creating such an explanation

judgment, n. An opinion as to the value or worth of something; an evaluation or assessment

key idea, n. phrase. A part of a piece of writing that is central to its meaning; an important or crucial point

literary element, n. phrase. A part of a literary work, such as its plot, setting, mood, or theme

literary technique, n. phrase. A special device used in a literary work. There are literary techniques related to meaning, such as metaphors and similes; literary techniques related to sound, such as alliteration and onomatopoeia; and literary techniques related to structure, such as the surprise ending or the beginning *in media res* (in the middle of the action).

logical, adj. Based upon sound reasons and arguments; supported by facts and by the relationships among the facts

main idea, n. phrase. The most important, key, or central idea in a piece of writing, also known as the thesis or the controlling idea

objective, adj. Based upon fact, not opinion; provable by reference to the facts or evidence

opinion, n. A judgment, belief, prediction, or other statement that cannot be proved, absolutely, by observation but that can, if the opinion is sound, be supported by facts

organization, n. The arrangement of ideas in a piece of writing

organize, v. To arrange ideas so that they follow logically from one another and so that the relationships among the ideas are clear to the reader. Common methods for organizing writing include chronological order, order of importance, and spatial order.

paraphrase, n. A restatement in other words

passage, n. A short selection from a piece of writing, ranging in size from a couple of sentences to a few paragraphs

proposition, n. A statement of fact that can be proved by definition, by observation, or by consulting an authoritative expert or reference work

recommendation, n. An opinion as to what someone else should do or think, usually based on specific facts or evidence presented in support of the opinion

relationship, n. A connection or association between two people, things, or ideas

APPENDICES

relevant, *adj.* Related to the matter or issue being discussed; pertinent

response, *n.* A reaction to something. For example, an essay might be a response to an essay question.

review, *v.* To examine something carefully and make a judgment about it based on the examination

selection, *n.* A part of a literary work or other piece of writing; a complete work that is part of a collection or anthology

show, *v.* To give evidence

specific, *n.* Particular, not vague or general. When an essay prompt asks you to be specific, you are being asked to give precise, detailed facts or evidence in your answer.

statement, *n.* Any short, meaningful writing or speech, such as a sentence, opinion, proposition, etc.

structure, *n.* The form and organization of a piece of writing. For example, an essay might have a five-paragraph structure, consisting of an introduction, three body paragraphs, and a conclusion. A short story might be structured as a series of flashbacks to an earlier time in a character's life.

subjective, *adj.* Based upon the opinions or internal, private experiences of an individual rather than upon observable facts that can be verified by others

summarize, *v.* To restate in fewer words

support, *v.* To provide evidence to back up an assertion (a statement of fact or an opinion). In a paragraph, the sentences in the body support the topic sentence. In an essay, the paragraphs of the body support the thesis statement, or controlling idea.

table, *n.* A kind of chart in which information is presented in list form in columns and rows

unified, *adj.* A piece of writing is unified if its ideas are all related to a single controlling idea and all contribute to creating a single dominant impression on the reader.

Appendix B: Literary Terms

allegory. A work in which many of the elements, such as the characters or the parts of the setting, symbolize, or represent, things beyond themselves

anecdote. A very brief story told to illustrate a point

article. An extended piece of nonfiction writing of the kind found in newspapers, magazines, and newsletters

autobiography. The story of a person's life, written by that person; a type of nonfiction

ballad. A simple narrative poem in four-line stanzas, usually meant to be sung

biography. The story of a person's life, written by someone else; a type of nonfiction

blank verse. Unrhymed poetry written in iambic pentameter

body. The part of an essay or composition in which ideas are presented to support the main idea presented in the introduction

character. A being who takes part in the action of a literary work

comedy. Originally referring to any literary work with a happy ending, this term is now used, primarily, of plays, screenplays, or other dramas that are light-hearted or humorous or in which the main character meets a pleasant fate.

conclusion. The final portion of an essay, often a single paragraph, in which the writer sums up his or her thoughts

conflict. Struggle in which the characters are involved. Conflict can be *internal* (inside a character) or *external* (with a person or force outside the character).

criticism. The act of interpreting and/or evaluating a literary work

description. A type of writing that has as its purpose presenting a portrait, in words, of some subject

diary. See *journal*.

drama. Writing that presents events through the dialogue and, sometimes, the movements and actions, of characters. Types of drama include stage plays, screenplays, radio plays, and reader's theater. Drama can be read or performed by actors.

dramatic dialogue. A dramatic poem in which two characters speak

dramatic monologue. A dramatic poem in which one character speaks, often to another character who is present but silent

dramatic poem. A verse that presents the speech of one or more characters in a dramatic situation

elegy. A formal poem about death or loss

epic. A long story, often in verse, involving heroes and gods and providing a portrait of a culture, of its legends, beliefs, values, laws, arts, and ways of life. Examples: the *Iliad,* the *Aeneid, Beowulf,* and *Paradise Lost.*

epistle. A letter, which may be in verse. A novel written in letters is known as an *epistolary novel.*

epithet. A disparaging nickname. *Shrink* is an epithet for a psychiatrist.

essay. A brief work of prose nonfiction. A good essay develops a single controlling idea and is characterized by unity and coherence. A *narrative essay* tells a story. An *autobiographical essay* is one in which the writer tells a true story from his or her own life. In a *biographical essay,* a writer tells a true story from someone else's life.

expository writing. Writing that has as its major purpose presenting information about a subject. Expository writing, also known as informative writing, presents facts, not opinions.

expressive writing. Writing that has as its major purpose describing personal feelings, attitudes, ideas, values, or beliefs. Personal essays are a kind of expressive writing.

fable. A brief story with animal characters told to illustrate a moral

fantasy. A literary work that contains highly

unrealistic elements, such as Swift's *Gulliver's Travels* or Lewis's *The Chronicles of Narnia*

farce. A type of comedy, often satirical, that depends heavily on so-called low humor and on improbable, wildly exaggerated characters and situations

fiction. A literary work, in prose, that tells about imaginary people, places, and events. Examples of fiction include short stories, novellas, and novels.

flashback. A section of a literary work that presents an event or series of events that occurred earlier than the current time in the work

folk tale. A brief story passed by word of mouth from generation to generation

free verse. Poetry that avoids the use of regular rhyme, rhythm, meter, or division into stanzas

genre. One of the types or categories into which literary works are divided.

image. A word or phrase that names something that can be seen, heard, touched, tasted, or smelled

imagery. The collective images used in a work

informative writing. See *expository writing*.

introduction. The opening part of a piece of writing. In a nonfiction essay, the introduction should grab the attention of the reader and present the subject and main idea, or thesis. In a short story, the introduction generally presents the setting, provides necessary background information, and introduces the protagonist and the central conflict.

irony. A contradiction, such as a difference between appearance and reality or a difference between what is said and what is meant.

journal. A day-to-day account of events; a diary. Such an account may be true (nonfiction) or imaginary (fiction).

legend. A story, which may be partially or wholly true, about a hero or heroine. Stories about the exploits of King Arthur and Annie Oakley are examples of legends.

lyric poem. A short, highly musical verse that expresses the thoughts and emotions of a speaker

Magical Realist fiction. Fiction that contains both realistic and fantastic elements, intermingled

melodrama. A drama containing exaggerated characters and events characterized by excessive and often sentimental emotion

memoir. An account of events from the past, told by someone who took part in those events; a synonym, with slightly different connotations, of the term *autobiography*.

mood. The emotional quality evoked by a literary work

motivation. A force, object, or circumstance that impels a character to act as he or she does; the act of being impelled to think or do something

motive. A reason why a character acts as he or she does

myth. A fanciful or fictive story dealing with a god or goddess or with supernatural occurrences. Often myths explain the origins of natural phenomena. The Greek story of Prometheus the fire-giver is an example.

narrative. Any work of prose, poetry, or drama, fictional or nonfictional, that tells a story

narrative poem. A verse that tells a story

Naturalist fiction. Fiction that presents characters as subject to biological or natural forces beyond their power to control

nonfiction. Any of a wide variety of literary works, generally in prose, that present factual information or that present actual people, places, and events. Examples of nonfiction include speeches, essays, memoirs, autobiographies, biographies, textbooks, and reference works.

nonsense verse. A kind of light verse that contains elements that are silly, absurd, or meaningless

novel. A long work of prose fiction

novella. A short novel or long short story

parody. A literary work that imitates another

work for humorous, often satirical purposes

periodical. A magazine, newsletter, or other publication that appears on a regular basis (e.g., monthly or quarterly)

personal essay. A short nonfiction work about a single topic that is autobiographical or biographical in nature or that expresses a subjective, personal view of a subject

persuasive writing. Writing that has as its purpose convincing others to adopt some belief or to take some action. Persuasive writing presents opinions.

position paper. An essay in which the writer presents his or her position, or opinion, with regard to some issue and backs up that opinion with factual evidence and/or persuasive rhetoric

prologue. An introduction to a literary work

proverb. A short, memorable statement that is passed by word of mouth from person-to-person, usually over many generations. "You can lead a horse to water, but you can't make it drink" is an example of a proverb.

psychological fiction. Fiction that emphasizes the subjective, interior experiences of characters, often fiction that deals with emotional or mental anguish or disturbance

purpose. The aim, or goal, of a piece of writing. Common purposes for writing include to inform, to persuade, to describe, to compare, to contrast, to define, to classify, to entertain, to express personal thoughts or feelings, and to make a proposal or recommendation.

Realist fiction. Fiction that attempts to present an accurate, often critical, portrayal or imitation of reality

review. A type of nonfiction essay in which a critic presents an interpretation and evaluation of a work or group of works such as a play, movie, novel, concert, or exhibition of paintings

romance. 1. A medieval story about the adventures and loves of knights; 2. a novel or other work involving exotic locales and extraordinary or mysterious events and characters; 3. nonrealistic fiction in general; 4. a love story

satire. A humorous literary work, in prose or in poetry, in which a writer pokes fun at something in order to point out errors, falsehoods, foibles, or failings

setting. The time and place in which a work of literature occurs

short story. A brief fictional work dealing with a central conflict and creating a single dominant impression

stage play. A kind of drama, consisting of stage directions and dialogue, that is performed on a stage by actors who portray characters

stanza. A recurring pattern of grouped lines in a poem

subplot. A subordinate story told in addition to the main story in a work of fiction

summary. A restatement, in other, fewer words

suspense. A feeling of curiosity, expectation, or anxiety created in the reader by questions about the outcome of the events in literary work

tall tale. A story containing wildly exaggerated characters and events, like the stories about Paul Bunyan and Pecos Bill

theme. A central idea in a literary work. Often the theme is a lesson learned by the protagonist.

thesis statement. A statement of the main idea of an essay. The thesis statement appears in the introduction and may be a single sentence or more than one sentence.

tragedy. A type of drama in which the main character falls from a high to a low estate due to some failing, or weakness, known as a tragic flaw. The term is sometimes used, as well, of other types of literary work in which the main character meets a negative fate.

Appendix C: Common Spelling Errors

A
absence
absolutely
accidentally
accommodate
achievement
acknowledge
acquaintance
adequate
ambiguous
analysis
ancestor
announcement
answer
anticipate
antique
anxious
apology
apparently
approximately
arguing
argument
article
artificial
asked
assessment
assistance
audience
average

B
beggar
beginning
believe
biased
break
brilliance
business

C
calendar
can't
candidate
career
ceiling
certainly
challenge
changeable
coming
commitment
committee
committing
comparable
comparative
comparison
competent
competition
competitor

conceive
concentrate
conference
conscience
conscious
consequently
continuous
convenience
courageous
criticism
criticize
cruelty
curiosity

D
debt
deceitful
defense
definite
despise
devise
dialogue
dictionary
disappear
discouragement
disillusioned
disloyal
dissatisfied
does
dramatize

E
eighth
elaborate
eliminate
embarrass
emphasis
encourage
enormous
enough
environment
essential
exaggerate
exceed
excellent
excessively
excitement
existence
explanation
extraordinary

F
familiarize
fascinate
feasible
fickle
fierce
figuratively

finally
flexible
foremost
foreshadow
foreword
fortunately
forward

G
gauge
genre
gracious
grammar
grateful
guarantee

H
half
having
height
heir
heritage
heroes
heroine
hoarse
humorous
hypocrisy

I
identity
imagination
imitate
immature
immediately
inadequate
inconceivable
incredible
independence
individual
influential
information
initiative
instead
integrity
intelligence
intention
interpretation
intriguing
irresistible
irresponsible

J
journal
journey
juvenile

L
legend

license
literally
loneliness
loose
lose
loveliness
loyalty

M
magnificent
maintain
maintenance
making
maneuver
marriage
masterpiece
meant
medieval
metaphor
minimum
minute
mischievous
misinterpret
misspell
misunderstood
monologue
moral
morale
morality

N
narrative
negative
neighbor
neither
ninety
nonsense
noticeable
nuisance

O
obnoxious
obstacle
occasion
occurrence
offense
often
opinion
opportunity
optimistic
ordinary
organization
original
outrageous

P
pamphlet
paradoxical

parallel
partially
peculiar
performance
permanent
physical
piece
playwright
possess
possessive
practical
prairie
preceding
precious
preface
preferred
prejudice
pretense
prevalent
primarily
privilege
proceed
prominent
propaganda
publicity

Q
quiet
quite

R
reciprocate
recommendation
recurring
regretted
relief
repetitious
resemblance
resolution
responsible
rewriting
rhyme
rhythm
ridiculous
routine

S
sacrifice
sarcastic
scenery
seize
separate
separation
sequence
similar
simile
sincerity
skillful

sophisticated
specific
spectacle
spectacular
statistics
straight
studying
successful
superb
supersede
surprising
syllable
symbol
symbolize
synonym

T
temporary
thinness
thorough
though
through
tonight
tragedy
tragic
transferred
transparent
treachery
tremendous
truly
twelfth

U
unbearable
unconscious
uncontrollable
usually

V
valuable
various
viewpoint
villain
visualize

W
warrior
weight
weird
whether
whole
wield
witnesses

Y
yield

Index of Concepts and Skills

A
achievement tests, 48
action words, 143, 145, 155, 178, 242–244
ad hominem, 131
aim, 120, 121
alliteration, 102, 108
analysis, 118
analysis chart, 151
analysis essay, 137–138
analyze, 83
analyzing, a literary text, 116
anecdote, 99
antagonist, 112
antecedent, 130, 170
antithesis, 122, 133
antonym, 76
apostrophe, literary 101
apposition, 76
aptitude tests, 47
author, 61
autobiography, 98

B
ballad, 99
bar graph, 84, 89
base words, 77
biographical criticism, 117
biography, 98
body, of a written piece, 62, 123
body paragraph, essay, 184–186, 188
boldface, 62

C
capitalization, 166, 171
caption, 88, 89
cause, 93, 137
cause and effect, 93
cause-and-effect chart, 150
cause-and-effect essay, 137
cause-and-effect order, 122
character, 101, 112
characteristics order, 122
chart, 88
chart of similarities and differences, 147–148
chronological order, 122
classification essay, 136–137
classification order, 122
climax, 113
clincher sentence, 62, 154
cluster chart, 152
column graph, 85, 89
column, in table, 87
comedy, 99

communications triangle, 121
compare, 147
comparison, as context clue, 76
comparison-and-contrast essay, 137
comparison/contrast chart, 146–147
comparison/contrast order, 122
compound words, 77–79
conclusion, 62, 123, 184–186, 188
conflict, 93, 113, 136
consequent, 130
context, 76
context clues, 75–77
contrast, 146
contrast, as context clue, 76
conventions, 169–176, 183
couplet, 103
crisis, 113
criticism, 116–119

D
decoding vocabulary, 75–82
deconstructionist criticism, 117
deduction, 94
degree order, 122
dénouement, 113
dependent variable, 84
description, 120
descriptive essay, 100
descriptive writing, 120
details, supporting, 71–74
diagram, 88, 89
dialogue, 120
diary, 98
didactic criticism, 117
direction line, multiple-choice, 53
double negative, 170
draft, 177
drafting, 181, 190
drama, 97, 99
dramatic poem, 99
dynamic character, 112

E
editorial, 126
effect, 93, 137
either . . . or argument, 131
elegy, 99
elements, of narrative, 112–113

end mark, 171
end rhyme, 103
endnotes, 62
epic, 99
eponym, 80
essay, 135
essay of definition, 138–139
essay, structure of, 184–185
evaluating, 118, 165–168, 193
evaluation, in writing process, 183
evaluation, of literary text, 118
evidence, 128, 158
evidence, citing, 144
examples, as context clues, 76
excerpt, 61
exposition, 113, 120
expository writing, 121
expressive writing, 121
external conflict, 113

F
fable, 98
fact, 126–127
fallacy, 130–132
fallacy of composition, 131
fallacy of decomposition, 131
fallacy of omission, 132
falling action, 113
false analogy, 130
false dichotomy, 131
feminist criticism, 117
fiction, 97
figurative language, 101–102
figures of speech, 101–102
final draft, 184
first-person point of view, 112
five-paragraph theme, 186, 187
flashback, 101
flat character, 112
focus, 183, 184
folk tale, 99
footnotes, 62
foreshadowing, 101
formal criticism, 117
fragments, sentence, 170
free verse, 103
Freudian criticism, 117
Freytag's Pyramid, 113

G
genres, of literature, 97, 120
genres, of nonfiction, 124
genus and differentia, 138
grammar, 165, 169–170
graphic organizers, 146–153
graphic organizer, for essay, 186
graphics, 83–92

H
heading, 62
heptastich, 103
historical criticism, 117
hyperbole, 101

I
icon, on map, 88
illustrations, 62, 88
image, 100
imagery, 100
inciting incident, 113
independent variable, 84, 85
induction, 94
inference, 94
inference, in decoding vocabulary, 77
infographics, 83, 89
informative essay, 100
informative writing, 121, 135–141
internal conflict, 113
internal rhyme, 103
interpretation, 118
introduction, 62, 123, 184–187
irony, 101
italics, 62

J
journal, 98
judgments, 95, 127

K
key, in graphics, 86, 88, 89
key question, 142
key terms, 62
key words, 93

L
leader line, multiple-choice, 53
legend, in graph, 86, 88, 89
legend, literary, 98
line graph, 83, 89
literary elements, 100–105, 245–247

INDEX

Answers to Who's Who, page ii:
1. C   2. A   3. B   4. G   5. E   6. D   7. F